LOUD AND CLEAR

LOUD AND CLEAR

LOUD AND CLEAR

LOUD AND CLEAR

LOUD AND CLEAR

LOUD AND CLEAR

Lake Headley
with William Hoffman

A Donald Hutter Book
HENRY HOLT AND COMPANY

Published by Henry Holt and Company, Inc.,
115 West 18th Street, New York, New York 10011.
Published in Canada by Fitzhenry & Whiteside Limited,
195 Allstate Parkway, Markham, Ontario L3R 4T8.

Library of Congress Cataloging-in-Publication Data
Headley, Lake.
    Loud and clear / Lake Headley with William Hoffman.—1st ed.
       p.   cm.
    "A Donald Hutter book."
    ISBN 0-8050-1138-2 (alk. paper)
    1. Murder—Arizona—Phoenix—Investigation—Case studies.
2. Bolles, Don.   I. Hoffman, William.   II. Title.
HV6534.P55H43 1990
364. 1′523′0979173—dc20   90-4170
                                                               CIP

Henry Holt books are available at special discounts
for bulk purchases for sales promotions, premiums,
fund-raising, or educational use. Special editions
or book excerpts can also be created to specification.
For details contact:
Special Sales Director, Henry Holt and Company, Inc.,
115 West 18th Street, New York, New York 10011

First Edition

BOOK DESIGN BY CLAIRE NAYLON VACCARO

Printed in the United States of America
Recognizing the importance of preserving
the written word, Henry Holt and Company, Inc.,
by policy, prints all of its first editions
on acid-free paper.♾

10 9 8 7 6 5 4 3 2 1

To Terri Lee Headley. If this story has a hero, it is Terri Lee, and not just because she paid a far greater price for the investigation than anyone else.

L. H.

To Judy Hoffman. If the writing of this book has a hero, it is Judy, a great talent and my great love.

W. H.

In memoriam: Don Hutter, an inspirational and kindly, firm guiding force throughout this book. We miss him, and owe him so much.

L. H. and W. H.

Contents

Acknowledgments

Sincere thanks are extended to Lake III, Anthony, Rod, and Tammy Headley; and William, Joe, Terri, and John Hoffman.

Also, deepest gratitude to George and Nancy Vlassis, who proved once again to be lifelong friends during this harrowing investigation; Don and Naomi Devereux, people with heart and courage, magnificent investigators; Jim Robison and Max Dunlap, honorable, *innocent* men; Jonathan Marshall, whose *Scottsdale Daily Progress* gave us a crucial window to the world; Reji Contreras, who typed a thousand letters, dried a million tears, and held my hand through dark, dangerous times; and, of course, the Dunlap Committee, who believed in Max when no one else did.

Others played important roles in this story: the Phoenix fire department, to which we owe our lives; Phoenix Baptist Hospital; the marvelous people in the Maricopa County General Hospital burn unit; Jon and Glynna Robinson, my good friends from Goshen, who provided a sanctuary whenever the pressure became too great; Bill Helmer; Molly Ivins; *Playboy* magazine; Eric Protter; John and Anita Reeves; Charles Ced; Rudy Ced; Betty Duke; Leonard and Bess McBrayer; and Ruby Reeves.

Literary agent Janet Wilkens Manus believed in the book from the beginning.

Many others. Mike and Sandy Stuhff, for an enduring friendship that began with the Bolles case; Dominic P. Gentile, who helped me return to my home in Las Vegas; and Nick and Becky Behnen, dear friends who made that return home a lot easier.

Also, Joe and Linda Lewandoski; the Blackledges in Gulfport, Mississippi; Jerry and Jane Shields; and Oliver.

I especially want to thank Victoria Cerinich, whose emotional support and critical readings of the manuscript-in-progress made the entire project seem worthwhile.

LOUD AND CLEAR

Introduction

THE BOMBING

DOWNTOWN PHOENIX, ARIZONA. JUNE 2, 1976. 11:32 A.M.

The big, forty-seven-year-old newspaper reporter with a resemblance to Clark Kent walks out of the front door of the Clarendon Hotel, turns right, and heads south on the narrow sidewalk toward the rear parking lot where he left his new Datsun thirty minutes earlier. Today holds pleasant promises; he isn't going to allow being stood up by a potential news source to spoil his plans. His mood is good, his step light.

11:33 A.M.

He ignores the boiling desert sun, the heavy heat. Awaiting him this night are a rare quiet dinner out and taking in a movie with his wife, Rosalie, in celebration of their seventeenth wedding anniversary. They plan to see *All the President's Men*. A topnotch investigative journalist himself, he believes it will be fun (maddening, also) to watch what he expects to be Hollywood's trivial and inaccurate portrayal of his profession.

11:34 A.M.

He opens the car door and proudly slides inside. He has saved hard for this automobile (without the fame of a Woodward or a Bernstein, most investigative reporters spend a lifetime behind the wheels of secondhand clunkers). Surely he thinks of Rosalie, for the next time he speaks it is of her. He turns the ignition key and the Datsun starts immediately. He backs the car out one foot, a foot and a half. His world explodes in a giant orange fireball.

"Telephone my wife. They finally got me. The Mafia. Emprise. Find John Adamson."

These were the last words of Don Bolles, uttered to attorney Max Klass and others who rushed to his side after they heard the bomb go off. Klass had run by a "ball of flesh," part of the reporter, and found him lying facedown in the Clarendon Hotel parking lot, the remains of his burned, mangled body half-inside, half-outside his demolished Datsun.

The tremendous explosion had shaken the ground with earthquake force, smashing windows hundreds of feet away, sending parts of the Datsun and pieces of Bolles atop a four-story building across six lanes of Central Avenue.

The assassins, who had planted the explosive device underneath the car, directly below the driver's seat, must have calculated that six sticks of dynamite would blast a human body apart. They couldn't have dreamed that the reporter would live, much less be able to gasp three key words: *Mafia. Emprise. Adamson.*

Bolles survived eleven days, but never spoke again. Doctors amputated his leg, an arm, the other leg, but the reporter clung to breath as tenaciously as he had pursued his investigative stories. When he finally died on June 13, his personal physician, Dr. William Dozer, said, "He put up the most courageous fight I have ever seen any person put up for his life."

Friends closest to Don Bolles could have predicted it. Even

his enemies—and he had many—didn't doubt his courage. For almost a decade and a half in Arizona, this devoted father of seven children had been a one-man crusade against organized crime and corrupt politicians, the two groups often working hand in hand; and this in a wide-open, gun-happy, let-the-sucker-beware state that more resembled the Old West than the new. He had exposed wrongs against Native Americans on the big Navajo reservation, atrocities committed against migrant workers in the Arizona citrus fields, and hoaxes perpetrated on retirees in fraudulent land schemes.

Bolles joined the *Arizona Republic* in 1962, and just three years later was nominated for a Pulitzer Prize, journalism's highest award, for a brilliant series of stories about political corruption. In 1974 his peers voted him Arizona Newsman of the Year. He was intelligent, persistent, and incorruptible.

The Bolles family was known for such traits. His grandfather had been a progressive U.S. congressman from Wisconsin, his father a respected AP bureau chief, and his brother an Episcopal priest who wrote best-selling how-to books. Even Bolles's wife, Rosalie, showed uncommon courage. Her support never wavered when the 1960s trickle of death threats against herself, her children, and her husband became a raging river in the mid-1970s.

For a short time after his death, it seemed that the politicians, at least, were trying to make it up to Don Bolles. Phoenix Mayor Margaret Hance proclaimed, "Don's fight for life was an inspiration to all of us. He lost his fight, but I pray that we will not forget him or what he was trying to do—create a decent, safe environment for all the citizens of Arizona."

Governor Raul Castro ordered the flag flown at half mast, saying "My memories of Don Bolles as a personal friend, and his many contributions as an investigative reporter and a citizen, will remain bright. His death is a searing reminder of tasks which remain to be done. It is a tragedy that his zealous pursuit of justice resulted in his death. We are all poorer because of his death, the same as we are all better because of his unshakable commitment to justice."

President Gerald Ford sent a telegram to Bolles's widow and seven children:

> Mrs. Ford and I and millions of citizens across the nation were deeply shocked by the senseless criminal violence that tragically deprived you of your husband and our free press of a prize-winning investigative reporter.
>
> Our thoughts are with you and your children as we pray that God will give you the courage to persevere through these difficult days. We hope that you and your family will find sustaining comfort in the knowledge that your husband dedicated his life to the search for truth and that the integrity he brought to his profession will endure as an inspiration for his colleagues for a long time to come.
>
> Your children can find reflected in their father's career the finest principles of our way of life to guide them through their formative years. They have been cruelly robbed of a devoted parent, but they also have been blessed by a memory that is truly worthy of being cherished and emulated. It is a memory that invokes qualities of personal character and civic responsibility which strengthen not just their lives but the life of our democratic society.

Then the journalism establishment tried to make it up to Bolles with a pile of posthumous honors. He received the prestigious John Peter Zenger Award for "distinguished service in behalf of freedom of the press and the people's right to know." Customarily, four hundred editors and publishers from around the world vote on their choice for the Zenger, "but this year [1976]," the *Arizona Republic* reported, "there was no need for a ballot."

And at first, when the search for his murderers began, it seemed that Arizona justice was also trying to make it up to him.

Just two and a half hours after Bolles died, the police picked up local hoodlum John Harvey Adamson and charged him with murder. Adamson had been mentioned in the reporter's dying words, and the prosecution quickly built an airtight case against him, including proof that he had lured Bolles to the Clarendon with the promise of an important story and personally planted the bomb under the reporter's car.

But who had hired Adamson?

In what would turn out to be a critically important decision, Jon Sellers, a police detective, granted immunity to a close associate of Adamson's, attorney Neal Roberts, in exchange for Roberts's theory of who masterminded the bombing.

Lawyer Roberts, thoroughly immunized, fingered Phoenix building contractor Max Dunlap and one of Arizona's richest men, rancher Kemper Marley. The *Arizona Republic*, Bolles's own paper, featured the Roberts theory in a major story.

Adamson waited seven months, then, in a plea bargain, named Max Dunlap and Kemper Marley as his accomplices, plus a local plumber, James Robison, who Adamson said had detonated the bomb.

Based almost entirely on the testimony of confessed murderer John Adamson, Robison and Dunlap were indicted and, on November 6, 1977, convicted of first-degree murder. Subsequently both were sentenced to die in the Arizona gas chamber. Marley wasn't even indicted—"not enough evidence," said the prosecution.

It appeared as if Arizona justice had done its job. A book written by Martin Tallberg about the killing—*Don Bolles, An Investigation into His Murder*—was published in December 1977 and proclaimed: "It soon became clear . . . that the real reason Adamson was willing to confess and turn state's evidence was the meticulously thorough and brilliant investigation conducted by the Phoenix police department."

Which was where the matter stood when a group of Max Dunlap supporters—old, close friends frightened by the probability of his execution—asked me to take a look at the case.

1

Discovery

Almost twenty-nine months after the savage, deadly bombing of Don Bolles, I met with representatives of the Max Dunlap Committee for Justice. The November 21, 1978, conference had been arranged by my childhood pal George Vlassis and was held in his Phoenix law office, thus bringing together two graduates of the Goshen (Indiana) High School class of '48, George and me, with our counterparts from Phoenix North High School's class of the same year.

Representing the Dunlap Committee were Dr. Ken Olsen, a psychologist, businessman Harold Bone, tire store owner John Sullivan, and attorney David Fraser. I had met Fraser the day before and been told he wanted to retain me to investigate the Bolles murder but needed approval from other committee leaders.

The Dunlap Committee numbered some three hundred supporters, many from that class of '48, whose president, captain of the football team, and most popular student, Max Dunlap, awaited the gas chamber on Arizona's death row. As Al Martinez wrote in the *Los Angeles Times*, "Arizona has never seen an effort like this on behalf of one man, even during the 1960s when causes were popular and crowds formed quickly."

Pillars of the Phoenix middle class, this "strange army"

—that's what newspapers called them—didn't believe for an instant that Dunlap had had anything to do with killing Don Bolles. "Really good guy," "salt of the earth," "nicest person you'll ever meet."

"I like him myself," admitted Jon Sellers, the chief police detective assigned to the homicide, "but he's guilty as hell."

I had handled hundreds of defense investigations, but the Bolles case with its worldwide notoriety ranked was unique because Dunlap's friends had rallied to his side after the conviction. Usually supporters make a big noise before a trial and start fading away once the verdict goes against their man.

None of the committee members had expected the jury to find Dunlap guilty of murder. This buddy of theirs, this family man, had to be innocent, the accusation a bizarre aberration, and justice would take its course. The first-degree murder verdict and subsequent death sentence came like a jug of ice water thrown in their faces.

"Gentlemen," said David Fraser, "this is Lake Headley. He's a private investigator from Los Angeles and a lifelong friend of George Vlassis. I've talked to him about our needs in the Dunlap matter, and having seen his résumé I believe he fills the bill. I think, for your own satisfaction, you should ask him questions."

We sat in highback leather chairs around a large mahogany table. Vlassis, one of Arizona's best-known and most successful lawyers, owned the entire distinctive N-shaped building on West Thomas Road near Encanto Park. For fourteen years he had served as general counsel to the Navajo Nation. On display throughout his office were valuable Native American hand-crafted dolls and rugs.

"Lake," said John Sullivan, the tire store owner, "I've known Max Dunlap a long time. I love and respect Max and know in my heart he couldn't commit murder. Killing is diametrically opposed to his nature. My question is: How can you help?"

"I'm not sure yet. But I know you need a thorough investigation that might unearth exculpatory new evidence to persuade an appeals court to grant a new trial. We're starting very late in the game, and I don't even know the salient facts of the case yet. But I will."

"I've been on top of everything since Max was charged," said the psychologist, Ken Olsen, his voice cracking with emotion. "All of us on the committee share a gut feeling that he had no part in this crime. But how can we prove it? How can *you* prove it?"

"I don't know I can, but the procedure is simple enough. I'm going to learn the case inside-out, I need to meet Dunlap's lawyer, and Robison's, and—"

"Robison? This is the Dunlap Committee. Don't we have enough problems just helping Max? You want to take on Robison?"

"Dunlap and Robison were co-defendants. By helping one, you help the other."

"I know Max is innocent. I'm not so sure about Robison."

"The state hasn't been able to split them, and we shouldn't try. We'll need complete cooperation from both men, and their lawyers, to have any shot at success. I want to interview Robison, which will require his attorney's assistance. I can't imagine any conflict of interest, and I understand Max and Jim have become friends since the indictment. Learning the state charged them as co-conspirators, even though they never met until their joint arraignment, knocked my socks off."

"Well then," said Harold Bone with a disgruntled chuckle, "prepare to pick cactus spines out of your bare feet because you'll lose all your socks walking through this case. There are a whole bunch of things that don't make sense." Shifting his weight in the chair, Bone said, "Mr. Headley, I think we'd like specifics on how you plan to start your investigation."

"I'll go to Arizona State Prison to see both men and let them decide if they want my help. All the players in a criminal case are subject to substitution—committees, lawyers, the judge, the prosecutor—with one exception: the defendants. Dunlap and Robison have to want me. Once that's decided, I'll urge them to commission a joint investigation. Then—"

"How will you get in? They're on death row. None of us have been allowed to visit."

"I've interviewed numerous death row inmates. Unless Arizona law is different, I'll interview these. In the past, a letter from the attorneys saying I represent the defense got me through the gate."

I tried to explain that my job involved pressuring the appeals court by getting favorable stories into print—assuming such existed—and if access couldn't be gained to the convicted men, I'd sound ludicrous to reporters. " 'Those two guys are innocent,' I might declare. 'How do you know?' would be a legitimate query. 'You own a crystal ball?' 'I just know,' I could say, dodging. 'Ever talk to them?' a reporter surely would ask. 'Well, no, but ...' "

"The committee members," said David Fraser, "still don't understand what you do, how you proceed."

Dunlap's friends seemed to be thrashing about, not sure how to help Max, wondering if hiring an investigator was a good idea in the first place. I needed to be patient and compassionate, but not raise false hopes.

"I can't say how I'll proceed. The facts will dictate my actions, but the first step is routine. I'll obtain the discovery material from the lawyers representing Dunlap and Robison."

"What is discovery material?" someone asked.

"Copies of all police reports supplied by the prosecution to the defense. I have to study them carefully."

"I've seen the discovery," said the attorney, Fraser. "It's a mountain of paper."

"Then it's a mountain I have to climb before I can intelligently discuss the case with anybody."

"And then you'll visit Max and Jim?"

"Correct." I sensed that my deliberate approach didn't thrill anyone. Understandably, committee members wanted Max Dunlap home with his family, today if possible. I didn't have the heart to tell them that statistically they faced horrendous odds. From my memory of cases this famous, I couldn't recall a single instance of conviction reversal.

Fraser shook his head. "I've never heard of a private investigator visiting death row inmates. George," he said to Vlassis, "do you know of this happening in Arizona?"

"No."

"Anyway, *if* you see them, what will you do next?"

I wasn't getting my message across. "I won't know until I talk with them."

We discussed money. The committee agreed to pay me $2,500 a month, no expenses. Usually I charged $50 an hour, *plus* expenses, but this case was one I might have worked for nothing. The murder victim had been a particularly admirable individual, and if innocent people had indeed been convicted, that meant . . . anyway, there were several national magazines I believed would contribute on the chance of obtaining an important story. Also, my good friend Vlassis had performed numerous favors for me, and I knew he wanted me to take on the investigation. The committee itself, at considerable expense (one woman had mortgaged her home for her friend Max), had already made major outlays, largely for ads in area newspapers to proclaim Dunlap's innocence.

But not in the two biggest newspapers, the *Arizona Republic* and *Phoenix Gazette.* Both papers, jointly owned by the Pulliam family (whose current member of note is Vice President Dan Quayle), had refused to sell ad space to the committee. Don Bolles had been nominated for a Pulitzer Prize during his fourteen trail-blazing years on the *Arizona Republic,* and putting the best face I could on the *Republic* and *Gazette* positions, I had to assume that they thoroughly believed Robison and Dunlap guilty and didn't intend to do anything—even accept paid ads—to support an opposing view.

I had run across similar problems in other cases. Sometimes they could be ironed out by reasoning with the publisher, explaining that the First Amendment guarantees of a free press shouldn't be limited to those wealthy enough to own a press. Other honest, righteous people can hold differing views and should have the right to be heard.

As the meeting neared a close, emotions became heated. These law-abiding, solid citizens typical of modern suburbia, many of whom probably had never been committed to a cause before, had become zealots, crusaders with a mission.

"Let me tell you about Max Dunlap," said Ken Olsen. "Outwardly he was a rugged kid, captain of the football team; but on the inside he was a sensitive, caring person. In the summertime when swarms of pesky June bugs bothered us, Max was the only guy who refused to kill them. He'd carefully brush them off, so we nicknamed him Juney. Why, Max wouldn't even swat a fly. That's the kind of gentle man the police say blew up Don Bolles."

Everybody had a story. Harold Bone: "I've known Max most of my life. He's been a good friend to me, but more, to everyone in the community. I can't remember his ever refusing to lend a helping hand, and often unsolicited. When you meet him you'll see: he's incapable of committing this crime."

John Sullivan: "I remember one year at the State Fair. A little girl had won the blue ribbon for her prize steer, but she was crying. Max asked her why. 'He's been bought,' she said. 'The new owners will slaughter him.' 'It doesn't have to be that way,' Max told her. He topped the bid for the steer and gave it back to her."

Later I learned from Dunlap's wife, Barbara, and their seven grown children more about what a soft touch Max was, always willing to respond to a hard-luck story. Or do someone a favor, like the one that landed him on death row.

The next morning, November 22, 1978, I went to the office of John Savoy, Dunlap's local defense attorney and another class of '48 graduate. A member of the Phoenix establishment, tall and heavyset, Savoy dressed in western clothes that didn't disguise his linebacker build. During preliminary hearings Max had been represented by Savoy and the famed Percy Foreman, then in his seventies, but still capable of impressive alcohol consumption. At one hearing Foreman couldn't remember what city he was in. Attorney Paul Smith came in from Boston to replace him and joined Savoy in the trial defense.

"Lake," said the lawyer, "I don't know how familiar you are with this case."

"Not very, but I'm catching up. I met with the committee

yesterday, and there's no doubt how they feel. What I need from you is the discovery."

"I'll have my secretary photocopy it for you."

"How about the defense investigation reports?"

"There are none, as such. We had a few things looked into, but not much. The police did a very thorough investigation."

My ears would tire from hearing of the police's "thorough" investigation. The deeper I dug, the more astounded I would become that anyone believed it.

"I'll need a letter authorizing me as your investigator."

"No problem. When do you want to visit Max?"

"Tomorrow."

"That soon? I doubt the authorities will allow it tomorrow. You see, Lake, the case is on appeal right now. After the Arizona Supreme Court denies the appeal, we then have access to the federal system. We can delay Max's execution for a long time, and who knows? Maybe Congress or the Supreme Court will outlaw capital punishment."

His remarks didn't fill me with optimism. I considered the defense's meager investigations appalling and from experience suspected that the police inquiry fell far short of the super job Savoy described.

Savoy's pessimism might have been warranted—no prisoner in Arizona history had ever walked off death row—but it nonetheless was discouraging to hear him refer to the state supreme court's confirmation of the guilty verdicts as a given. Were Robison and Dunlap so obviously culpable that they stood no chance?

"Why do you expect a denial on the appeal?"

"Arizona is a big place that harbors a clannish, small-state mentality. You'll soon get a bellyful of the unfriendly climate we face. The whole community was whipped up by the *Arizona Republic*, which exerted terrific pressure to get this murder out of the way. I doubt the state supreme court has the guts to overturn."

• • •

Next I saw David Derickson, Robison's court-appointed lawyer, a savvy, street-smart barrister, the flip side of the conservative Savoy. Derickson, dapper, slender, handsome, shared two traits with Savoy: a penchant for western wear and pessimism about his client's future. "Jim says he didn't do it, and I halfway believe him," Derickson offered, "but the evidence was very strong."

"I need your discovery material."

"If Savoy's giving you his discovery, you'll have it all. But I'll be happy to write that authorization for you to visit Jim."

"You conduct any defense investigation for Robison?"

"We had a few things checked out. Mainly concerning his alibi for the time around the bombing."

Derickson's respect and sympathy for his client impressed me, and I decided to lay it on the line. "Do you think Dunlap and Robison killed Don Bolles?"

The lawyer took his time before answering. "No. In fact, I'd bet they didn't. But that doesn't mean we're going to win. I doubt we will. All the forces in this state are arrayed against Jim and Max. I said I don't think they're guilty; but if you ask me who is, I'll have to say I don't know. We'll probably never know."

"The Dunlap Committee drew me a thumbnail sketch of Max, but Robison's a total blank. Tell me about him. What's he like?"

"A helluva individual in no way resembling the monstrous brute described by the press. His biggest problem is his appearance, mainly a deep scar on his forehead that makes you think he lost an ax fight. Actually, he sustained the injury as a kid in a diving accident. The press called him Jimmy the Plumber, to convey a Mob connotation. Hell, he really is a plumber, a blue-collar guy who works with his hands."

"How about schooling?"

"Jim is totally self-educated. I'm not given to dishing out praise, but he has a brilliant mind, and he's the best-read individual I've met. Shortly after being appointed to represent him, I asked if he needed anything. He said, 'Some good books would be nice.' Then he grinned and added, 'This place isn't exactly a center for cultural enlightenment.' Well, that day I received four

Book-of-the-Month Club selections. When I carried them over
to the jail, he said, 'Thanks, but I've already read these.' Since
then I've taken him scores of books, and he's usually read them,
too."

Late that night I sat in Room 217 of the Westward Ho Hotel
with the discovery papers up over my head. I had rented a room
in the spacious, marble-columned hostelry—where Calvin Cool-
idge spent part of his retirement—because of its proximity to
courthouse, lawyers, library, and post office.

Important finds in a complex murder case usually come after
long, tedious digging, but right away I happened upon a double
bonanza: the clear weakness of the police version of the murder,
and evidence in the discovery material of a vast, largely un-
tapped mother lode for the defense.

First, the police theory. The name *Adamson* was one of the
last words Bolles said after the bomb exploded beneath his Datsun. This referred to John Harvey Adamson, a.k.a. Cocaine John,
local thug, arsonist, enforcer, con man, fixer—a walking-around
definition of the word *sleaze*—who turned himself in to police
on June 3, 1976, the day after the bombing, on an unrelated
"defrauding an innkeeper" charge. He got released in two and a
half hours on a hundred dollars bail, but when Bolles died after
eleven days of excruciating pain and suffering, the police charged
Adamson with first-degree murder, a crime punishable by death
in the Arizona gas chamber.

The prosecution quickly built an ironclad case against Adamson, but the police conveniently forgot Bolles's other two words:
Emprise. Mafia.

And Adamson couldn't have acted alone. Someone must have
hired him. With much of the nation outraged by the murder of
a fighting reporter, the police and prosecution were pressured to
bring all principals to justice. To do so, they offered Adamson a
lenient sentence, new identity, and a hundred thousand dollars,
put up by the *Arizona Republic,* to name who helped him and/
or hired him. Ironically, this man who evidently planted the

bomb under the reporter's car stood to collect a reward from the victim's employer for solving the case.

Phoenix police detective Jon Sellers headed the murder investigation, and two days after Bolles's death Sellers found his scenario, one he would follow to the very end. In a critical and, I thought, outlandish move, Sellers, a *police detective*, gave immunity to an associate and close drinking buddy of Adamson, attorney Neal Roberts, in exchange for his "theory of the crime." Roberts's theory, promptly printed in the *Arizona Republic*, speculated that Max Dunlap, acting under orders from multimillionaire rancher Kemper Marley, hired Adamson to kill Bolles.

Ever since Max Dunlap's high school days, he and the financially and politically powerful Marley had shared a father-son relationship, with the rich man providing advice and loans to further Dunlap's career.

Marley's motive for wanting Bolles dead? Revenge—"rangeland justice" Neal Roberts called it—in retaliation for articles written by Bolles months before, which Roberts said cost Marley a post on the Arizona racing commission.

While Adamson debated whether to accept the generous plea bargain offer and read in the *Republic* of his friend Neal Roberts's theory, Governor Raul Castro shifted responsibility for prosecution from the Maricopa County attorney's office to the Arizona attorney general, Bruce Babbitt—later governor of Arizona and a 1988 presidential candidate. Babbitt suggested a slightly different deal: Adamson would receive a sentence of 54 years, with parole *guaranteed* after 20, to be served outside Arizona; and immunity from 33 confessed felonies (punishment for which totaled $80,000 in fines and 325 years in prison, plus two separate life sentences and death in the gas chamber). Not to overdo it, Babbitt's offer did not include the $100,000 reward.

Adamson readily accepted the new deal, agreeing to plead guilty to the Bolles murder and name his accomplices. He also agreed to testify "truthfully and completely at all times whether under oath or not." If he didn't speak truthfully and fully, the plea bargain read, the entire agreement became "null and void and the original charges automatically reinstated."

On December 28, 1976, more than six months after his arrest, the con man finally gave the prosecution his story, and it fitted perfectly with Neal Roberts's "theory": contractor Max Dunlap, calling Kemper Marley "Mr. Smith" and acting as a go-between for the crusty, colorful rancher, hired Adamson to kill Bolles; and James Robison, a plumber with electrical experience and an acquaintance of Adamson, built the bomb Adamson planted, then triggered the blast.

Like almost every state in the United States, Arizona law required corroboration of accusations against a defendant. In this instance, however, the Arizona legislature expeditiously passed a special measure—to become known as the Adamson Act—which eliminated the need for corroboration and permitted the prosecution to obtain death sentences based solely on one man's testimony, that man being John Harvey Adamson.

Putting aside my sense of wonder about Arizona justice, I couldn't imagine a weaker motive for murder than the one attributed to Kemper Marley. Would an individual contract a murder because of *articles already published,* a fait accompli? A far more likely motive would have been *to stop a planned story.*

But there was a problem with this more logical line of reasoning: the *Arizona Republic* maintained Bolles had burned out, becoming a mere shell of his former dynamic self. So he had been taken off the investigative beat. Prior to his death he had been covering the rather staid proceedings of the state legislature.

From reading the discovery I gleaned glimpses of what had happened at the trial of Robison and Dunlap. Adamson, without whose testimony *no* case existed, had invoked a selective memory to shore up his testimony. "It may have been that way," he often said. Or, "I'm not saying it didn't happen like that, I'm just saying I don't remember."

And when even selective memory failed him, Adamson simply took the Fifth Amendment. This netted him several contempt-of-court citations, but neither William Schafer III, the assistant attorney general and chief prosecutor, nor Jon Sellers professed much uneasiness with Adamson taking the Fifth, despite his broad immunity deal and his sworn agreement to testify "truthfully and fully" at all times.

The second point that grabbed me as I read the discovery was the massive supply of defense ammunition stockpiled therein. What follows is a police report of June 5, 1976 (three days after the bombing, when Bolles still clung to life), written by Phoenix police detective G. Marcus Aurelius:

On 6/5/76, at 1:30 A.M., investigator made telephone contact with Betty Funk Richardson through the Balboa Beach Club number. Mrs. Richardson identified herself as the ex-wife of a Bradley Funk, of the Funk-Jacobs-Emprise Corporation organization. She is presently married to a Bill Richardson and living with him at the Balboa Beach Club, Balboa, California.

Emprise! The name itself was enough to rivet my eyes to the police report. It had come from Bolles's own lips, and he surely knew best who might want him dead.

Mrs. Richardson advised having married Bradley Funk due to an unwanted pregnancy while Bradley Funk was a student at the University of Arizona, approximately 1960. She subsequently separated from him in 1961 and was subjected to continuous harassment and financial disregard by Bradley Funk. During this period she lived with her children in the Phoenix area, and due to the lack of financial support, she was required to exist on Welfare funding. During the course of years, she met and became friends with Don Bolles.

What Aurelius wrote was unfolding like a true-crime thriller. First Emprise, now Bolles.

Mrs. Richardson subsequently met and married Bill Richardson, her present husband. She has been separated and divorced from Bradley Funk approximately 14 years.

Her children are described as being both afraid and totally indifferent to Bradley Funk, which is a source of irritation to him. Reportedly, on one occasion, he and David Funk attempted to have sexual relations with the daughters. She characterized Bradley Funk as an only child, spoiled, very demanding, vindictive and mean, especially when he does not obtain things he wants. She indicated having walked out on him, and because of her independence and the actions of the children, Bradley Funk has been especially mean and vindictive toward them. Don Bolles in the past has written newspaper articles concerning the Emprise Corporation which prompted Bradley Funk to make a statement in a news article, "We're going to have to get him off of our back"; reportedly a 1972 article. She advised Bradley Funk has expressed vengeance toward Don Bolles in the past and she believed it to have been prompted not only by the newspaper articles but also by the fact Don Bolles has appeared in various court trials on her behalf in opposition to Bradley Funk.

I had never heard of Bradley Funk prior to reading this police report, but the statement about getting Bolles "off of our back" merited scrutiny. If Robison and Dunlap were innocent, other people committed the crime, and although finding these persons didn't constitute my job—I'd been hired, after all, to prove the innocence of the convicted men—I'd be remiss if I overlooked other suspects. Detective Aurelius's report picked up speed:

Mrs. Richardson advised of a pending 1.5-million-dollar lawsuit she has instigated against Bradley Funk for invasion of privacy and harassment. The lawsuit is presently being prepared by a Mr. Bill Stevens in Phoenix. Reportedly, Bradley Funk is not aware of the suit; however, a number of coincidences have occurred recently. Originally, she was utilizing an attorney by the name of Pulumbo in the Bill Stevens firm. He unexpectedly left the firm, with Bill Stevens taking over the lawsuit's prepara-

tion. On 5/10/76 she had telephone contact with Don
Bolles during which time she mentioned the pending lawsuit. This information was in confidence and provided because of their close association. On 5/12/76 she received
an anonymous phone call threatening her welfare, at the
Balboa Beach Club residence phone. The caller was not
identified.

The information Betty Funk Richardson provided Detective
Aurelius pointed to a stronger motive than the one attributed to
Kemper Marley. Moreover, as soon as her attorney filed that
lawsuit, with its allegations of harassment and sexual impropri-
ety, it became a matter of public record—and Bolles could publish it.

On 6/2/76 during the afternoon hours, Mrs. Richardson received a telephone call from her attorney, Bill Stevens. He inquired of her who in Phoenix did she mention
the lawsuit to. She advised Stevens she had informed only
Don Bolles. Stevens then asked, "Do you know what they
did to him?" She responded "No," and he remarked,
"They just blew up his car." This was her first indication
Don Bolles had been injured.
She advised having no knowledge as to the suspect's
identity; however, she suggested investigators consider
Bradley Funk as an instigator. She repeated her character
description of Bradley Funk as being mean and vindictive;
however, she offered her opinion that he had "blown a
fuse" and should be in a mental institution. She believes
Bradley Funk had become so insanely jealous and vindictive due to the indifference toward him of his daughters
that it is quite possible for him to have privately engaged
the services of a subject to harm Bolles. She described Bolles
as being the only person, other than the lawyers, knowing
of the pending lawsuit. She offers no suggestion how others
may have learned of the lawsuit other than bugging the telephone of Don Bolles, or through Pulumbo.

Wiretapping Bolles's telephone seemed extravagant. I was to learn, however, that the reporter's phone had been tapped before, and by none other than Bradley Funk.

Mrs. Richardson explained not wanting to sound like a vindictive ex-wife; however, she advised being very familiar with the Funk family and of course Bradley Funk, and to what extremes they would go to obtain what they wanted. She described them as barbarians, as animals, with Bradley Funk in his present state of mind very capable of causing injury to Don Bolles.

Mrs. Richardson advised that Don Bolles had been fighting the Emprise Corporation for the last several years, almost on his own, without real support from other agencies or people. She advised being aware the Emprise Corporation and the Funks are well protected and are involved with a number of socially prominent personalities. Among the names mentioned were Judge Bernstein, the Paul Fannin and Joe Hunt families, Barry Goldwater, and Rosenzweigs. She expressed her understanding it was very difficult to get to the Funks because of how they have shielded themselves with such personalities. She advised, however, because of the Don Bolles bombing incident, if the Funks are involved, if Bradley Funk specifically is responsible, all of his friends, and associates, will stay away from him and may provide information to investigators. She indicated the bombing of Bolles to be totally out of character for the syndicate, and if the Funks, or Bradley Funk specifically is responsible, he has made an irreversible mistake. She then repeated her desire to be properly understood as not being vindictive towards him but felt investigators should understand that Bradley Funk in his present state of mind has a motive to hurt her and the family by destroying Don Bolles. She also expressed the opinion that John Adamson, a subject she is not familiar with, should also be in danger because he flubbed the job. She advised "they" are probably trying to find him because Bolles is still alive and Adamson's identity is known. She suggested that Adamson would be better off in police custody than free on the streets.

It was far too early to form opinions—I had only started the case this afternoon—but on the surface, merely scanning the discovery, I had already found a stronger motive than the one tagged to Kemper Marley. Bolles evidently had been a thorn in Bradley Funk's side for years, and the distinct possibility existed that just before the bombing the two adversaries were again set to square off over accusations that could ruin Funk.

I read early into the morning, growing increasingly alarmed by what I learned. The attitude in Phoenix after the murder had been, "Solve this case fast, get that national spotlight away from us," and the predictable result was a completely blinkered investigation ignoring any leads other than those provided by admitted killer John Adamson. Many in Arizona officialdom, including prosecutors, a police detective recklessly handing out immunity, and a state legislature passing the Adamson Act, abetted the single-minded rush to judgment of Robison and Dunlap.

I knew of no other state with a criminal provision such as the Adamson Act, whereby the naked, unsupported accusations of even a notorious liar, hoodlum, and murderer were considered adequate to send two defendants to the gas chamber. What made the law all the more repugnant was the fact that it had been enacted solely to facilitate prosecution in the Bolles case.

It had been a long day, and I couldn't keep my eyes open any longer. At this point I had no idea whether Jim and Max were guilty, only that I wouldn't lack, as the committee feared, things to do.

2

The Patsy

I drove the rental car southeast on Interstate 10 toward Tucson, exiting on 387 to reach the town of Florence and the Arizona State Prison. I hardly expected to find a model of the modern maximum security penitentiary jutting out of the sand, but nothing in my experience had prepared me for the abysmal hell-hole I found.

Convict labor built the Florence "correctional facility" from remnants of the Old West's notorious Yuma Territorial Prison, moved some two hundred miles—literally stone by stone—across the desert.

Inmates sweltered in sizzling slow summers and shivered when whistling winter winds chased in all manner of wilderness vermin through gaping cracks and crevices. Its only appearances of "modernization": razor wire and closely spaced guard towers topping the institution's ugly stone walls.

Death row, where Robison and Dunlap existed in six-by-ten-foot cells, came equipped with aggressive rats and a menagerie of small, shyer creatures skittering across the floor, over grungy walls, and along a crumbling ceiling that leaked copiously when-ever the rains came. Except for a few minutes of fresh air and outdoor exercise in a hurricane-fence enclosure called the "dog run," inmates stayed locked down twenty-four hours a day.

Death row also served as a deterrent to crime *within* the prison. When inmates from the general prison population committed some serious infraction (say, knifing a guard), the harshest punishment authorities could dole out was a stint on death row— suffering the same misery Dunlap, Robison, and several dozen others convicted of capital crimes had to endure from their first day.

I had called ahead, and after a wearisome row with Carolyn Robinson, a warden's assistant, had obtained an okay to visit Max and Jim. I suspected the battle hadn't ended, however, and sure enough, as soon as I'd entered the administration building, a surly captain with the walleyed stare of a fish told me, "You can't be here."

"I'm already here," I pointed out, and attempted to reason with the man. He griped that what I wanted was "something out of the ordinary." Logic seemed beside the point as I tried to convince this "screw" that he had no say in the matter—one of his superiors had already granted permission—until at last he called Carolyn Robinson. (I grew to know her well in the next year and a half and almost became fond of hearing, "You back again?") Although she was still riled that I'd gained entrance into their domain—she must have checked around and learned that (1) I couldn't be legally stopped and (2) my reputation suggested I would sue if they tried—she told him to send me through.

After the captain searched my pockets, briefcase, tape recorder, and self, then had me walk through a metal detector, a trusty escorted me to another building and into a minuscule attorney/client room containing all of one tiny table and two small chairs. Through a window I spotted Max Dunlap being led across the yard, knowing he would undergo a strip search before and after seeing me.

I looked him over when we shook hands. He stood six feet tall, weighed around two hundred and thirty pounds, and at forty-eight years already had a full head of steel-gray hair. My instant impression: an outdoors type with a permanent Huckleberry Hound expression on a guileless face that radiated openness, honesty and, yes, simplicity. Even if I hadn't talked with the committee, I would have judged this man a valued, trusted neighbor in middle-income suburbia; in a hustler's milieu, he'd be an out-and-out sucker.

And clearly a staunch family man. Soon as we'd introduced ourselves—I with a brief oral résumé, he wondering if I'd met his wife and children—he said, and I didn't doubt it, that he could accept his fate, but "It's terrible what this has done to Barbara and the kids."

Dunlap's sun-weathered face made it easy to picture him as a contractor supervising workmen at a construction site and still wearing his hard hat after 5 P.M. in the good-time atmosphere of a neighborhood bar, drinking beer with friends before heading home for dinner.

He spoke softly and earnestly, ignoring the yellow pads I brought for him to write on, in case we had listeners. Already convinced that the Arizona authorities had artfully maneuvered him onto death row, I assumed they'd consider bugging his visitor conversations a small matter.

"Max," I said, "I think the toughest area you have to overcome is that money you delivered to Adamson. And your relationship to Kemper Marley. Without Marley, you had no motive at all for the killing."

Dunlap's delivery of cash to Adamson had evidently cinched the jury's decision to convict. I knew the story by heart from the reading I did the night before, but I wanted to hear it from my client's lips.

"You need to remember," Dunlap began, "that Neal Roberts was in my high school class. Through the years after graduation we stayed in touch, and I used him on a few small land deals. Well, eight days after the bombing, he called and asked me to do him a favor: deliver some money to Adamson's lawyer, Tom Foster. Neal said it would be in hundred-dollar bills, which I should change into tens and twenties. I said, 'Why can't you do this yourself?' He said he knew Adamson pretty well, and since Adamson was already a prime suspect in the bombing, he didn't want to get involved any deeper. Really, it was a favor I didn't mind doing."

This fit the profile provided by his friends on the committee. Good old Max would help *anybody*, especially a former high school classmate.

"The next morning," Dunlap continued, "very early, just as I was leaving for work, a car pulled up in my driveway. The driver said, 'Neal sent me,' handed me a paper sack, and left. Marty Fogelsong, who dates one of my daughters, was at my house that morning. He witnessed everything that happened. Anyway, I went to my bank later in the day, changed the five thousand eight hundred dollars into lower denominations, and took it to Tom Foster's office. His receptionist said Tom had gone to court, but John Adamson was in the conference room and I should give the money to him."

"Did you?"

"Yes."

"What did you say to Adamson?"

"Nothing. I handed him the money and went about my business."

The prosecution, after Adamson testified that the money came from Kemper Marley, understandably imputed the most sinister of motives to Dunlap's delivery of this cash.

I watched in the close quarters we occupied as Max struggled to find the right words to explain. "Lake," he said finally, "would you do a favor like that for George Vlassis, if he asked?"

My turn had come to think, but only for a moment. "In a hot second," I said, "without looking back."

"That's how I felt."

I remembered again what those committee members said about Max, always ready to help a pal. That's why they had come together at the eleventh hour: to try to do something for him.

"Describe the man who brought the money."

"I think he was Mexican. One of Neal Roberts's gofers. Neal always had a lot of people around to run errands."

"What kind of car did he drive?"

"An older model. I really don't remember. It might help if you talked to Marty Fogelsong." (This I did. Fogelsong confirmed Max's story and passed a lie detector test. I also had him put under hypnosis, and he remembered a partial license plate number; but I never did locate that bagman.)

"Tell me about Kemper Marley."

"He's been my friend since I was in high school. I wrote him a letter in my freshman year—a history teacher told me Kemper enjoyed helping ambitious youths—and this started a friendship that has lasted to the present day. He's provided guidance, both business and personal. He enjoyed, vicariously, whatever small successes I achieved. Kemper's got millions of dollars and zillions of projects. He's also an old man, and thick-skinned from this desert heat. It's important for you to understand Kemper's personality. He's a rough old cob—races horses and likes cockfights—and he didn't give a flying flip what Don Bolles or the *Arizona Republic* said about him. Remember this, too: Kemper knows everybody. He'd never use someone like me to arrange a murder. I'm a pushover, the last person in the world he'd associate with violence. And besides, Kemper's not the underhanded sort who hires people to do his dirty work. If he wanted Don Bolles dead, he would have killed him himself, right on the courthouse steps."

The possibility that Dunlap told the truth—his straightforward, a-train-just-ran-over-me demeanor differing from any innocence-vowing defendant I ever met—was overwhelming, alerting everything in me to my responsibility to ferret out the facts. If Dunlap was innocent, he was living a Kafkaesque nightmare, awaiting execution for a crime to which he was only remotely and unwittingly connected—doing a favor for a high school chum, the same man now safe under a grant of immunity in exchange for the very theory that put Max Dunlap here in the first place. Mr. Perfect Patsy, merely in the right place at the right time—for Neal Roberts, John Adamson, and who knew how many others.

"Are there areas I should avoid?" I asked routinely. The query was one way to determine if he had anything to hide.

"Lake, do anything you want. Go anyplace. Talk to anybody. Even if you think it's leading to me, keep heading forward, because it can't lead to me. I'm innocent."

"Well, the state wants to execute you, and your best hope is my operating unshackled."

"You need to understand, only recently has the state become serious about killing me. They didn't aim for that before, but they're doing it now. Police officers, guards, prosecutors, and plenty of others have told me, 'You know what we want. Give it to us. You've got the key to your cell in your pocket.' What they're after, of course, is Kemper's head on a silver platter. And for the life of me, I don't know why. I suppose someone that rich and powerful has stepped on a lot of toes. But, no sir, I refuse to play their game. Kemper's my friend, and I won't lie and blame him for a crime he didn't commit. I wouldn't frame anyone the way Adamson framed me."

"You've been offered a deal if you'll finger Marley?"

"Many times. I've been told they'll go lighter on me than they did on Adamson."

"Sounds as if I should stay clear of Marley. If they see or hear me getting together with him, they're going to figure there *is* something between you. Unless you think he knows something that might help us."

"Lake, he doesn't know anything. *I* don't know anything. Except for delivering that money to Adamson, which I've tried to explain, Adamson's lies were the only testimony against me."

He was right—Adamson's *was* the only testimony against him. Later, reading the trial transcript, I would confirm that the Dunlap I saw was the Dunlap everybody got. Ed Carson, president of First National Bank, called Max's reputation for honesty "excellent." "A reputation for peacefulness," said Leo J. Baumgartner. "His reputation was, in my opinion, spotless." Said longtime friend Charles Mann: "I have found Max to be a very honorable gentleman, very upright. He's a very peaceful sort of man."

Honest and peaceful, that's what witness after witness told the jury. *Never* violent, they all stressed. Wouldn't hurt a fly. Or a June bug.

"Max, about my investigation." I needed to make this point clear. "What if the committee has a different agenda?"

"I can't worry about the committee. They're a bunch of nice

people, but they're not in my spot. You work for me, and I'm giving you carte blanche. I'm the guy who wakes up every morning just fifty feet from the green door."

"When did you first meet Jim Robison?"

"The day we were arraigned. Isn't that a kicker? I was indicted as a co-conspirator for first-degree murder, and I'd never met my supposed partner. That's what was so bizarre, Lake. They convicted me of conspiring with a man I didn't even know. Actually, he remained a stranger—we were totally separated during the trial—until we reached Florence and were put on death row."

Since then, however, they had become good friends, two completely different men—Dunlap, naive, open, warmhearted; Robison, tough and shrewd—bonded by a shared disaster. And I would learn they had something else in common: resentment toward John Adamson, that *he* wasn't the one on death row. But because of Adamson's cushy plea bargain, that could never be.

Or could it?

"Do you have much chance to talk with Jim?"

"I do now. Controls have been relaxed, and inmates can converse more with one another. I take some credit for that. I began interceding for other prisoners with the guards. It was a horrible situation before, with the inmates unable to communicate with them. The cons just didn't know any better. When they wanted something, they would 'motherfucker' and 'cocksucker' the guards, and of course this gained them nothing. So I began presenting their beefs in a human-to-human approach. It worked wonders."

Max told me if he ever got released, he would devote his spare time to prison reform, with special emphasis on training guards, whom he described, without rancor, as mentally dense and/or sadistic. "But whoa," he said, "I'm getting off the track. You asked me about Jim. He's a genuinely intelligent man, and I have the greatest respect for him. *I* couldn't roll over on Kemper Marley. He's my friend. Actually, more like a father, as I'm sure you've heard. My own dad died when I was thirteen. And that's when Kemper came into my life. So I couldn't accuse him falsely, but Jim Robison sure could, if he wanted to save himself. Kemper Marley is just a face in the crowd to him. Jim could snitch him off in a minute and save his own neck, but he won't. It's a matter of principle. He and I realize we're in this together, and we've become like brothers. Shared experience, I guess you call it. There's nothing I wouldn't do for Jim Robison, and I'm sure he feels the same way about me."

A guard knocked on the door, indicating we had five more minutes. I asked if Max had anything special he wanted me to do.

"Tell Barbara I say 'hi.' Tell her I love her very much. You should go by the house. They'll be glad to know someone's working on this. And don't forget to give the kids my love."

"I'll do it." Barbara visited every week, and sometimes the children came along, but Max wanted them to know they were always in his thoughts.

"Anything else?"

"No, except to say I'm grateful. I know you're operating on short money, and if I ever get out, I'll take care of you. Unfortunately, I'm broke now, this case has cost me everything, but maybe I'll get a chance to build a new nest egg."

I sensed in Dunlap a desire to accept me as a potential savior, a tough role to play, but even in this open, straightforward man there lurked suspicion of anyone connected with the case.

I had learned little from Dunlap about the Bolles killing because he claimed *not to know anything*. He said he had been framed, and that was it. From Robison I expected much more. Robison had known Adamson well, had been his confidant.

3

The Plumber

I ate lunch at a small diner in Florence, surrounded by sullen citizens bristling at what they considered a one-man invasion of their turf.

The prison constituted Florence's main industry, and word had spread about the stranger, the p.i., paying a visit such as none of his type had ever made. What did these suspicious people think? That I'd disrupt their way of life? From the waitress slamming a plate down in front of me to the unfriendly stares singeing my face, the folks in this backroads desert town weren't exactly dusting off the welcome mat.

With time to kill, I cruised the bleak landscape until I found a cemetery, an apt place for my mood, spread out a blanket, and read more of the discovery. Before this long, complicated, dangerous case ended for me, I would set a record for visits to the Arizona State Prison—seventy in all—and the quiet graveyard would become a regular resting spot between morning visits with Max and afternoon sessions with Jim.

What I read that day in the few hours before I was scheduled to see Robison was even more mind-blowing than my reading of the night before.

It began with Hank Landry, a one-legged card cheat and buddy of Neal Roberts and John Adamson. I read the story from a police report penned by none other than Jon Sellers:

On 4/11/78 at approximately 3:00 P.M., Hank Landry
was contacted by telephone. The purpose for the contact
was to determine what knowledge Mr. Landry possessed
of the Bolles incident. At this time Mr. Landry related
to investigator that he was present at a Memorial Day
weekend picnic of 1976 at Neal Roberts's house at 90 W.
Virginia. He further stated that during this picnic there
was a conversation between Neal Roberts and John
Adamson concerning the [Anarchist] cookbook, as well as
explosives. He said that during the conversation, Don
Bolles's name was mentioned, and that he interceded in
the conversation asking, "Why not just use a gun and get
it over with?" He said that as a result of this statement,
Neal Roberts replied he wanted it to be loud and clear.

I read this report four times before convincing myself that
my eyes weren't deceiving me. The *weekend before* Don Bolles's
car exploded, Adamson and Roberts had talked about blowing
him up—using dynamite for a "loud and clear" warning that
other reporters should keep their noses out of sensitive investigations. The ramifications absolutely chilled me.

As did Sellers's next report, which threw all his professed
beliefs into a cocked hat. Evidently amazed by what the one-
legged gambler had told him, Sellers conducted a second interview with Landry:

On April 13, 1978, at approximately 1:00 P.M., Mr.
Hank Landry was interviewed at the Organized Crime
Bureau of the Phoenix Police Department. During this
interview, Mr. Landry related things that he remembered
happening prior to the incident, the day of the incident,
and the days following the incident.

Mr. Landry related that he believes he arrived in Phoenix on Friday, May 30, 1976. He said his purpose for
coming to Phoenix was to attend Robert Letierre's wedding. Mr. Landry stated that he had originally intended
to stay with Dink Miller. However, he wound up staying

at John Adamson's apartment. Mr. Landry stated that on Saturday he took a ride with John Adamson and they went to the *Arizona Republic* parking lot looking for Don Bolles's car. He said that during this occurrence, Adamson told him that he was going to blow Bolles up for $50,000. He also stated that Adamson told him that he had other work to do after this was done.

The Robert Letierre referred to in Landry's statement would later testify that Adamson had asked him to help kill Bolles, only to have Letierre refuse.

Adamson told Sellers his "other work" involved murdering Alphonso "King Al" Lizanetz—a former Marley publicist and eccentric who dressed in funny costumes and seemed convinced of his own royalty—and Attorney General Bruce Babbitt: a three-murder deal, said Adamson, contracted by Kemper Marley.

Adamson claimed Marley wanted Babbitt assassinated because he feared the attorney general was investigating him, and Bolles was merely the first of three hits. But why kill King Al, widely regarded, with considerable justification, as the Town Clown? Because, said Adamson, Lizanetz had gone around Phoenix hinting at skeletons in Marley's closet.

Hogwash! All of this made no more sense than the motive given for Bolles's murder. Babbitt wasn't any threat to Marley, and no one in Arizona took King Al seriously. He was a nut. His organization—Unity with Humanity for All—wrote letters over a "King Alphonso" signature to Kurt Waldheim at the United Nations, calling Al himself Robin Hood and Waldheim "a real gem of God." Al passed out recipes on Phoenix street corners for "King Alphonso's Freedom Cake" and "Freedom Icing," concoctions so heavily laced with alcohol they might indeed convey a sense of freedom. However, more important to me than the obfuscations of Adamson—no one even considered prosecutions in the "conspiracies" to murder Babbitt, the attorney general, for heaven's sake, and Lizanetz—was the information Landry provided Sellers:

Landry also related to investigator that on Memorial Day, he went with John Adamson to a black barbecue place and purchased some ribs which they ultimately took to Neal Roberts's home and ate. He said that some of the people he remembered being present at Neal Roberts's home on Memorial Day were John Adamson, Mary Adamson and her son, Neal Roberts, a young couple who he described as living in one of Neal Roberts's apartments, and possibly Barbara Gant. He said he remembers doing card tricks for them.

Landry stated that during the afternoon hours he was present when John and Neal were talking about dynamite, and explosives, and how a person could buy normal items in a store to make a bomb. He said at this time he asked Adamson, "Why do it with a bomb? Why not just shoot him with a gun?" Adamson replied, "My people want it done with dynamite."

He said that during this same conversation Neal Roberts also said, "I want it to be loud and clear." Landry also stated that at some point in the conversation, Roberts indicated Bolles was a son of a bitch anyway.

The more I read the report, the more I wondered why Sellers, after interviewing Landry, hadn't come forward with arms waving to demand a dig-out-the-truth investigation. Was it to avoid egg on his face for having immunized Neal Roberts who, according to Landry, had prior knowledge of the bombing? Or was he simply obeying orders—something like "go through the usual detective routine, but don't make waves"— that he'd followed from the beginning of the case? Why didn't Sellers employ the Landry information to paint in missing parts of the picture instead of dwelling on nit-picking points? For example:

Upon reading the transcribed interview with Mr. Landry, which was taken on April 15, 1978, it was noted that investigator had failed to bring out with Mr. Landry as he had on April 13, 1978, which word Neal Roberts actually used when he said, "I want it loud and clear." As a result of this, investigator contacted Mr. Landry on April 25, 1978, and queried him as to his memory of the words that Neal Roberts actually used when he said, "I want it loud and clear." Mr. Landry stated that he could not remember for sure whether Neal Roberts used the word[s] "I want it loud and clear," or whether he used the words "We want it loud and clear."

Hell's bells! What's the difference? By using either word, "I" *or* "we," Roberts included himself, and Sellers should have been on the attorney's doorstep asking for an explanation.

On the morning of April 26, 1978, Sellers contacted John Adamson, described thus in his report:

At this time Adamson was advised by investigator that further information had been learned concerning the Bolles incident. . . . He was asked if he remembered taking Hank Landry to the *Arizona Republic* parking lot and looking for Don Bolles's car. He stated he did not remember doing this. He said he also did not remember confiding in Landry that he had a contract to kill Don Bolles. Adamson was asked whether or not it happened, or he just couldn't remember; and he stated that he would not say it didn't happen, but that he just couldn't remember it.

I had to wonder about Adamson's lapse of memory in the Landry matter when compared to the gambler's passing a police-administered lie detector test, but by then it was time for me to go see Jim Robison.

Again a hassle slowed my entrance into the prison that afternoon (this song and dance never changed—the guards, bent on not bending, figured if they threw up enough roadblocks, I'd tire and back off), but after forty minutes I found myself in the tiny visitor's enclosure sitting opposite Max Dunlap's convicted co-conspirator.

Jim Robison stood five foot seven, weighed 220 pounds, and had big bulging shoulders and forearms and gnarled hands, which had wrestled for years with rusty pipes and clogged drains. A long scar zigzagged through a deep dent on his forehead, as if someone had struck him with a sledgehammer and *then* wielded an ax. A rough character.

It was soon apparent that whereas the gods had blessed Dunlap with hundreds of friends and a loving, supportive family, Jim Robison had nobody. Unlike Max, who wore "easy mark" stamped all over his face, the rugged, powerful Robison could hardly be mistaken for a pushover.

Robison opened the conversation by interviewing me. What had I done? Where had I been? Who did I know? Finally, "Why do you think you can do something for Max and me when nobody else has?"

In day-to-day life I had more friends who resembled Robison than Dunlap. Robison, wise in the ways of the alley, would think twice and three times before agreeing to help a Neal Roberts. Yet I was to discover that Jim wasn't a selfish or venal man. Once you got past his forbidding exterior, there was a sensitive, extremely learned individual.

I had to halt his barrage of questions. He possessed good cause to want information about me, but *I* wasn't on death row, and we had limited time. "Jim," I said, "I've read a good deal of the discovery, and it looks like you know more about Adamson than anybody else. Tell me about him. It's critical."

"John Adamson is the smartest s.o.b. connected with this case."

"Why do you say that?"

"He got everything he wanted, didn't he? He has the cops backing his story. The prosecutors cut him a deal made in heaven. Remember, he admitted planting the bomb. Max and I are on death row, when it's really Adamson who belongs here. I'd call that being a smart s.o.b., wouldn't you?"

"I need to know what he's like."

"Everyone thinks he's a crude street hustler, lots of noise and bombast. Not true. He's a damn good con man. For years he avoided both arrest and a job by cultivating friends at all levels of Phoenix society: judges, doctors, lawyers, politicians, pimps, dope dealers, whores. A cocaine junkie—people called him 'Cocaine John'—and always in a shadowy alcoholic haze. But still, even the upper crust sought him out, for his conversation, his wit, his free-spending camaraderie, but most of all for his services. He'd sell a hot coat at a fraction of its value. Get them dope. A woman. Beat the shit out of someone for them. Several of his closest acquaintances—I don't think he has any friends— said under oath at our trial that Adamson shouldn't be believed under any circumstances. Yet that cop, Sellers, and the assistant a.g., Schafer, bet our lives on his word, and won."

"How did Adamson obtain stolen merchandise?"

"Boosters."

"What do you mean?"

"He had connections with big-time shoplifters in San Diego. One was called San Diego Ralph, and of course Adamson had ties with the Mob."

Mafia. Emprise. Adamson. Bolles's last words. I had just stepped into the investigation, on a trail almost two and a half years cold, but already those three names loomed ever more prominent. I became silent, eyes downcast, and Robison must have thought his new investigator had turned catatonic.

But I needed to get my thoughts together. What with all my reading of last night and today, and interviewing both alleged co-conspirators, too much was coming at me too quickly. I flashed back to the accounts I'd read and heard of concerning those days immediately following Bolles's death, recalling the futile efforts to solve the case.

The police knew Adamson had not acted alone; he'd had no motive and no technical expertise. After several months thrashing about, and a suspiciously channeled investigation (everything focusing on Roberts's theory and the hope of Adamson plea bargaining—why no close look at Bradley Funk?), Jon Sellers was no closer to the answers of "who" and "why" than he'd been on the day the bomb exploded.

Pressure from the public, politicians, and media mounted as time dragged by. Because of the Bolles killing, CBS's "Sixty Minutes" cast an unwelcome eye on wheeling/dealing Arizona. Where were those additional promised arrests? Perhaps fearing what a real investigation might reveal, the state waited for Adamson to accept its generous offer.

Gone were the final words of the murdered reporter. Forgotten were those critical clues, replaced by the clever "evidence" of con artist John Harvey Adamson.

The Schafer-Sellers position couldn't be condoned, even with the best possible face put on it: they feared, without the testimony of Adamson—who insisted on implicating Robison and Dunlap—that the case could not be solved. Worse, Schafer and Sellers needed no foresight to realize, once they'd embraced the hoodlum's version, that they were stuck with it forever.

I had to caution myself to avoid forming my own theories too soon. It wasn't my role to play prosecution or police. Still, the short time I'd spent with that unappetizing mound of discovery material had convinced me that the stampede to accept Adamson's plea bargain covered with a cloud of dust all leads not connecting Dunlap and Robison to the crime. Somehow, I had to bring the case back to Bolles's last words: *Mafia, Emprise, Adamson.*

"Tell me more about San Diego," I said to Robison. In the discovery material I had read the previous night, Adamson's girlfriend, Gail Owens, traveled with Adamson to San Diego and financed his purchase of the remote-control device used to trigger the bomb. Gail Owens, who stored the dynamite and detonator in her apartment, had received immunity from the prosecution, despite her full knowledge of Adamson's intentions to kill Bolles.

"Adamson knew a guy in San Diego called Frank," Robison said. "He was killed in a phone booth."

"Frank Bompensiero?" A major San Diego Mafia figure. Adamson dealt in the big time if he rubbed elbows with Bompensiero.

"That's the one."

"Who else?"

"You heard of Jimmy the Weasel?"

"Jimmy Frattiano."

"Well, Frattiano and Adamson put their heads together and came up with a drug rehab scam. That pair, believe it or not, intended to get into the drug rehabilitation business. They figured to rake in fat federal grants."

"Okay, so Adamson sold cocaine. What did he have in mind, treating the addicts he supplied?"

"That's about the size of it. Adamson told me rehab was more profitable than selling the stuff. Anyway, I've harbored a serious suspicion for quite a long time, and I'd like to lay it out. I think Frattiano played the role the police assigned to me in the Bolles killing: detonating the dynamite. He's been an FBI informant since 1970 and has received immunity for seven murders, including Danny Green in Cleveland. Green died when dynamite got set off under his car by a remote-control device, the same m.o. used to murder Bolles. You know, the police keep harping the Mob doesn't use bombs, they pump a bullet in your head and stuff you in a car trunk. That's Hollywood bullshit. The Mafia sure as hell didn't blow Danny Green and his car to bits with a bullet."

"Was Frattiano questioned?"

"Hell, no, he wasn't questioned."

"Why not? He was Adamson's business associate."

"Jon Sellers knows the answer. He headed the investigation and made that rotten immunity deal with Neal Roberts. Did you ever hear of a *cop* giving immunity?"

No, I hadn't. I also thought it unusual for Sellers, still only a detective after twenty years on the police force, to be picked to head up the most famous murder case in Arizona history.

A single thought recurred, as it would for the entire year and a half of my investigation, and I voiced it aloud to Robison. "The motive's no good—that Bolles was killed for stories he'd already written."

"It's ridiculous, and I'll tell you what. Bolles was close to something: poking around, asking questions, scaring the daylights out of somebody. The guy had a reputation for printing what he uncovered. And he was stubborn as a government mule. Couldn't be bought off or scared off. I believe someone found out he was close to a big story, and stopped it right then, no questions asked."

"What do you think Sellers overlooked, or covered up?"

"Well, the Hank Landry information, for sure."

It was what I'd been waiting for. Quickly and easily, Robison related the same basics I had just read in Sellers's police reports.

"How did Adamson and Landry get hooked up?" I asked, when Robison had finished.

"I don't know how they met. But John invited Landry to cheat in a big gin game at the Arizona Club. Neal Roberts got Adamson into the club, and Adamson brought Landry."

"Tell me about your relationship with Adamson."

"He's a sick braggart. The kind of guy who steals paintings, hides them in his basement, and is compelled to show them to someone. He needs credit for what he's done but is smart enough to choose a person who doesn't drink and can keep his mouth shut. Well, I was that guy. Adamson confided in me. He told me a lot."

"How did you meet him?"

"Through my girlfriend, Betty, who knew Adamson's wife, Mary. Adamson liked me, began to trust me, and soon told me about many of his harebrained schemes. I listened, and commented when appropriate."

I had to approach this juncture carefully. If I leaned too hard at this first meeting, I might look like a cop to Robison, who had good reason not to trust anyone. Exploration of "harebrained schemes" was tempting, but I decided not to push and said simply, "Tell me more about you and Adamson."

"He came to my house on a regular basis, or to my job at Ashford Plumbing, crowing about his latest deals and capers. John was on duty twenty-four hours a day. He lived, breathed, ate, and slept hustling."

"What do you mean?"

"For instance, he kept a police scanner next to his bed. When he heard a promising report, he hit the ground running."

"Give me a specific."

"I'll give you one he used to help frame me. When Ashford Plumbing burned down, I went over to assess the damage. Adamson was already there. He said he heard about the fire on his police band. But later, after Bolles, he claimed *we* torched that building. Of course, people saw us together at the fire, and their testimony 'proved' an ongoing criminal relationship. Then there was Tops Tavern."

"Tell me about Tops."

"Adamson knew I almost always stayed home, so he felt safe saying I went out ripping with him. Since I usually *was* alone, I had a flimsy alibi when he implicated me in one of his crimes. He said we burned down Tops Tavern, and I couldn't prove otherwise."

"Why would he implicate you in these arsons?"

"To sell the Bolles killing, by claiming we committed other crimes together. He almost messed up with Bolles."

"How's that?"

"He said I detonated the bomb he put under the car with a device like kids use to fly model airplanes. But the bombing occurred during the day, eleven-thirty-four, when I worked, and a hardware store clerk, Chris Stamps, testified I was buying a brass pipe coupling from him at eleven-fifteen in the morning. No way could I have driven all the way across town in nineteen minutes to detonate that bomb. Regardless, Adamson testified that I was with him at the Clarendon parking lot at eleven-ten."

"How did the prosecution beat the alibi?"

"They said to the hardware clerk, 'How do you know your watch wasn't five minutes fast?' Well, he couldn't know. Then the prosecution had a cop drive the distance, racing across town, flying through school zones, running red lights, a regular bat out of hell. He made it to the Clarendon Hotel with thirty seconds to spare. Phenomenal. Even with all that, though, I couldn't have been there at eleven-ten, like Adamson swore."

Robison shook his head, and I saw his fists and jaws clench. "So I guess I screeched to a stop at the Clarendon, probably sweaty and shaky, and in all of thirty seconds concealed myself in a spot that provided an unobstructed view—the device had to be pointed directly at the vehicle to explode the dynamite—and blew him up."

The condemned man had been talking quickly, agitated by the memory, but now he slowed. "So you see, both Tops and Ashford were at night, when my only alibi was being home reading a book. Bolles happened during the day. My lawyers messed up bad by not making a bigger fuss over the cop's time trial. Mario Andretti probably couldn't have beat it."

Robison had been portrayed to me as thoughtful and self-educated. That seemed accurate enough. He had lived almost as a hermit (because of his fearsome appearance?), happy with his books and himself.

His attitude toward death row confinement differed from any other I encountered: "They sentenced me to death, and I want them to carry out the order. The judge didn't mention one word about torture, yet this is it—a terrible fucking place with subhuman conditions. Dying here is preferable to living. They say they want to kill me, and they should have the guts to do it."

The interview drew to a close. "Jim," I said, "I'd like to know, did you have anything at all to do with killing Don Bolles?"

"No. Absolutely no. But remember, when Adamson asked me about metallurgy and the mechanics of plumbing, I often explained them to him. He might have used my answers to construct a bomb. I don't know. But I had nothing at all to do with the murder."

A guard knocked on the door. We had five minutes left.

"I hope you do some good," Robison said, not a trace of emotion in his voice, "but I'm afraid you're Don Quixote off on a tilt with windmills."

"Maybe not," I said.

"Anyway, I look forward to your coming back, and I certainly enjoyed this conversation. I know I'll be more helpful to you than poor Max—he's just in a state of total confusion—and there's other information I may give you. But I think you understand."

I thought so, too. He needed to trust me more before opening up completely.

. . .

On the outskirts of Florence, headed for the freeway, a red light
flashing in the rearview mirror short-circuited my afterimages of
Max and Jim. I slowly pulled to a stop on the shoulder, fumbled
out my driver's license, and walked toward an enormous red-
faced block-of-granite state trooper making like Rod Steiger of
In the Heat of the Night—mirrored sunglasses, hand on holstered
pistol.

"What did I do wrong, officer?" I asked, handing him my
license.

"What you've done wrong would make a list longer than your
arm." He returned to his car with its light flashing and initiated
a record check on the radio. A few moments later he came back
and stared down on me again. "You have any outstanding warrants?"

"No, sir, I don't."

"Well, if you do, you're going to jail."

"Yes, sir. I know the drill."

"What do you do for a living?"

"I'm an investigative journalist."

"Then why did you say at the penitentiary that you're a private investigator?"

Most cops hate people in my profession. Worse, I didn't have
an Arizona p.i. license, though I did in Nevada and California.
Getting credentials in Arizona, I figured, would mean eternal
red-tape delays by a state apparatus not eager to see the Bolles
murder rehashed. No, I hadn't yet contracted a magazine assignment for this story, but I'd done investigative pieces before, so
the title "investigative journalist" fit. The truth was I didn't want
to sit on my hands, possibly for months, waiting for the state to
decide if it wanted me investigating how it screwed up the Bolles
case.

Regardless, I had to tread gingerly with this big cop.

"A person can," I said, "be both p.i. and investigative journalist. I'm wondering. How do you know what I told them at the
joint?"

"Listen, asshole. I ask the questions. You may be a whiz in some circles, but you ain't shit on this road. I'm king out here. This is my highway, and I'll ask the fuckin' questions."

The radio crackled. "Stand where you are," he ordered and headed back to his car to see if I was a wanted man.

"Well, no warrants." He looked disappointed. "I'm not putting you in jail this time, so you can go now, Mr. Private Investigator, or Mr. Investigative Journalist, or whatever you call yourself. But I'm gonna give you some advice: we don't like people who murder reporters in this state, or the scum who work for them. Since you like those killers you just left, we'll do everything we can to see that you join them. If you're half as smart as I think you are, you'll climb in your vehicle, drive off, and never come back. If you do return, you ain't gonna like it."

4

Creating Havoc

George Vlassis lives in Encanto Park in a large, comfortable, Spanish-style house with a two-car garage full of model boats he built. He and his wife, Nancy, who was his high school sweetheart, keep a full-size pool table in the living room and have ten cats they dearly love.

George and I played both ways as guards for the Goshen High School football team, on a line featuring center Doug Weaver, now athletic director at Michigan State, and Ken LaRue, business manager for the Los Angeles Raiders. George spent summers as a gandy dancer for the New York Central Railroad, and I worked in my dad's grocery store.

We had just finished a late dinner and sat reminiscing about our Indiana childhoods. He talked about my father, many years police chief in Goshen, a strong but gentle man nicknamed Modoc, after an elephant in the Ringling Brothers Circus. His strength, legendary in Goshen, usually made physical force unnecessary: I don't think he ever had to fire his gun. As a boy, Modoc had had to forfeit his grab for the brass ring, a football scholarship to Notre Dame offered during Knute Rockne's recruitment of the legendary Four Horsemen, to work and support his mother and six siblings.

George talked about my dad; I talked about his. Peter Vlassis, an industrious Greek immigrant and a bar owner who never drank, always had an abundance of Cokes and sandwiches for George and the kids he brought around to the rear of the saloon.

I admired George and his father. The adult George, in fact, represented my idea of success. A good father and provider, he prospered by helping people. As general counsel to the Navajo Nation, he enjoyed unmatched respect from tribal members, becoming a virtual father confessor to any one of them with a problem large or small.

George helped right many wrongs inflicted upon the Navajos. He'd been instrumental in negotiating a contract with Peabody Coal—which previously paid the tribe a paltry five cents per ton for coal mined on the reservation—whereby the Indians became equal partners. A sizable chunk of the electrical power for Los Angeles came from energy generated on the massive Navajo reservation, and George secured them a cut of this income, too.

Much as I enjoyed talking to my fellow Hoosier, he, not I, was working the tight schedule that made relaxed conversation almost impossible. George knew the real purpose for my visit, and it wasn't long before he asked my first impressions of the case.

His eyebrows lifted when I told him about the Betty Funk Richardson interview with the police.

"The Funks are a wealthy and powerful family in Phoenix," George said, and certainly he stood in a position to know. A Phoenix insider, Vlassis knew as much about the city and its people as anyone. But he was also a cautious man, normally the most discreet and circumspect of individuals. George would, I believed, open up to me.

I told him I couldn't buy the motive for the murder, that Bolles was killed because of articles he wrote about Marley. "Still," I said, "Bolles's own paper said he was washed up as an investigative journalist, that they'd had to reassign him to the legislature."

"That's a false claim by the *Arizona Republic*," said George. "Bolles interviewed me not long before his death about a plane crash on the reservation, the one in which three Navajo council members died. I found Bolles rather abrasive, not someone you'd invite to dinner, but very determined and effective. When he came around asking questions, people got antsy. He kept digging and digging until he reached the truth, and there was plenty to sniff out. Lots of back-room deals."

"Like what?"

"Traditionally, land fraud. Lake, this is no exaggeration. In the last decade, land fraud has escalated to the number two industry in Arizona, second only to tourism. Remember, we're the fastest-growing state in America, and Phoenix is the fastest-growing city. We had a hundred and six thousand residents in 1950, one point two million now, all flocking to the Grand Canyon State for its great climate and natural beauty. But some of it isn't so appealing. More would-be homesteaders have been saddled with worthless Arizona desert than with Florida swampland."

"What about politics? If Robison and Dunlap are innocent, politics must have had something to do with putting them away."

"The good-old-boy system originated in Arizona, which in many ways is still part of the frontier. We have the laxest gun laws in the country, restricted only by a requirement that you *don't* conceal your weapon. As for political power, it's wielded by Barry Goldwater and a half-dozen families, not the least of them the Funks."

"Tell me about Goldwater."

"He's from an old-line family himself, as are the others who run the show here. From personal experience I can assure you Goldwater doesn't like Peter MacDonald [the Navajo chairman]. That's why I'm sure the *Arizona Republic* had it wrong about Bolles, because I know he worked on Navajo stories right up to the time of the bombing."

"Who should I see about that?"

"Claude Keller. He's a lawyer I've done a few favors for, including putting him to work for the Navajos when nobody wanted to give him a job. Coincidentally, Keller moved into Neal Roberts's office a few days before Bolles got bombed."

Now I recalled. It came from a police report, dated June 24, 1977, which I had read.

According to the report, Claude Keller said he had seen Joe Patrick visiting with Neal Roberts on several occasions. Keller also said he sat in on a meeting between Patrick, Harry Noy, and Neal Roberts some time in May 1976, and at that time Patrick was involved in an anti-MacDonald campaign on the Navajo reservation, which he was doing for a politician. Keller told the investigator he wasn't sure, but he believed Patrick was working for Barry Goldwater. Roberts himself told Keller that he had frequent conversations with Senator Goldwater.

"You should also talk to Keller about Neal Roberts," Vlassis continued, as if reading my mind. "And about how Roberts and Goldwater wanted MacDonald replaced as tribal chairman."

I asked him to tell me what he knew about Roberts and Goldwater.

"Goldwater considers himself a friend to the Navajos, and he's sold himself to Senate colleagues as the top expert in the country on Indian affairs. He's not close, not by a long shot, but he sincerely believes he is. Anyway, a long time ago, Goldwater invited MacDonald to a social affair the senator considered important, and MacDonald didn't show. Goldwater openly proclaimed this an affront—you come, no questions asked, when an old-line Arizonan summons—but a more weighty reason for his animosity is that MacDonald is a man he can't control. There's uranium, coal, oil, and gold on the Navajo reservation, a vast fortune. Goldwater planned to replace MacDonald with a person named Tony Lincoln, and his first step was to insinuate an old air force buddy of his, Joe Patrick, onto the reservation as an advisor, in reality a spy. You'll want to interview Patrick, and I can help you with him. But don't forget, Neal Roberts is part of this whole effort. And Adamson."

"How's that?"

"Roberts wanted my job. As you know, not much happens on the reservation that I don't hear about. I've made a lot of friends these last fourteen years, and a few enemies. The Navajos come to me with every conceivable problem, from financing a car to getting their kids into college, and I try to help them. I knew about the plot to oust MacDonald long before Bolles got killed, and so, I think, did Bolles. Roberts had arranged for Adamson to create havoc on the Navajo reservation. If Roberts and Adamson succeeded, Goldwater could say Mac-Donald had lost control of his people and arrange to replace him with Tony Lincoln. Lincoln intended to appoint Roberts to the post of general counsel, my job, enabling Goldwater's big business friends to cut sweeter deals for the Navajos' natural resources."

"And you think Bolles knew about this?"

"He either knew, or was in a position to find out. After the plane crash, Bolles interviewed me, Claude Keller, and Joe Patrick, plus a lot of people on the reservation. If Bolles prowled the vicinity of a story, he got it. He was a real badger."

"What did you mean about Adamson 'creating havoc'?"

"Those were Adamson's words, printed in the *Arizona Republic*. Roberts planned to send Adamson onto the reservation to blow up some things, including MacDonald's car, and the campaign began with the attempted dynamiting of the Indian Health Services building."

This failed bombing in Phoenix, one of many crimes for which Adamson received immunity, resulted in convictions for Robison (as in the later Bolles murder, fingered by Adamson because of his knowledge of explosives) and Roberts based solely on the con man's testimony. The convictions were later reversed.

"That building," I said. "How does it connect with the reservation?"

"There's a common misconception that the Navajos own the Indian Health Services building. In fact, Roberts partially owned it. If the bombing succeeded, it would work two ways: Roberts would collect the insurance, and the Navajos would receive the heat. Creating havoc also meant inciting civil disorder to make it appear MacDonald had lost control."

"How did you find out all this?"

"Shortly before the Bolles bombing, Roberts met in his office with Adamson, Tony Lincoln, and half-a-dozen tribal council-men to discuss the plan." George smiled. "One of them is a good friend of mine."

"What happened to the plan?"

"Adamson chickened out. He didn't like the idea of driv-ing around the reservation with dynamite in his car. Too risky, he said. So they chose the Indian Health Services building in Phoenix."

Back in my room at the Westward Ho Hotel, I returned to my treasure trove of discovery documents and found another gold nugget: the police report of an interview with Mary Adamson, the killer's wife, conducted shortly after the bombing. Mary told the police she didn't know where her husband was but sug-gested they "look for him at the Apache Junction dog track, because he works for Emprise." She would later deny making the statement, but the police officer, Harry Hawkins, said he was quite sure he had heard correctly.

Before calling it quits at the end of a long day, I also skimmed through a book George Vlassis gave me just before I left his house—*The Arizona Project: How a Team of Investigative Re-porters Got Revenge on Deadline*, by Michael F. Wendland, pub-lished in 1977. Wendland had been one of the so-called IRE team, the letters standing for Independent Reporters and Edi-tors. Headed by Bob Greene, a two-time Pulitzer Prize–winner from the Long Island newspaper *Newsday*, this crew of thirty-six, professing shock at the murder of a comrade, came to Ari-zona with two goals.

> First, the team attempted to pay tribute to a slain col-league by finishing what he had started, by getting to the heart of the political corruption and organized crime in Arizona that had made Bolles's killers believe that murder was a logical response to a reporter's work. Second, by clearly demonstrating the solidarity of the American press, the team effort would reemphasize the old underworld

adage: "You don't kill a reporter because it brings too much heat."

Wendland ends *The Arizona Project* with the convictions of Robison and Dunlap, and the words: "The media had done their job. Arizona's ills had been exposed, and justice, though not yet complete, was slowly being done. It was the future that was the story now."

Done their job? I wanted to vomit. Their self-proclaimed job involved finishing what Bolles started. How could they possibly accomplish this when they bought the *Arizona Republic's* line that Bolles wasn't doing anything of merit? How can you finish a job when you don't know what it is?

In the course of doing *my* job, I would investigate these investigators and become increasingly disgusted as I learned that many members of the IRE team spent much of their time playing celebrity, claiming to be knights on white horses, and getting drunk and boasting to other patrons of the Adams Hotel bar. Of course much worse was the team's decision, right from the start, to leave the question of *who* killed Don Bolles up to the police. That subtitle of Wendland's book about getting revenge made me feel like laughing and crying at the same time.

I had breakfast the next morning with Claude Keller at the Gaslight Restaurant. A tall, heavyset man, the crusty Keller said he would be happy to cooperate with any friend of George Vlassis. Keller had worked in Roberts's office right up to the time of the bombing.

"Neal," said Keller, "had this redheaded English secretary, Eileen Roberts—no relation—who got Barry Goldwater on the phone. After Roberts talked to him, I heard him tell Eileen that Goldwater asked, 'How much is this going to cost me?'"

"What tie did Goldwater have with Roberts?" I asked Keller.

"The Navajo reservation. It stuck in Goldwater's craw that MacDonald, through George Vlassis, had a strong hand in Indian business deals with big corporations. They waged an ongoing war with Peabody Coal to increase the Navajo share, and Goldwater took static from the Peabody bosses."

"Is any of this—what was going on between Goldwater and Roberts—a matter of general knowledge?"

He smiled. "Depends on what you mean by 'general knowledge.' Hell, publicly Goldwater and Roberts deny even knowing each other. But there's one thing I'm sure of. Don Bolles was following the story very closely."

"The *Arizona Republic* says Bolles only covered the legislature."

"Nonsense. I knew Don. He wouldn't have accepted that humiliating beat without something on the back burner. He was hopelessly addicted to investigative reporting. I know he did articles for the *Gallup Independent,* a paper in New Mexico. Why don't you give their editorial office a call?"

Leaving my car in a handy loading zone—which provided me not only with quick access to the Westward Ho but also a total of sixty parking tickets during the investigation—I phoned New Mexico and reached John Zollinger, publisher of the *Gallup Independent.*

"Mr. Zollinger, my name is Lake Headley, and I'm looking into the Bolles murder for the Max Dunlap Committee for Justice. I'd like—"

"Another investigator? Won't that thing ever go away?"

"If I do my job right, maybe we can put it to rest. That's why I'm calling."

"What can I do for you?"

"I've been told your newspaper ran stories by Don Bolles about the Navajo reservation almost up to the time of his death."

"Yes, we did."

"What was his capacity?"

"Free-lance journalist. He sent us good copy."

"Did the *Arizona Republic* know Bolles was writing for you?"

Zollinger became huffy, as if I had accused him of violating Fourth Estate ethics. "What kind of operation do you think we run here? Of course the *Republic* knew. I called his editor and received an okay. I can tell you, also, that Bolles was stringing for *Newsweek*."

"The national magazine?"

"The same. Bolles was a good journalist."

Newsweek. An exposé in that media powerhouse could plant fear in anyone.

"What did he do for *Newsweek*?" I asked Zollinger.

"I don't know, but I'm sure the *Republic* could tell you. Bolles wouldn't keep secrets from them. He was the most upfront person I ever knew, nothing devious about him."

I thanked Zollinger, said good-bye, and released the phone receiver from an ever-tightening grip.

There it was! Right out in the open. A revelation that left me more angry than satisfied. I grew hot thinking about the ridiculously weak bill of goods the police had sold as Kemper Marley's motive, and the *Arizona Republic*'s deliberate evasiveness about a reporter who gave that newspaper fourteen years of his life. Oops, I thought, glimpsing *The Arizona Project* on my night table, and let's not fail to stuff the IRE into this mental punching bag.

Before returning to the parking ticket downstairs, I cooled off and made calls to Dunlap Committee members more familiar than I with the overall scope of the case.

What I learned from them placed the *Arizona Republic* in an even more shadowy light: Bolles had written stories on Emprise, on the Funk family, and particularly on Bradley Funk, linking him to organized-crime control of Arizona dog tracks. Funk had sued, and as part of the lawsuit settlement, the *Republic*—which up to then had backed Bolles's well-documented stories— promised to take its star reporter off the investigation of the Funk/Emprise racing empire.

But Bolles didn't stop, I learned in going back over the discovery papers. His widow, Rosalie, told the police that right up to the time of the bombing he pursued "the involvement of the Funk family into organized crime." She and Don, Rosalie said, "were greatly concerned" about the Funk investigation. Said the

police report: "Mrs. Bolles explained that this particular investigation was a continuous one for her husband, and since the
investigation started, they have received numerous threatening
phone calls."

In just a few days I had uncovered concrete inconsistencies
that cried for further investigation, but the information didn't
help if it remained locked in my head. I had to relay it to the
public, and to do that I needed an ally in the media.

I could forget the *Arizona Republic* and *Phoenix Gazette*,
the area's major papers, both hostile from the beginning to Dunlap and Robison, but Dunlap Committee members had mentioned the *Scottsdale Daily Progress* and its publisher, Jonathan
Marshall, as potentially receptive to new revelations on the Bolles
case.

The more I thought about the Scottsdale paper, the more
ideal it seemed. It served a rich, influential community, and its
circulation extended to Paradise Valley, home of Barry Goldwater. I suspected the *Progress* also had readers on the Arizona
Supreme Court, now considering the appeals.

Committee members provided some background on Marshall. He came from a wealthy eastern family, with an industri-
alist father and a progressive mother with outspoken ecological
views. The elder Marshall may have assessed his son as less than
a shrewd financier, but Jonathan had exhibited an aptitude for
journalism, so the family bought the *Progress* for him. Possessing
a bit of his father's business acumen, combined with his mother's feisty outlook, Jonathan Marshall had done a good job with
the newspaper.

"Mr. Marshall," I said after introductions, sitting across from
him at his working desk, "the Dunlap Committee is firmly convinced Max Dunlap had nothing to do with killing Don Bolles.
I've interviewed Robison and Dunlap, and I have doubts about
the guilt of either man."

"What makes you say that? I've followed the case from its
inception, and I believe Robison is guilty, though I admit grave

reservations concerning Dunlap. The prosecution withheld evidence, I believe, specifically a statement from that secretary—Eileen Roberts—about her boss Neal Roberts raising money for Adamson's defense. Also that one-legged gambler. And James McVay."

Clearly, Marshall had done his homework. "Who is James McVay?" I asked.

"You haven't come across him yet? McVay was in the Maricopa County jail with Adamson, after the arrest but before that disgraceful plea bargain. McVay said Adamson told him he was going to frame Dunlap. There's no question the entire story of this murder hasn't come out."

"I agree."

I intended to agree with Marshall about a lot of things, and to that end I needed to size him up rather quickly. Medium height, slender, balding, with his glasses askew in typical preoccupied professorial fashion, I judged him to be a practical intellectual, someone to whom a combination of reason, a cause, *and* potential profit would prove irresistible.

The bottom line: Dunlap and Robison needed fair, nonbiased press attention. If I started out challenging Marshall's belief that the police did a thorough job, I could close a door I needed kept open. But I felt on safe ground shoveling dirt on rival newspapers. I approached the subject obliquely. "Let me say this, Mr. Marshall. The motive doesn't make sense, that Bolles got hit for previously written articles. I think he'd more likely be killed to stop a story."

"What story? He covered the state legislature, hardly a beat brimming with cloak-and-dagger material."

"That wasn't all he worked on." I looked at Marshall, waited for him to bite.

"What do you mean? The *Arizona Republic* said he was strictly state legislature."

"That may be true for the *Republic,* but he didn't work solely for them."

"What are you talking about?"

"I called John Zollinger at the *Gallup Independent,* and Bolles free-lanced for him on Navajo stories. He was also stringing for *Newsweek* magazine."

"You sure about this?"

"Yes."

Marshall leaned back and thought. I waited. "I'm sure the *Republic* didn't know about this," he finally said.

"Wrong, Mr. Marshall. They knew. Zollinger talked with Bolles's editor at the *Republic*. Zollinger was very sensitive about this point."

Marshall let this perk. "Well, that means ... geesus, that means the *Arizona Republic* lied."

Bingo.

"Why would the newspaper lie?" he asked, more to himself than me.

"I don't know the *Republic*'s reason, but this is just one of several things I've stumbled onto that I want to share with you." With which I opened my little can of worms.

Some of them he already knew. I told him about the Betty Funk Richardson interview with Detective Marcus Aurelius; here was a real motive, I emphasized, unlike the Kemper Marley story. I told him about Rosalie Bolles's concern about the ongoing investigation of Bradley Funk; Neal Roberts's "loud and clear" remark uttered several days before Bolles got bombed; and that the reporter might have been digging into the Navajo reservation story involving Roberts, Adamson, and possibly Barry Goldwater. I could have told him more, but he interrupted to show his business side.

"Lake," he said, "I don't have time to retry the murder in this office. Frankly, I'm only interested in one thing."

"What's that?"

"As you probably realize, no one has ever interviewed James Robison. We got a scoop of sorts interviewing Dunlap, and I must say the man impressed me. So do his friends, the people who call me and assert his innocence. But Robison—nobody has talked to Robison. You claim you have access to him. Well, if you can arrange an interview, we might take a fresh look. Remember, Phoenix has been inundated with Bolles stories. People are sick of them. But something new—an interview with the silent man, Robison—could be good for us."

I suspected Marshall played a hard-to-get game, and I should return in kind. "That's a pretty tall order, Mr. Marshall," I said.

Actually, I figured it would be no sweat. Robison and Dunlap needed fair press coverage, and the *Scottsdale Daily Progress* fit the bill perfectly. By making an exclusive with Robison seem difficult to arrange, I might put Marshall in my debt. "I'll sure give it a try," I said, certain that Robison, if for no reason other than self-interest, would agree.

But it turned out not so easy. Robison also had a demand: a guarantee of accurate quotes.

Wonderful, I thought. How can I control what someone else writes?

Ultimately, my own promise to be present all through the interview, plus the *Progress*'s assurance that their piece would stick strictly to the truth (What else would any newspaper say?) persuaded the prisoner to proceed.

"Robison's agreed to the interview," I said, back in the newspaper office a few days later. Marshall wore a tie—he always wore a tie—in combination with a tweed sport coat.

"You sure? I guess you are."

"That's what you wanted. Will you conduct the interview?"

"No. I'll send a reporter named Don Devereux. He's an expert on the Bolles case. Don was a member of the IRE team. You'll like him."

Marshall turned out to be correct, and then some, though at the time I couldn't imagine liking *anyone* who had been on the IRE team.

"I'll have to accompany him to Florence," I said. "They won't let him in without me."

"Okay. I think Devereux is here now. Let me get you two together."

In his late thirties, slender, light brown hair with a graying beard, Devereux turned out to be one of the heroes of the Bolles

investigation. And his wife, Naomi—a brilliant, good-looking, extremely well-educated lady who concocted crossword puzzles for
The New York Times—would also play a key role in our murder
inquiry.

Don Devereux, I would learn, was a true investigative journalist, one of the best. He'd left his job at a Santa Fe paper to
join the IRE team, outraged by the murder of Bolles. Extremely
idealistic, his specialty had been uncovering the disgraceful conditions endured by migrant laborers in the Southwest.

Quiet, though with a fire burning inside, especially when relating the plight of *braceros,* Devereux didn't smoke or drink, and
his devotion to Naomi and their four children was total. Obtaining riches didn't appear anywhere on the list of Don's priorities,
and he possessed the admirable qualities of rigid honesty, integrity, and a workaholic's total attention to detail. During the
course of our long relationship, he made me think that if Don
Bolles could be said to have a successor in Arizona, he was
named Don Devereux.

5

Three Stolen
Vehicles

"I know you're working for Dunlap and Robison," Devereux said, "so I think it's fair to tell you I believe this case is largely resolved. I think Robison did it, and maybe Dunlap, and it's my opinion the police did a thorough job under the circumstances."

I had picked up Devereux at the entrance to the modern stucco building where the *Scottsdale Daily Progress* was written and printed, and now I wheeled onto I-10 for the drive to Florence.

"When I came to Phoenix to work with the IRE team," Devereux continued, "Bob Greene told both the police and us that he didn't intend for us to stick our noses into the homicide itself—the cops were qualified, we weren't. We were there to demonstrate that killing a reporter didn't stop his work."

Bob Greene wasn't sitting in the car with me, so I aimed my favorite question at Devereux: "How could you continue his work if you didn't know what it was?"

"Greene went to the *Arizona Republic* and found out what Bolles did before being transferred to the legislature."

"What was that?"

"Migrant farm workers, my field. Land fraud. The dog track business. Items that were his staples, what he worked on in the past."

"And that's what the team concentrated on?"

"Yeah. We went through the motions, I guess you could say."

Not Devereux, I would learn, and even now I admired his use of the word *we*.

"I haven't learned many good things about the IRE team," I said.

Devereux winced. "I suppose some of the editors and reporters used the time in Phoenix as a vacation. If we served a purpose, it was as a show of force."

"What did you do?"

"My specialty. The migrant farm labor situation. Barry Goldwater's brother, Bob, is one of the big exploiters of Mexican workers. Anyway, there's plenty to accomplish in the area, and I'm doing what I can. Those people are not only underpaid and overworked, they're forced to live like animals."

"You getting anywhere?"

"It's uphill. The ones running the show don't want change. Some of them profit from the status quo. I just wish the public could see for itself."

"You came here from New Mexico?"

"Yeah. I stayed in Phoenix when the IRE team left. I divide my time between the *Progress* and the farm labor union in Glendale."

"What do you do for the union?" Conversation helped pass the time, and I was measuring him for a very serious proposal.

"Some organizing. I help with legal affairs. I've arranged an attorney for the union. Victor Aranow. Maybe you know him."

"I do, and I like him." Although my history with Native Americans didn't date back as far as George Vlassis's, it was considerable, and I tried to keep updated. I switched the subject. "Are you working on the Bolles case for the *Daily Progress*?"

"We haven't done a lot. Most people in Phoenix consider it over."

"What if the supreme court overturns the convictions?"

"Are you kidding? In this state? In this political climate? The supreme court's not going to overturn them."

"Well, that's my goal. That's why the committee hired me, and why we're going to Florence."

• • •

The *Scottsdale Daily Progress* article about this first Robison interview—the paper also ran a second story—began as follows:

> James Robison looks like an arch criminal in a cartoon
> strip. He is short and heavy set, with muscular arms, a
> bull neck and a deep scar over one eye. He gives an initial
> impression of being a sullen man. . . . When Robison spoke
> and became relaxed, it was apparent that first impressions
> are deceiving. Instead of the crude, oafish character we
> had expected, we found a well-read, self-educated and ar-
> ticulate man with an excellent vocabulary and a sense of
> humor.

Devereux's interview with Robison started a drumbeat of press
coverage that couldn't possibly hurt the defendants, I figured.
And it might help them. True, Marshall's *Progress* stood alone
in Arizona, but as Laurie Dunlap, one of Max's daughters, told
me rather poetically, after reading seemingly endless negative stories about her father: "In the land of darkness, you lit a candle."

During the interview Robison rehashed for Devereux pretty
much the same things he told me. He used a lot of the time not
to defend himself, but Dunlap. He asked, rhetorically, why it
took eight days for that damaging $5,800 to be delivered to
Adamson. "I think," he said, "Roberts had to wait for the money
to come from San Diego. With plenty of money at the time he
could easily have got it from his bank. He didn't have to wait
eight days."

Robison pointed out that, despite the most massive investigation in Arizona history, *none* of Adamson's allegations about
his involvement had ever been corroborated. He called Adamson's Fifth Amendment cop outs "outrageous" and said the con
man had lied when he stated Robison did demolition work in
the navy. "The FBI said it couldn't find my navy records to
verify or refute Adamson's claim. I never did demolition work.
All I used was a typewriter."

After the interview, the *Progress* called Assistant Attorney General William Schafer to ask if the Bolles murder case remained open. Schafer replied affirmatively. Without offering a time frame, Schafer said he expected additional indictments. It was the same thing he'd been saying since the case began.

"Robison's an interesting guy," Devereux said when we were back in the car headed to Phoenix. "Nothing like I'd been led to believe. Still, and I know you won't like this, I think he did it. The police couldn't be that far wrong."

"Don, let's do this. When we get to Phoenix, we'll have something to eat, then go to my 'office' at Westward Ho. I've found some police reports plus other information I'd like you to take a look at. I think it might change your mind."

It was time for the proposal I'd been considering. "Here's what I'll do, Don," I said, "and I mean every word: If you look at the material, and still feel the way you do, I'll forget this case, pack up, and leave Phoenix."

"I'll be damned," Devereux said, putting aside another sheaf of papers. He had been sitting on the bed for hours, surrounded by paper, and this, if I maintained an accurate count, was his fourth "I'll be damned."

It had to be the information I'd recently uncovered about Neal Roberts. Enlightening as the discovery had been, I suspected the Phoenix police hadn't provided everything, so I had called a police officer friend of mine in Los Angeles and asked him to run a computer check of Neal Roberts. Roberts, along with Bradley Funk, deserved the closest scrutiny, and in that spirit I had asked my friend for a favor.

"Three vehicles," Devereux said, shaking his head in disbelief. "My God."

On the day of the bombing, Roberts had reported three vehicles that he owned stolen from his office parking lot.

"What do you think the odds are," I asked, "against two cars and a pickup truck being stolen from one guy in one day? In a classy neighborhood? On the day he's a hot suspect in a major bombing?" I was wound up. "I don't think something like this has happened in the history of the world. Three vehicles? On—"

"—the day Bolles was hit," Devereux completed.

He began to pace the room. "What do you think this is all about?" he asked.

"Let's start with the Cadillac. Adamson told Robison— remember, Adamson called him a few days after the bombing— he took that car and headed for Havasu, where Roberts had made reservations for him at the Rodeway Inn. The trip was rushed, because one big thing went wrong: Bolles didn't die right away. He lived, and he was talking, and surely he named Adamson. So Adamson and his wife, Mary, were making a quick getaway, but the Cadillac overheated. They caught a ride back to Phoenix, and I believe Adamson screamed bloody murder at Roberts about the car. Roberts feared Adamson, with good reason, and to placate him he chartered a plane to Havasu." I took a breath. "That accounts for the first vehicle. Of course, Robison's story is corroborated by where the Cadillac was found: I-10 in the direction of Havasu."

"What about the pickup?"

"Vehicle number two. The cops recovered it at Sky Harbor Airport. Check the color of that pickup: green and white. Witnesses at the bombing scene recall seeing a green and white pickup, never located by the police. Obviously, whoever took that pickup caught a plane and got out of town."

"And the Chrysler?"

"Vehicle number three. Never found. Maybe it ended up in San Diego. Or was abandoned in the desert. I can't put a fix on that car, but I can on the pickup and the Cadillac. They were getaway vehicles. Probably not in the original plan, but Bolles's living changed the entire scenario, to the point Roberts got left with his absurd multiple robbery story. I suspect all three people involved in the bombing returned to Roberts's office. We know from later statements to Sellers that Roberts believed he was under almost immediate surveillance. He would want to get those three people out of town. He—"

"What do you mean, three people? I've always thought there

were two. Adamson, to plant the bomb; Robison, or whoever, to detonate it."

"Don," I said, "I'll give you a theory. Remember, it's just a theory, but I'll want immunity even if it's dead wrong."

We both laughed at my parody, though it wasn't funny, not under the circumstances: Roberts walking away a free man.

"Go ahead," Devereux said.

"I think a daylight bombing in a crowded metropolitan area, with a number of potential witnesses around, is too risky for just two."

"I don't see that. You need number one: someone to plant the bomb; and number two, someone to trigger it."

"I labeled this a theory. But all my experience, everything I've learned, makes me believe a third person was involved."

"For what purpose?"

"A lookout, what burglars call a point man. The one team member who is absolutely clean. Adamson has to plant the bomb, and the second person carries the detonator. But this third individual has nothing. He can just sit there, maybe in that green and white pickup. If the police show up unexpectedly, or witnesses interfere, the point man distracts them so the others can escape. This man has to resort to any tactic necessary to take attention away from the other two. If a patrol car happened by, he might have to ram it."

"If he had a vehicle."

"He had to have one. Adamson was well known to the police and couldn't risk being seen as he strolled over to the Clarendon Hotel carrying a bomb under his arm, or when he attached the dynamite to the car's underside. The third individual—there to intervene if anyone ambled by—also served as wheelman to get the others away from the scene. Imagine what these killers faced shortly after the bombing. They were desperate when Bolles survived the blast. Surely he pointed out that Adamson lured him to the Clarendon. It's not difficult to picture these three hard cases telling Neal Roberts, 'Get us the hell out of here, asshole,' and Roberts replying, 'Take my cars.' Don," I concluded, "if there weren't three people, there should have been."

Devereux said nothing, apparently lost in thought. I fished out the police reports quoting Hank Landry as saying he drove with Adamson to the *Arizona Republic* building, and Adamson asked a guard where Bolles parked his car (Landry's motive for cooperation: after passing a police-administered polygraph examination, he received immunity for thirty felonies, including his witnessing, but not reporting, the "loud and clear" remark). Landry said he and Adamson also went to a Datsun dealership where Adamson crawled underneath a car identical to the one Bolles drove and studied where to plant the bomb. In addition, they drove to the state legislature to look for the reporter's vehicle.

Devereux had become almost eerily quiet. Pensive.

"Well, Don," I said, "you now know everything I know. Should I pack my clothes?"

"Lake, I'm not convinced Max and Jim are totally innocent, but I am convinced something is terribly wrong here. Let's you and me take a very close look at this."

And what a look we did take.

Though I couldn't have known it at the time, the investigative team that became such an irritant to authorities in Arizona was almost complete. It consisted of Devereux, his wife, Naomi, myself, and a young, attractive woman about to come into my life.

Research ranks as one of the most boring facets of any investigation—especially when you have an important new witness, as I did, to interview—yet meticulous information-gathering is critical. Although I could let my fingers do the walking, research never counted as a favorite of mine. I'd much rather be face-to-face with John Harvey Adamson, trying to squeeze the truth out of him about the Bolles murder, than wading through a back-issue search of magazine and newspaper stories about Bradley Funk and the Emprise connection.

It was early December 1978 when I sat in the Phoenix Public Library, having already made a paper mountain that towered above the discovery foothill.

I was tired, the hour was late, my eyes hurt and burned. The

Bolles case consumed me, kept me plugging, but this night I was exhausted. My head bent forward and my eyes drooped shut; I dreamed of the fiery explosion and a dying reporter screaming and . . .

"Excuse me. Are you okay?"

I felt a hand on my shoulder gently shaking me awake. Looking up, I saw concerned brown eyes pouring compassion from a lovely face.

"You look very tired," she said. "Maybe you need a cup of coffee."

"I'll say, but I hate to drink alone. Will you join me?"

"Would you rather have something stronger?"

"No alcohol. That coffee sounds great."

"There's a place across the street."

Her name was Terri Lee Yoder, age twenty-five (far too young for me, I mused sadly), and after a brief marriage, she was currently putting herself through Phoenix City College—majoring in photography—by working five nights a week as a bartender. Luckily for me, she had come to the library on this night off to research film speed and developing techniques.

I learned Terri was not only pretty—almost statuesque, lovely features—but razor sharp mentally. A native Phoenician, familiar with the town and its people, she was well-read and informed. Good looking, intelligent, a nice person. I considered it a real coup when I left the restaurant with her phone number and the okay to call.

Over coffee I told Terri a bit about the Bolles investigation. She said she always had been intrigued by private investigators, the work they did, the way they lived. She called it a fascination, and offered to help if I needed anything done.

Why not? I didn't have much hope she could provide assistance (which proved a remarkably bad judgment), but I said she could try. Devereux had mentioned stories Bolles wrote about Bradley Funk and Emprise, and I'd been planning to find them. Would Terri be interested in doing that?

She would.

I had that witness to see, and told her I'd call in a few days.

6

''My People Don't
Give Immunity''

I sat in the county jail making small talk with a Texas Ranger until guards brought James McVay to the visiting room. The trip to this Texas town of eighty thousand (considered "expenses," not paid for by the committee) constituted a shot in the dark.

I'd obtained McVay's name from the first meeting with Jonathan Marshall, who'd done some reading of police reports himself. McVay had been a trusty at the Maricopa County jail during the six-plus months between Adamson's arrest and confession. His assignment—pushing the feeding cart—guaranteed daily contact with Adamson, who only infrequently left his isolation cell for exercise and court appearances.

Adamson, uptight and paranoid during those six months (to save his skin he needed to hone a convincing story without telling the truth), early on struck up the only friendship he made at the Maricopa facility: McVay. McVay became the one person Adamson allowed to bring his meals; he refused to eat if another trusty served the food. To humor the murderer, jailers acquiesced, hoping for a confession and naming of accomplices. It seemed instructive that the accuser of Dunlap and Robison feared being poisoned or otherwise killed by *every individual, except James McVay*, with whom direct contact might be required.

McVay, in the mode of all snitches, capitalized on Adamson's trust to relay the information he received to the police. Adamson told McVay he had been offered a reduced sentence, intended to grab it, but found himself in a quandary because, to receive immunity, he needed to name his accomplices.

"I don't see a problem, John," McVay responded. "Take the immunity and give them your accomplices."

"You don't understand," Adamson replied. "I can't do that. My people don't give immunity."

What "people don't give immunity?" Dunlap, Robison, and Marley? Or the Mafia?

I didn't trust the police to include everything McVay told them in the report, and thus the trip to Laredo. Helpful to Dunlap and Robison as I believed the "My people don't give immunity" crack to be, there might be more.

Tracking McVay down had finally required another favor from my Los Angeles police officer friend with access to the computer. After release from the Maricopa County jail, McVay journeyed to Ohio and got busted for burglary. He escaped from custody and was picked up as a fugitive in Laredo, where he awaited extradition.

"James," I said to McVay as we sat alone in the visitor's room, "I've come here from Phoenix to talk to you about John Adamson."

"You working for Dunlap and Robison, the two guys convicted for offing that reporter?"

"Yes. And the deeper I dig, the less sure I am of their guilt."

"Well, I'll tell you anything I know. I should be able to help. I have a large personal interest in this." McVay seemed nervous; his eyes darted about to detect listeners.

"What personal interest?"

"Jon Sellers tried to kill me, you know."

No, I didn't know.

"It was here in Laredo."

"Why would Sellers want to kill you?"

"What else? The information Adamson gave me about the Bolles murder. There had to be big powerful names involved in that."

"What happened with Sellers?"

"He tried to shoot me a couple weeks ago. I was coming out of a liquor store and saw him standing by a parked car."

"Did you talk to him?"

"Fuck, no. I was a fugitive. I'm not talking to no cop who knows me. I made a left turn, started to walk away, like I hadn't seen him, and he yelled, 'McVay! Freeze!' "

"You sure it was Sellers?"

"I saw Sellers's mug almost every day for six months, all the times he came to visit Adamson. Fuck yes, it was Sellers. When he yelled 'Freeze!' I started running, and I heard a gunshot. I glanced over my shoulder and saw him stretching across the hood of the car holding his pistol in both hands. I really started haulin' tail out of there. I heard another shot, ducked into an alley, up a fire escape, and onto the roof of a building. I got away from him, but Jesus, he really wanted my ass."

"What did you do then?"

"I went to my hotel room, picked up the few things I own, and moved."

"Why didn't you leave town?"

"Not enough money. I called my mother in Ohio to wire bread so I could get away from that crazy son of a bitch. I was busted picking it up at Western Union."

"Who busted you?"

"The Rangers."

"How do you think they found you?"

"Sellers, I guess. Maybe he had a flag on me at Western Union. How did *you* find me?"

"A records check through Los Angeles."

I finally brought the conversation with the frightened convict around to his relationship with Adamson during the months in the Maricopa County jail.

To the "My people don't give immunity" line, McVay added that Adamson said he intended to "frame Dunlap" as part of a scenario "his people" found acceptable.

"He said 'frame Dunlap'?"

"Yes."

"Did he mention Jim Robison?"

"No. I didn't hear anything about Robison."

I found it interesting that Roberts's theory, printed in the *Arizona Republic*, hadn't mentioned Robison's name.

"Will you take a polygraph regarding what you told me?" I asked.

"Absolutely."

But McVay didn't, though I never stopped pushing for it, and he remained willing, even eager. The reason: he was always in custody, and the needed permission couldn't be obtained from authorities. Still, I hadn't seen the last of James McVay.

Confronted with McVay's accusation that Sellers tried to kill him, the detective replied, "If I'd shot at James McVay, I'd have hit James McVay."

7

Going Public

Some thirty reporters, radio and TV newsmen, and cameramen representing the local media, plus a small contingent from papers in New Mexico, gathered December 19 at the Phoenix Press Club when I went public with my findings in the Bolles case.

Max's family was there, as well as committee members, and, I suspected, several Phoenix undercover cops.

I considered this press conference an important part of my job. Indeed, a major reason the Dunlap Committee had retained me was to obtain media coverage. Dunlap's friends never doubted that whatever I found would point away from Max, but the developments I had reported were astounding and rekindled hopes long dormant.

The turnout pleased me. It was vital the media show up and not just read a press release, because on display were affidavits, statements, and police reports of unimpeachable authenticity they needed to examine. I hoped the presence of AP and UPI reporters meant nationwide coverage.

But what would be the tenor of that coverage? Not many of the newsmen present would want to deal with a new can of worms in the Bolles case. They had invested too much time and too many words supporting the police version of the murder.

While committee member Harold Bone held forth on stage

introducing me as "a noted criminal consultant," I stood in the wings arranging my papers one last time. Suddenly someone told me I had a phone call.

"I'm busy," I said. "Get a number."

"The caller says it's urgent. An emergency."

Urgent I could blow off. Emergency I'd better find out about.

"This Lake Headley?"

"Yes."

"Jordan Green here. I'm one of Max Dunlap's attorneys."

"I know who you are, Mr. Green." He had worked with Savoy at the trial.

"I don't want you to hold that press conference."

"You're too late, Mr. Green. The camera lights have come on. I don't have time to talk to you."

"Then I'll make this simple: if you go ahead with the press conference, I'll sue your ass off."

"I'll be just as clear. Max and Jim signed authorizations for me to conduct this news conference, and I don't give a fuck what you do."

I hung up and headed for the dais.

Later, Max Dunlap, delighted by one "up" day after a seeming eon of downers, asked Green what provoked the lawsuit threat. Green said he didn't think the timing was right. The timing wasn't right? In a convoluted way, Green had a point: the correct time to release this information would have been during the trial, preventing a lot of misery for Robison and Dunlap.

I opened my presentation with a letter dated October 29, 1976, from the Maricopa County prosecutor to the chief of the Phoenix police department. It said in part, "There is still a lingering doubt in my mind as to the political implications which may be motivating the attorney general's decision" to take the case away from local prosecutors and place it with the attorney general.

There were questions implicit in that letter, most of them indeed political: What *did* motivate Attorney General Bruce Babbitt, now Governor Bruce Babbitt, to handle the prosecution? The opportunity to make a national name for himself?

This certainly would be political. Or to make sure the probe didn't touch important Arizonans possibly involved in the murder? Which also could be called political, among other things.

The replaced prosecutor also wrote, "Furthermore, if the attorney general prosecutes the Adamson case in Maricopa County after standing up in court and stating that the defendant could not get a fair trial because of adverse publicity generated during the months prior to the trial, then it is my legal opinion that there is a great possibility of reversal."

Adamson had simply slid into his cozy plea bargain, but Dunlap and Robison, much vilified, were tried in Maricopa County where—associated with Adamson by his own kiss-of-death testimony—they stood little or no chance, given the lack of a solid defense investigation.

My audience sat stonefaced. Could the PA not be loud enough? I wondered. Or maybe their antennae weren't tuned in to me yet. Whatever, this should wake them up: I pointed to police reports showing that John Adamson and Neal Roberts took and failed police-administered polygraph examinations. This information was never released to the press. By contrast, when Max Dunlap, a man never convicted for so much as a traffic violation, failed a polygraph, the *Arizona Republic* prominently featured the story. (Max, unnerved at the time, later did pass the polygraph.) What police officer or prosecutor, I asked, withheld the Adamson and Roberts polygraph results, while releasing Dunlap's?

The prosecution truly didn't want to hear what came next: Robison had been offered immunity, money, relocation, and immediate release from death row if he corroborated Adamson's story of Kemper Marley contracting the murder. In short, the state now wanted to execute a man to whom they offered immunity.

I called attention to affidavit after affidavit (which reporters could read, touch, take home) shoring up my observation that with absolute blind faith in John Harvey Adamson's version—and after an ensuing year-long investigation by the Arizona attorney general's office—the FBI and the Phoenix police department failed to establish any evidence substantiating Adamson's accusations against Marley.

I had a lot to cover. I talked about the three vehicles reported stolen on the day of the bombing from the immunized Neal Roberts, information withheld from the defense (and which would still have been unavailable had I not gone into the police computer via my Los Angeles friend).

Again I discerned no reaction from reporters, sitting on the other side of the podium as expressionless as a gathering of zombies at high noon.

I introduced a sworn statement from Rosalie Bolles, the slain reporter's widow, stating that her husband, contrary to what the *Republic* said, pursued investigative work, including the Funk/ Emprise connection, right up to the time of the bombing.

After producing articles Bolles wrote for the *Gallup Independent,* I challenged those in attendance to call John Zollinger in New Mexico if they still believed the *Republic's* claims.

The Betty Funk Richardson police report and the Hank Landry statement detailing Neal Roberts's "loud and clear" remark were entered into evidence in my tribunal.

I told them about James McVay, who said Adamson had confessed to him that he framed Dunlap.

Closing what I considered a calm, coherent, well-documented presentation, I opened the floor to questions. Immediately I learned that what I'd mistaken for woolgathering had been a grimly silent collecting of ammo to shoot me down. The reporters were irate all right, but not at the outrages committed by the police and prosecution.

"Isn't it true you're being paid by the Dunlap Committee?" the first questioner asked, as if I hadn't made the point at the start of my presentation.

"Yes," I said. I didn't point out that my expenses already exceeded my salary.

"How can you claim to be impartial, when you're working for the Dunlap Committee?"

"The evidence is impartial. It speaks for itself, and I urge you to read it."

"What makes you think you can do a better job than the police?"

"If the police, with all their resources, had conducted an objective investigation, I don't for an instant imagine I could have competed with them. A few others and myself are operating on a shoestring. But to answer your question, you have a large amount of hard evidence in front of you pointing away from Robison and Dunlap and directly at others."

"Why are you so hostile to the police?"

Good grief. "I'm not; I've been a policeman. Now you have the evidence. Please. Study it. If you concentrate on only one thing, let it be the remark Neal Roberts made, three days before the attack on Don Bolles, your brother, that the reason for using dynamite was to send a message 'loud and clear.' "

"I don't understand the importance you attach to those stolen vehicles."

A reporter, and he didn't understand this?

"It's an inconceivable coincidence for three vehicles to be stolen from the back of a principal suspect's residence on the day of a high-profile murder."

Of course Assistant Attorney General William Schafer had said he didn't understand either. Asked why the information hadn't been included in the discovery, Schafer had said, "Auto theft is a separate crime. We worked a homicide." A preposterous remark. Thus, I suppose, a speeding car, racing away from a just-committed bank robbery would, according to Schafer, be a matter for Traffic to investigate.

The questions kept coming, none of them (except when Devereux introduced queries to emphasize a salient point) indicating a thirst for enlightenment. For example: "The *Arizona Republic* has said all along that Bolles only worked the legislature. Why should we believe you instead of the newspaper?"

"I'm not asking you to believe me about anything. I don't expect you to. I want you to check everything *yourselves*. Do what I did. Read Bolles's articles I gave you. Call John Zollinger at the *Gallup Independent*."

"You're accusing the *Arizona Republic* of lying?"

"I'm telling you what happened. I'm asking you to join me in a search for truth. If Don Bolles were here, he would."

Committee members began pitching in, trying to lighten the mood so information could be exchanged, but the venom in that room was palpable. I was practically begging them to look at the evidence. Uncomfortable as a supplicant, I pleaded, "Don't you care? Don't you want to find out who killed Don Bolles?"

I even brought up Rosalie Bolles's name again, quoting the respected widow about how right up to the end her husband worked on investigative pieces, and how numerous threats warning him off the Funk/Emprise investigation were received shortly before the bombing. "We remember Don Bolles gave us three clues to identify his killers. Mafia. Emprise. Adamson. The police forgot the Mafia and Emprise part, but we shouldn't. And there was a fourth phrase Bolles used. 'They finally got me.' Think about it. 'Finally.' Bolles was telling us he'd been expecting this. He'd been expecting it because of those threats relating to Funk and Emprise, whom he'd been investigating for years."

This didn't move the media, either. Their attitude seemed to project: So what?

I began to realize that these reporters were resisting because of an inescapable implication in my presentation: *Look, guys, you did a sloppy job, and you know it.* No one threw this verbal barb, of course, or gave even the slightest innuendo. But they had to know, and they flailed at me instead of examining themselves.

"Why haven't the police done all this work?" one of the disbelievers asked.

"They either did, and covered up, or they didn't because of tunnel vision caused by pressure to solve the murder. That's it. They either did or they didn't."

I suspected the former.

The nastiness continued to the finish, and when it ended I wondered if even one mind had been opened. I closed the press conference with a call for the U.S. attorney general's office to join the Dunlap Committee in our ongoing investigation into the murder. A U.S. attorney, I pointed out, could impanel a federal grand jury with the power of subpoena and might less likely be swayed by local politics.

I felt better when Harold Bone shook my hand and Laurie Dunlap hugged me. "I can't thank you enough, Mr. Headley," Laurie said. "You don't know how much this means to my family." She started to cry.

"Well, thank you. I'm glad you feel that way."

"This is the first time since all this began that anyone said something nice about my father."

A vehicle followed my rented car for the next two days as I made my rounds. Through contacts established with several Phoenix police officers unhappy at what they viewed as a department coverup of the Bolles case, I learned the brass deemed me worthy of surveillance. The tailing would become a constant fact of life.

As Christmas approached, I felt a sentimental urge to trade sun, sand, and palm trees for the more traditional Currier and Ives snowdrifts of my home state Indiana. Chestnuts wouldn't taste right from an open fire in Phoenix, nor would Jack Frost nip at my toes in the desert. And a break would do me good after five nonstop weeks on the case. Besides, my staying couldn't accomplish much during the holidays what with lawyers, judges, courts, and others I needed to visit out on semivacations.

But no matter how justified a brief hop to the Midwest, a guilty conscience kept attacking with thoughts of Max and Jim spending another Christmas behind bars.

I did want to stay in Phoenix long enough to hear the U.S. attorney's reaction to my proposal that he join in the investigation, and to see firsthand the kind of media coverage the press conference generated.

It generated plenty, leading off virtually every local TV newscast. A mixed bag: the reporting generally graded out as unfriendly, but points were stressed here and there to a public that up to then had considered the matter closed. Most important, we stirred up something, demonstrated that at least a handful of people didn't buy the official version. Maybe someone would come forward with important new revelations.

The newspaper articles hit the street the next day. Except for the *Scottsdale Daily Progress*, none of the stories was particularly favorable. The worst appeared in the *Phoenix Gazette*, written by Pat Sabo, which used code words to tell readers I shouldn't be believed.

The lead paragraph read: "A self-styled investigative journalist claims new evidence has surfaced in the murder of newsman Don Bolles and he called for the case to be reopened."

I could tell where this story headed without going any further. "Self-styled"? Sabo could have checked with *Playboy*, from whom I had received several assignments, or with any of a half-dozen other magazines. Would she begin an article about Bruce Babbitt by calling him the self-styled attorney general?

"Claims new evidence has surfaced"? I *handed* Ms. Sabo the evidence.

Sabo continued in the same vein in her second paragraph: "Lake W. Headley, who said he is a licensed private investigator in Los Angeles, outlined the alleged new evidence Tuesday at a press conference called by the Justice for Max Dunlap Committee."

Said I'm a licensed private investigator? She could have verified my credentials with a call to California. And if she wondered about my competence, she might have asked Vince Bugliosi, Manson prosecutor and *Helter Skelter* author who, however generous with his praise, called me "the best p.i. in the world."

Alleged new evidence? Again, I *handed* it to her. ("Alleged" is probably the most oft-used code word in the hands of a biased reporter.)

And so the article continued, in the sister newspaper to the one Bolles worked for, filled with "Headley claimed" and "Headley alleged."

One thing I "claimed," police reports about Neal Roberts's stolen vehicles, Sabo dismissed by writing, "Former Phoenix Police Detective Jon Sellers, who is now a special investigator for the state attorney general's office assigned to the Bolles case, denied that any information of significance was withheld from the defense."

Ridiculous. The stolen vehicle reports *were* withheld. Case closed. (And there would be a lot more, a veritable Niagara of information I had yet to discover.)

U.S. Attorney Morton Sitver, thanks to pressure from Jonathan Marshall (Sitver might dismiss me, but he could not so easily dismiss an important publisher), responded rather quickly—the next day, in fact—to the suggestion he become involved in the Bolles investigation. "It depends on exactly what they are requesting," Sitver said. "At first blush, it doesn't seem a matter we would have jurisdiction over, but we could look at what they are claiming."

Good. And I didn't think jurisdiction should be a problem. The FBI, after all, had involved itself from the beginning. Sitver said he would look at our evidence, and I had an eyeful to show him.

So with mixed emotions, I decided to go back home to Indiana for the holidays. I knew Devereux, Naomi, and Terri Lee would keep digging in Phoenix, and besides, I had a rather glamorous Bolles-connected appointment to keep before reaching Goshen.

8

A Visit to *Playboy*,
A Goshen Christmas

A taxi from O'Hare dropped me off at the Playboy Building—across North Michigan Avenue from the Drake Hotel, next door to the Knickerbocker, just north of the famous Chicago Water Tower, the only structure to survive the Great Chicago Fire of 1871.

From the lobby, which resembles a small bank with old wooden door elevators, I went to *Playboy* magazine's editorial offices on the tenth floor to see Bill Helmer, senior editor in charge of the Forum section.

Helmer was no stranger; we had worked together before. Today he showed me around the facility, which was decorated with an impressive collection of valuable art. I don't know which sank in first: the contrast of an aging building with the thoroughly modern interiors, or the unisex rest rooms.

"This place was erected in 1936 as the Palmolive Building," Helmer said with the ring and smoothness of an experienced tour guide. "A thirty-six-story architectural marvel topped off with a penthouse and the Lindbergh Beacon that, so I'm told, on clear nights reached all the way across the lake to the Michigan shore. In the fifties high rises began dwarfing what had been for decades the most imposing structure on this side of the city. But neighbors complained, and they finally had to shut it down for good about ten years ago."

Helmer explained that Hugh Hefner now resided almost ex-clusively in the Los Angeles Playboy Mansion, but still kept a close eye on the magazine. Using state-of-the-art electronics, Hefner on the West Coast could exactly duplicate Chicago light-ing to view and discuss a picture with one of his editors at the Playboy Building.

Efficiency seemed the watchword for the editorial staff, and those putting the magazine together displayed an enthusiasm akin to that of college students I remembered organizing antiwar demonstrations. This was a get-the-job-done place of work—jeans, sweatshirt, and sneakers—unlike the Chicago and Los An-geles mansions, which exuded an ambience of glamour.

I'd visited both of these mansions when Helmer hired me to investigate a serial murder case in Ohio that resulted in a *Play-boy* story titled "Close Call for Claudia." Partly due to a joint investigation I conducted with Austin, Texas, p.i. Russ Million, a woman suspect was cleared and released from custody. During the Ohio investigation, I met Hugh Hefner and his daughter, Christie, in the Los Angeles mansion at a political fund-raiser for Democrat Willie Brown.

Obviously a magazine publishing genius (though not so suc-cessful when he branched into other fields), Hefner took ex-treme pride in his California estate with its sprawling grounds, exotic pool, flamingos walking free, tall palms towering above everything, all of it smack in the middle of West Los Angeles.

What I remember most was the bevy of truly beautiful women swimming in the grotto section of the pool, and the many show business celebrities: Jack Nicholson, Robin Williams, James Caan, Caan's brother, the producer (and pool sharp) Ron-ald Caan, and Peter Falk.

Near the end of my tenth-floor tour of the Chicago head-quarters, we came upon Christie Hefner. "You probably don't remember me," I said. I really didn't think she would, or should.

"Of course I do, Lake." Her smile and hug made my day.

Before getting down to business, I talked with my friend and business associate in his small, cluttered office. "Unusual" best describes this Forum editor, particularly as he sat behind his desk, flanked on one wall by an antiwar poster and on another by an EAT MORE BABY SEAL bumper sticker.

Helmer projected the image of a 1920s newsman, hard-drinking and apparently cynical. A reformer at heart, he enjoyed poking fun at "knee-jerk liberoid do-gooders."

Before moving to Chicago, he, like so many good writers (Larry McMurtry, Gary Cartwright, and others), had written for *Texas Monthly* magazine and *The Texas Observer* in Austin. A bullet fired by Charles Whitman had grazed his neck and struck another student during the Texas Tower massacre at the University of Texas in 1966.

Bill Helmer joined *Playboy* in 1969 after working on the National Violence Commission in Washington, D.C. He had written a book, *The Gun That Made the Twenties Roar*, which was the definitive work on the Thompson submachine gun, and out of that research he became an authority on John Dillinger.

I liked the one-of-a-kind Forum editor. He always cracked me up when his thin, five-foot-nine body went into its Lone Star shitkicker routine: belching over a longneck beer while listening to the nasal twang of melancholy country music about drinking, unfaithful wives, and lives gone down the drain. (Though I never did cotton to his habit, in fancy restaurants, of ordering a bacon-wrapped filet mignon with a bottle of ketchup.) He went around Chicago in western garb long before *Urban Cowboy* made it fashionable . . . until local pimps adopted cowboy hats, when Helmer shelved his and switched to gangster-style fedoras.

Much as I enjoyed his company, I had to keep in mind the reason for this visit: Helmer sat on the board of the Playboy Foundation and I needed his help.

"Lake," he said, "what do you see as *Playboy*'s angle in the Arizona story? It's not sex or drugs, and we don't usually get involved in murder cases. How is this one different?"

"*Playboy* has always opposed the death penalty, and in my opinion Dunlap and Robison are the best arguments against it you'll ever find. I've interviewed them several times and believe they're innocent."

"Why?"

I ran it all down, adding that Dunlap Committee member David Fraser had provided me with a copy of a deposition taken from Eileen Roberts, Neal Roberts's secretary. She said that the *day before* the bombing, June 1, 1976, she overheard Neal Roberts, Hank Landry, John Adamson, and a fourth individual she couldn't identify (she said it wasn't Max Dunlap) discuss travel arrangements to Havasu, fund-raising efforts for Adamson, and model airplanes (requiring remote-control devices). Fraser said, and I agreed, that Eileen Roberts should have testified at the Robison/Dunlap murder trial.

I finished my minispeech to Helmer with an appeal—unsuccessful with those Arizona reporters at the press conference—on behalf of a fallen journalist. The chain-smoking Helmer seemed interested.

"Didn't Greene from *Newsday* take a team to Arizona?"

"They spent too much time partying in the Adams Hotel and wrapped up their 'investigation' with a declaration that the Phoenix police did an outstanding job."

"The Playboy Foundation—I'm a nonvoting member—tries to support financially what we support editorially. Put our money where our mouth is."

Helmer swiveled his chair and looked out the window. He sat thinking for a moment, then turned back to me. "I'd say this case falls within our parameters. I'd like you to run it by the Chicago head honcho, Arthur Kretchmer."

The view of Lake Michigan from Kretchmer's office, much bigger than Helmer's but more Spartan, almost took my breath away. The general clutter was the same, however, and in none of the offices did I see centerfold pictures.

Kretchmer looked like Abe Lincoln, craggy and gangly. Stern, unsmiling, direct, he had been in business with Hefner for a long time, and his number two *Playboy* masthead position as editorial director and associate publisher carried a lot of clout.

"Lake," he said, "you keep getting involved in the damnedest things. How did you come up with this one?"

He referred to Wounded Knee, I suppose, and the serial murder case in Ohio, and the Friar's Club gin rummy cheating case.

"Through George Vlassis," I said. "He's an old high school
and football-playing pal of mine who is now a lawyer in Phoenix
and has many friends on the Dunlap Committee."

"Why should *Playboy* be interested in this story?"

"You're against the death penalty. Here's the perfect case:
Arizona is going to execute two innocent men."

My own deep-rooted opposition to capital punishment
stemmed from working twenty years of murder cases and murder trials. The irrevocability of execution makes correcting the
mistakes of fallible judges and juries an impossibility. Also, the
plain fact that no wealthy person has ever been executed in this
country makes the death penalty clearly class-oriented.

I felt it vital that *Playboy* offer help—the *Arizona Republic*
and *Phoenix Gazette* clearly outgunned the courageous Jonathan
Marshall—but I didn't believe that a hard sell would be appropriate with Kretchmer. Still, mentioning that the majority of
people on death row are black, Hispanic, or Native American,
elicited a curt interruption.

"Don't tell me about minorities," Kretchmer said. "I haven't
always been on the tenth floor of the Playboy Building. I was a
Jewish kid, raised in an Italian neighborhood, and had to fight
my way out of Hell's Kitchen."

"Mr. Kretchmer," I said, "any financial support from the
foundation will be appreciated and put to good use. The Dunlap
Committee pays me twenty-five hundred dollars a month, no
expenses. That's not enough money for the size of the job.
There's travel, rental cars, hotel rooms. Photocopying charges
alone are in the stratosphere. But, more than the money, I need
the support of the magazine to legitimize my work in Arizona.
I've already taken heat from law enforcement over a p.i. license,
which would take a year and a lawsuit to obtain. What I—"

"You mean," Kretchmer said, "authorities are more concerned with the status of your license than what you find out
about the case?"

"That's right." In fact, it seemed they now investigated me
more than the Bolles homicide. Neal Roberts, Mr. Loud and
Clear, faced no threat of prosecution. I did.

"What I need is your authorization to state publicly that I'm working for *Playboy* as a journalist. Then I could claim an ex-emption to the p.i. license, in the same way the IRE did."

I told Kretchmer about going to the Arizona Department of Public Safety to get a work card, permitting me to operate as a p.i. on a friend's license (an ex-cop named Tom Atchinson). The DPS sergeant who gave me the forms volunteered that I'd never get licensed because of my "activities so far."

"That may be," I said, "but it's not your decision. I'll go to the Supreme Court if I have to. Besides, why didn't you jump on the IRE about this? How does my work differ from theirs?"

"They were reporters working on a story. You're a private investigator hired by the Dunlap Committee, and we know it."

"So it's where the buck comes from, not what I do, that determines whether I can conduct an investigation?"

The sergeant shrugged.

At this time Arizona also had a year's residency requirement before a p.i. could be licensed. In a year, Dunlap and Robison might be dead.

"Mr. Kretchmer," I said, "this battle, like so many others, will be fought in the press. Jonathan Marshall and the *Scottsdale Daily Progress* are in my corner, but that's a small paper up against the giants of the Pulliam empire. To be effective, I need affiliation with a powerful publication. *Playboy*'s what I need. And this case fits exactly *Playboy*'s own philosophy. What else can I say?"

Kretchmer made his decision quickly. "Okay. You're working for us. We'll back you on that. In the meantime, the next foundation meeting is January 18, and Bill Helmer will see about getting you some money. It sounds like you're on a good story that needs telling, and I wish you luck."

Hooray. I'd gotten what I needed, not a small triumph. With-out the *Playboy* backup, I figured, I would go to jail.

I figured correctly. Time and again the police would threaten me with arrest, and in each instance I would successfully bring the weight of the magazine to bear.

• • •

I arrived in my snowy hometown, Goshen, population twenty thousand, on Christmas Eve, moving in as a guest of high school buddy Jon Robinson and his wife, Glynna. Jon supervised city vehicle maintenance, and Glynna worked for Penn Electric Switch Company (now Johnson Control). These old friends lived in the sturdy house Jon was born in, and long ago they had designated a room there as "Lake's Room."

That evening I called Devereux in Arizona and he told me about the continuing fallout from the press conference. Then I phoned Terri Lee Yoder, who sounded excited about what she had dug up on Don Bolles, Bradley Funk, and Emprise. I had just arrived in Goshen, but like an old fire horse I yearned to return to the action.

Still, Goshen is a good place to spend an old-fashioned, homespun Christmas. The Mennonite College and a strong Amish community have firm roots in my hometown. Their closeness to nature and the plentiful supply of handmade articles brings Christmas gift-giving back to its original meaning, a meaning too often stifled in the big city by constantly ringing cash registers.

Hitching rails run along the fronts of supermarkets, where the Amish park their horse-drawn buggies. The Mennonites, who wear white bonnets, do drive cars, but the Amish, in their black hats, allow no mechanization. They milk by hand, churn butter manually, and employ windmills not to generate electricity but to pump water. The men remain clean-shaven until marriage, and all of them are totally nonviolent and law abiding.

I learned to speak a little Pennsylvania Dutch while working in my father's grocery store, and I know the Amish will help a person with almost anything he asks. They don't fight, steal, lie, or wage wars, though they might be tyrannical inside their own society. Gearing down to life among these peaceful people always makes coming home more enjoyable and relaxing.

Snow was piled deep this Goshen Christmas, and I enjoyed watching the horses and buggies crunch through the crisp white powder past stalled, abandoned cars.

I visited friends and relatives, including my mother's family, the Jacksons, the first settlers in Elkhart County, which encompasses Goshen and a place named for them, Jackson Township.

My days assumed a regular pattern. I'd get up early, drink coffee, call Devereux and Terri Lee, go to the Olympia Candy Kitchen for more coffee and talks with friends, then to the Holiday Inn for lunch and coffee. Lots of coffee. I know most of the people in Goshen, and we relived good times at Lake Wawasee and dinners in good restaurants like The Sleepy Cove. Then it would be back to the Robinson home for TV late into the night.

About a week into my visit Devereux called. His normally unshakable voice cracked, and I sensed his tension all the way from Arizona.

"The damnedest thing just happened," he said. "I went around to the back to start my car. It was dark. Down the alley I heard an engine crank and then tires screeching. I looked up and saw this pickup truck, its lights off, bearing down on me from less than thirty feet away. There was no doubt the driver wanted to run me down. I just managed to jump onto the trunk of my car, but it was a close call."

Geesus. Already there had been phone threats to Devereux and me, and the word on Phoenix streets was warning us to stay away from the Bolles case, but I hadn't expected action so soon.

"Did you report this to the police?"

"It just happened."

"I think you should report it."

"I'm pretty upset. Shaken."

"Any witnesses?"

"No."

"Why were you going out late?"

"To interview somebody. I don't duck things. I never thought this would happen."

"I warned you this Bolles investigation could be dangerous."

"I know. But talking is one thing; having it happen is another."

"What kind of pickup?"

"I barely noticed it was a truck."

"What color?"

"I have a sense it was red, but I'm not sure."

"Did you get a plate, or a partial?"

"No. I couldn't see anything. Not a light on inside or outside when it zoomed by."

"Could you see where the pickup went?"

"It turned right, at the end of the alley. I heard peeling rubber for three blocks."

"Cool it for a day or so. Be careful. There's a blizzard here, and I'll come back as soon as it lifts, and we'll stay a little closer together in the future. For now, don't go anyplace alone. Remember, you're an investigative journalist. That's what Don Bolles *was*."

9

Bradley Funk's Emprise

I couldn't return to Phoenix until January 4, 1979. A record-breaking blizzard caused the first extended closing ever of O'Hare.

"I'm glad you're back," Terri Lee said when she met me at Sky Harbor Airport. She wore jeans and a designer silk top. "I missed you. I've been thinking about you."

Wow. I loved the new open-type woman. "Well, I missed and thought about you, too. That could be dangerous."

That night Terri Lee and I ate at the Spaghetti Factory, a restaurant in downtown Phoenix designed to resemble an industrial plant: machine parts hung from the ceiling, all manner of wrenches and tools on the walls. We each ordered linguini with clam sauce, and then I leaned forward to hear what she had to say. Terri had brought a briefcase, which she opened with a key on a rabbit's foot key chain. I asked her about the rabbit's foot, and she said her father gave it to her for good luck.

Terri removed a four-inch-high stack of photocopies from the briefcase. "I don't know if this is what you wanted. I hope it helps."

• • •

Helps? I guess it helped. After reluctantly driving Terri to her home, in north Phoenix, I read her research for several hours at the Westward Ho.

I learned that Emprise, one of the last words on the lips of Don Bolles, began as a company founded in 1915 by Louis Jacobs, a man *Sports Illustrated* dubbed The Godfather of Sports.

Louis Jacobs became quite a success. As a little boy he sold popcorn at the Gayety Theater in Buffalo, New York, and peanuts at the baseball park. In 1927 he landed his first concession contract, with the Detroit Tigers, and he was on his way. Under the name of an Emprise subsidiary, Sportservice, he ultimately gained control of the concessions for six major league baseball teams—Detroit, Cincinnati, Milwaukee, Baltimore, the Chicago White Sox, Montreal.

Also, the concessions for four hockey teams: Kansas City, Buffalo, Chicago, St. Louis.

And five basketball teams: Chicago, Cleveland, Cincinnati, Milwaukee, Buffalo.

Plus eight professional football teams: Green Bay (at games played in Milwaukee), Buffalo, Baltimore, Washington, Chicago, Detroit, St. Louis, Cincinnati.

On May 26, 1972, *Sports Illustrated* revealed that Louis Jacobs's two sons, Max and Jeremy, Emprise's top two officers, had "the concessions at more than fifty horse and dog tracks in the U.S. and Canada, plus ten more in England and Puerto Rico. They had contracts with jai-alai frontons, bowling alleys, horse shows, golf tournaments, and ski lodges. In 1960 they were the concessionaires for the Rome Olympics.

"But more important," I read, "they had taken a further giant step, vaulting from behind the hot dog counter into the front office. In 1963 Jeremy Jacobs obtained controlling interest in the Cincinnati Royals and the Cincinnati Gardens, where the Royals played. The Jacobses owned stock (off and on) in the Buffalo Bisons of the International League and in the Buffalo franchise in the American Hockey League. Emprise holds stock, bonds, and debentures in at least nineteen separate pari-mutuel entities, including controlling interest in the Buffalo raceway; Finger Lakes raceway (N.Y.); Latonia raceway (Ky.); Miles Park (Ky.);

Southland dog track, in West Memphis; Daytona Beach (Fla.) Kennel Club; Daytona Beach Jai-Alai Fronton; Melbourne (Fla.) Jai-Alai Fronton; Centennial Turf Club (Colo.); and in Arizona, all six greyhound tracks and until recently two of the three thoroughbred tracks."

It was this control of the Funk-Emprise Arizona racing empire that Bolles first wrote about in October 1969 in a story titled "N.Y. Firm in Quiet Control of Most Racing Tracks Here."

"A huge New York firm," his article began, "is gradually getting control of all horse and dog racing in Arizona. The Emprise Corp. of Buffalo, N.Y., has majority stock control in six of the seven firms which run dog racing in the state, and is part owner of the seventh."

The deeper Bolles probed into Emprise, the more he learned: Sportservice alone (Emprise controlled at least 162 other corporations) by 1972 had become a hundred-million-dollars-a-year operation selling five million bags of peanuts annually, thirty million soft drinks, twenty million hot dogs, and twenty-five million containers of beer. Concessions seemed an even better deal than owning a major league franchise: for one thing, no highly paid ball players to negotiate with.

How did Emprise pull it off? Well, sports franchises, like individuals, often need loans. *Sports Illustrated* revealed that Emprise loaned two million dollars to the Seattle Pilots in exchange for a twenty-five-year concession agreement with Sportservice. Emprise loaned two million dollars to the Montreal Expos and received a thirty-year concession contract, with option to renew. It loaned twelve million dollars to the city of St. Louis to help finance Busch Memorial Stadium in exchange for a thirty-year concession deal. Often, when Emprise loaned money, it acquired partial ownership in the sports franchise.

When Louis Jacobs died, in 1968, ownership of Emprise passed to his sons, Max and Jeremy. A year later U.S. Congressman Sam Steiger of Arizona, fed information by reporter Don Bolles, began to make noise about the Funks and Emprise. On the floor of Congress, Steiger charged that Emprise did business with Sam Tucker of River Downs racetrack in Ohio, a member of the Mafia's infamous Purple Gang; with Moe Dalitz of Cleveland, named by the Kefauver Committee as a member of the Mafia; and with Raymond Patriarca, head of the New England Mafia. Steiger raged about Emprise's 12 percent interest in Hazel Park, on whose board of directors sat Anthony J. Zerilli, Giacomo W. Tocco, and Dominic P. Corrado, all named by the McClellan Committee as belonging to the Detroit Mafia.

Charges were also leveled that Louis Jacobs had financed Russell Bufalino in the purchase of four amusement parks in the Pittsburgh area, and that Jerry Catena, Vito Genovese's successor in the New York Mafia, arranged for Emprise to fund a Mob takeover of the Finger Lakes racetrack.

On April 26, 1972, Emprise was convicted of criminally conspiring to obtain secret ownership of the Frontier Hotel-Casino in Las Vegas, a verdict that threatened the entire Jacobs empire. Many states prohibit a convicted felon from owning shares in a pari-mutuel business, and other states prohibit felons from obtaining a liquor license. Still, Emprise's involvement with the Frontier wasn't its first move on Las Vegas. Louis Jacobs, during the fifties, arranged loans that permitted Moe Dalitz to gain control of the Stardust.

Sports Illustrated revealed deal after deal that Emprise made with Mafia figures and with major professional sports franchises. Louis Jacobs loaned money to Bill Veeck, chief owner of four major league baseball franchises, and even to the so-called Grand Old Man of Baseball, Connie Mack. Often owners regretted these deals when they tried to sell their teams, encumbered as they were by lengthy concession contracts with Emprise.

From Terri Lee's own research, I discovered that the purported fifty-fifty relationship between the Funks and Emprise didn't really exist. The Funks owed Emprise money, and as collateral pledged their 50 percent of the racing empire to the Buffalo conglomerate. The Funks remained as well-paid managers.

In 1971, Terri Lee's research revealed, Bolles was approached by a military school roommate of Bradley Funk's named George Johnson, who told the reporter that the previous year, 1970, Bradley Funk and Emprise had paid him sixteen thousand dollars to "dig up dirt" on Bolles and Congressman Steiger. Johnson said he had arranged for wiretaps on the phones of Bolles and Steiger, and had paid bank employees and phone company workers for personal information on Bolles.

Bolles checked the story out and printed it, whereupon the Funks sued, asking for twenty million dollars. The *Arizona Republic* countersued for harassment, and the case got settled in 1973, with no admission of wrongdoing on either side. Terms of the settlement weren't announced, though apparently one of them involved a promise by the *Republic* that Bolles would never again write about the dog tracks.

"As he told friends, including Steiger," the *New Times*, an Arizona weekly, reported, "he was bitterly disappointed. Friends remember he never forgave his newspaper for pulling the rug out from under him. 'I think when we filed the lawsuit, his stories just stopped,' Funk recalls innocently."

But, as I learned, Bolles didn't stop investigating the Funks and Emprise just because his paper, for whatever reason, took him off the story.

In May 1972, between the time (1970) when Bolles revealed the tapping of his telephone and various other illegal invasions of privacy, and his being pulled off the Funk-Emprise investigation (1973), he and Bradley Funk each testified before the Select Committee on Crime, chaired by Congressman Claude Pepper, on the influence of organized crime in sports.

Bradley Funk, questioned by chief counsel Joseph Phillips, testified first, and it didn't take long for Don Bolles's name to be raised:

> MR. PHILLIPS: Mr. Funk, as near as I can make out, you say there are individuals who are in some type of concerted action to destroy you and your family's interests; is that correct?
>
> MR. FUNK: That is our belief, sir. Yes.
>
> MR. PHILLIPS: Could you tell us who you believe are in this concert of action to destroy you and your family's interests?

MR. FUNK: Mr. Phillips, if I might, if I could answer that question as I feel it, with some explanation, I think I can give you a pretty good idea and help the committee understand why we feel this way.

MR. PHILLIPS: I did not ask you why you feel this way. I asked you who these people were who are in the concerted effort to destroy your business. I would like to know particularly, individually, who you have in mind as part of this concerted interest to destroy you, your family, and your business. The question is: Who is the group, so we can start off and know who we are talking about.

MR. FUNK: Primarily Mr. Donald Bolles of the *Arizona Republic*; Mr. Eugene Pulliam, publisher of the Phoenix Newspapers, Inc.; Congressman Sam Steiger; a man named Gene Mondue from Tucson, Arizona; a man named Sam Jenkins; and others that we are not sure who they might be.

MR. PHILLIPS: You don't include Mr. Osman in that particular category?

MR. FUNK: No, sir. I don't believe so. Although Mr. Osman has made some misleading statements also, to the press.

MR. PHILLIPS: Does the fact you disagree with a man on a statement indicate to you he is part of the conspiracy to destroy you?

MR. FUNK: Mr. Phillips, I believe in an article carried in the *Arizona Republic*, Mr. Osman stated that—

MR. PHILLIPS: I didn't ask you that. I am not asking you what he said. I am asking you, particularly, whether you think if someone criticizes you or makes some statement you have disagreement with, automatically he is in con-

> spiracy to destroy your family and business interests?
>
> MR. FUNK: Yes, sir; when they lie. I certainly do.
>
> MR. PHILLIPS: Anyone who lies about you is in conspiracy with Mr. Steiger and other people to destroy you; is that correct?
>
> MR. FUNK: They appear to have been working very closely together; yes, sir.

Bradley Funk's paranoia—for that's surely what it was—must have diminished somewhat when the Pulliams took Bolles off the Funk-Emprise story. Nevertheless, what he viewed as a conspiracy to "destroy" was simply Bolles doing stories he thought the public ought to know about. One of these, the payment to Racing Commissioner Frank Waitman by Funk-Emprise for construction work done at the Prescott Downs horse track, soon became a concern of the Pepper Committee.

> MR. PHILLIPS: Let's start with the matter involving payment to Mr. Waitman. According to the testimony of Mr. Osman, you paid $23,719.92 to Mr. Waitman. Is that correct?
>
> MR. FUNK: Yes, sir.
>
> MR. PHILLIPS: Do you regard it as a conflict of interest for a public official to be taking money from a person he is supervising?
>
> MR. FUNK: No, sir. If the work is performed by a public official, is paid for, and is done under the competitive prices. I see no conflict of interest any more than I see a conflict of interest where in the State of Arizona we have racing commissioners who have racing horses at privately owned racetracks which they supervise, and they earn purse money and breeders' awards, and everything else.

Next the Pepper Committee tried to pin Funk down on the varying figures his racing operation submitted to the IRS and the Arizona legislature.

MR. PHILLIPS: Do you think Mr. Osman deliberately mis-
stated his findings?

MR. FUNK: I believe Mr. Osman had some precon-
ceived notions and went about his—not audit—examination with a certain amount of
prejudice. Yes, sir.

MR. PHILLIPS: And you believe the staff Mr. Osman had
working on this particular report was also
so biased and prejudiced that they produced a distorted result?

MR. FUNK: No, sir; I believe if you queried Mr. Osman's staff, they felt quite the contrary,
that the report submitted wasn't quite what
they had examined.

MR. PHILLIPS: On what do you base that?

MR. FUNK: Talking to different people who worked for
the auditor's office, that it was doubtful.

MR. PHILLIPS: Would you tell us who told you that?

MR. FUNK: That was two years ago, sir. But I am sure
Mr. Osman knows.

MR. PHILLIPS: I would like for you to tell this committee
who said this report is invalid.

MR. FUNK: I said I don't remember the names, sir.

The Pepper Committee then turned to the bugging of Bolles's and Congressman Steiger's phones. As I read I remem- bered Betty Funk Richardson's suggestion that perhaps her ex- husband, Bradley, learned of Bolles's knowledge of her lawsuit by wiretapping.

MR. PHILLIPS: Did there come a time when you knew
George Harry Johnson?

MR. FUNK: Yes, sir.

MR. PHILLIPS: When was that?

MR. FUNK: I first knew George Harry Johnson probably about the third grade, fourth grade, Phoenix, Arizona.

MR. PHILLIPS: Would you say you were good friends?

MR. FUNK: Off and on, we went to different schools together. We went to Franklin School. We were pals there. We went to military school.

MR. PHILLIPS: So you have been longtime friends, is that correct?

MR. FUNK: Off and on.

MR. PHILLIPS: Did there come a time when you commissioned him to conduct an investigation?

MR. FUNK: I believe it was around February of 1970. We had been receiving a great deal of flak from the Phoenix newspapers, and George was around the track because he and I were developing a piece of property. We were also seeing each other socially. He was aware of the newspaper, the bad press we were getting, and he came to me one day, as I recall, and said he had a friend that had some information on Congressman Steiger that might help us put this conspiracy together, because Steiger was probably the key to the whole conspiracy. I don't remember exactly.

MR. PHILLIPS: What conspiracy are you talking about? Did you discuss the conspiracy prior to meeting Mr. Johnson?

MR. FUNK: Sir, I don't know exactly when it was filed, but in relation to the dog breeders' problem we were having, the lies that were being told about us, we felt somebody—we didn't know who it might be—was pulling somebody's strings, so to speak, to try to destroy us, take over our business. There was bad legislation to be considered, there were racing commission problems, there were all kinds of things going on, and George had also advised me of a pending strike months before it happened. I thought maybe, well, somebody is doing some things—and I thought, yes, very definitely, there is some kind of a conspiracy going on. I think that is probably the legal term, but there were people out working to destroy us.

MR. PHILLIPS: In retrospect, would you say that is paranoia?

MR. FUNK: I don't think—my sitting here today, it seems to me that from all that has happened to me and my family in the last year—that I was too far from wrong in 1970; no, sir.

MR. PHILLIPS: In other words, in 1970 you felt there was a conspiracy, and you presently feel there is a conspiracy?

MR. FUNK: I believe my being here is probably the result of that conspiracy, yes, sir; for one reason or another.

MR. PHILLIPS: Who else was a conspirator? Congressman Steiger was a conspirator, I take it?

MR. FUNK: Congressman Steiger was being very vocal.

MR. PHILLIPS: Don't you believe a man has a right to be vocal, especially a public official?

MR. FUNK: Vocal by innuendo, by traveling to other states and saying bad things when he wouldn't say it right in our own state. It kind of puzzled me—yes, sir—as to what his motives were.

With Congressman Waldie questioning, the Pepper Committee returned to George Johnson's wiretapping of Bolles and Steiger.

MR. WALDIE: In terms of the illegal activities in which Mr.
              Johnson admittedly engaged, what aware-
              ness did you have of those illegal activities?

MR. FUNK: Sir, I don't think Mr. Johnson did any illegal
              activities.

MR. WALDIE: Mr. Johnson said he solicited and got wire-
              taps. He solicited and got bank accounts. He
              solicited and got telephone records that were
              all confidential. Do you believe he did not
              get those illegally?

MR. FUNK: Well, by the number, sir. The phone rec-
              ords: George came to me one day, some
              time in, I believe it was April or May, and
              said that he had a friend at the telephone
              company who worked in the computer
              room. He was a manager or something. And
              that he didn't like what the newspaper was
              doing to us, and he was going to get him a
              list of telephone numbers called between
              conspirators. That is what Mr. Johnson told
              me.

MR. WALDIE: You did not construe that as being an illegal
              activity?

MR. FUNK: No, sir. I asked him if he had to pay the man
              anything. He said, "No," and I said, "OK."
              I assumed it was like a credit check, or any-
              thing else.

MR. WALDIE: What about bank accounts?

MR. FUNK: Bank accounts: George came to me again. I
              believe this was subsequent to—I believe it
              was subsequent to the telephone records. He
              says, "I have a hunch or lead or rumor that
              Steiger, or Steiger's backers, are paying
              Bolles to do these articles, and if I can get
              their bank records, we can prove, we can
              match this movement of funds from Mr.
              Steiger's account." I said, "George, leave off

that, we have a conspiracy suit going. When the time comes, we will subpoena them."

Bradley Funk testified that neither Max nor Jeremy Jacobs knew about the employment of George Johnson, but that he told Jeremy Jacobs about it after Johnson's activities ceased.

MR. WALDIE: What was Jerry Jacobs's response to that?

MR. FUNK: I don't recall, sir.

MR. WALDIE: Did he accept that as a proper activity on the part of the Funks?

MR. FUNK: Sir, Mr. Jacobs was very upset with the speeches that Mr. Steiger had made.

MR. WALDIE: Then, can I conclude from that remark that Mr. Jacobs was just as anxious as you were to determine something incriminating in Mr. Steiger's background?

MR. FUNK: Probably more so; yes, sir.

MR. WALDIE: It would appear—I really say this editorially—that Mr. Jacobs was just as aware as you were of what I have characterized as a shabby bit of business. I don't ask you to respond to that.

For all their vaunted mission to complete Don Bolles's work, the IRE had gotten very little on this important corner of that work. Bradley Funk's testimony left me with new, clearer impressions of the man. So too would I see Don Bolles more clearly when I read what he told the Pepper Committee.

10

Don Bolles's Emprise

Despite Bradley Funk's concern about being "ruined" and "destroyed" by the conspiracy involving the *Arizona Republic*, Don Bolles, Sam Steiger, and others, Funk, his family, and Emprise still held virtually an unthreatened monopoly of pari-mutuel racing in Arizona.

Bolles himself viewed his victories—getting the information into print—as Pyrrhic. Although, at great effort, he had exposed much about the influential Funk family and the gigantic Emprise, his adversaries remained as firmly in control as ever.

What good was exposé if nothing significant changed? I likened his 1972 situation to my own in 1979: a large amount of evidence had already reached the public, yet Dunlap and Robison remained on death row, apparently no better off than when I started the case.

Anyway, Bolles had hoped the Pepper Committee's inquiry into organized crime influence over professional sports would result in significant reform, and the reporter came well prepared for his appearance before the committee. Bradley Funk may have been paranoid when he railed about a conspiracy, but there was nothing delusional about Bolles's position. His remarkable testimony before the Congressional committee revealed near-encyclopedic knowledge of his subject, an excellent memory, and the rare ability to translate in-depth, complex information into laymen's language.

MR. PHILLIPS: Will you tell us what you did about investigating Emprise?

MR. BOLLES: About in the early winter of 1970, I went on an extended tour of many cities around the country at the request of my managing editor and looked at newspaper clippings and interviewed persons in connection with Emprise's role in racing.

MR. PHILLIPS: Would you tell us very briefly what you found as a result of this investigative trip?

MR. BOLLES: Well, there were several general conclusions I drew from the information I gathered. Before I give you this information, I want to say that it is basically what other people told me. Much of it has not come firsthand. We have tried as best we can to ascertain that this information is correct and accurate. If there is anything in there that is not accurate, we would be happy to have the Emprise people tell us so. I guarantee them that we will not repeat this again if it can be demonstrated it is not accurate. We have attempted very extensively to trace this information and ascertain that it is accurate. The first thing we found was a continual association with organized crime figures over a thirty-five-year period.

MR. PHILLIPS: You say there was a continual association on behalf of the Emprise principals?

MR. BOLLES: By Emprise and its officials.

MR. PHILLIPS: And would that have been Lou Jacobs, the predominant executive official of that organization?

MR. BOLLES: I would say that was so. The information we received was that Mr. Jacobs was the principal in most of the arrangements.

MR. PHILLIPS: Would you please elaborate on that finding?

MR. BOLLES: Well, here again, we started with second-hand information, but the first indication we had that Emprise might not be the finest people to have around was a book by a well-known crime writer, Hank Messick, who wrote a book called *The Silent Syndicate*. He reported that—this was in 1937—Lou loaned money to a Sam Tucker, reportedly of the Cleveland syndicate, and that in 1958 there was a temporary crisis in the Sportservice system and Lou borrowed money back again for a short period of time from Moe Dalitz and Sam Hass of the Cleveland syndicate.

MR. PHILLIPS: Did you make any other conclusions in your investigation of Emprise?

MR. BOLLES: Yes. We found there had been a seduction of public officials and use of well-respected front men to accomplish its objectives.

MR. PHILLIPS: Were there any other racketeering individuals who you determined were associating with Emprise or its officials?

MR. BOLLES: I don't allege that this next gentleman is a racketeer, but I will just give you the information I have. In 1952, John Masoni, who later tried to start a track in Coeur D'Alene, Idaho, with Jerry Jacobs, the current president of Emprise, was involved in an Ohio track called Randall Park. Masoni was in Randall at the time when Joseph C. Lombardo was in Cleveland and they kept having things happening to their various projects like bombs going off. The Thoroughbred Racing Protection Bureau notes one of the more serious allegations concerning these three partners is the manner in which they operated North Randall Park and employed persons with criminal records and hoodlum reputations to do the policing at the track. That same year of 1952, Masoni, along with an ex-convict named Paul Clellan and a New York nightclub operator named John Boggiano... started a dog track in North Carolina. Boggiano, according to the *Memphis Commercial Appeal*, which wrote about the situation in some detail, had held stock with the family of Steven Franze; but Franze, Boggiano's ex-partner, was slain gangland style in 1953 in New York. That same year, the wife of Vito Genovese, now dead, reported that her husband held financial interests in North Carolina and Virginia dog tracks.

MR. PHILLIPS: Vito Genovese has been identified as one of the family heads operating out of New York; is that correct?

MR. BOLLES: Yes. Vito Genovese is listed in the 1969 McClellan investigating committee report as having been on the commission of the Cosa Nostra in 1960, and also head of his own family, which reportedly is now headed by Geraldo Catena.

MR. PHILLIPS: You recounted to the committee the observation that Mrs. Genovese, in a divorce action, had testified Vito Genovese had owned dog interests in North Carolina and Virginia. Did you come across, in your inquiry, anything about Raymond Patriarca?

MR. BOLLES: In 1962, a track called Berkshire Downs was formed in Massachusetts. The information I have is that Sportservice, or Emprise, put a hundred thousand dollars in this track, loaned the owners of record three hundred and fifty-seven thousand dollars and got the concessions. FBI wiretaps revealed in federal court in 1967, I believe in Boston, that the real power behind Berkshire Downs was Raymond Patriarca, who is listed in the McClellan committee report as the leader of the New England Cosa Nostra.

MR. PHILLIPS: The next point you made, I think, was that Emprise used a pattern of seduction of public officials. Tell us about that.

MR. BOLLES: Well, what I know best is the situation in the Arizona Racing Commission. We had a racing commissioner by the name of Frank Waitman, of Prescott. Let me back up. There came a time a group of businessmen in the Phoenix area decided that they would try and start a competing track against the Funk-Emprise monopoly. They filed an application with the Arizona Racing Commission to create this track at Black Canyon, which is just north of the Phoenix area, across the county line, because there was a requirement you could not build two in the same county. As memory serves me, there were some "rinky dink" procedures in the racing commission which made it very, very difficult for this competing applicant to even get his petition heard. But then at one point, Mr. Waitman made an application that the Funks be allowed to build on that location, and Mr. Waitman was rewarded with a contract to install the plumbing at the Black Canyon Dog Track, which if memory serves me correctly, was in the approximate amount of twenty-three thousand dollars. State auditor general Ira Osman can give you the specifics on that. It was also a situation with Racing Commissioner Donald Butler, who was in a land syndicate in Yuma, and again Mr. Osman can give you the more detailed specifics of it because his mind understands all of those financial transactions better than mine. But the Funk-Emprise interest put twenty thousand dollars, as I recall, into that land syndicate.

MR. PHILLIPS: Just going back to the Waitman situation: Waitman was a racing commissioner and he was also doing business with these people he was regulating?

MR. BOLLES: That is correct.

MR. PHILLIPS: Apparently, that was brought out in the press by your particular paper; is that true?

MR. BOLLES: Yes. Also, later on, Mr. Osman recommended that the matter be presented to the proper authorities. I believe he branded it an apparent conflict of interest, which may be prohibited by Arizona racing law. To my knowledge, nothing was ever done about it.

MR. PHILLIPS: We were talking about a second racing commissioner who became involved with these racing interests?

MR. BOLLES: Yes. Donald Butler, formerly of Yuma, and now Tucson.

MR. PHILLIPS: Would you tell us about him, please.

MR. BOLLES: I think I gave you the information about their putting twenty thousand dollars into a land syndicate of which he was some kind of managing director or principal.

MR. PHILLIPS: Did this information ultimately reach the press?

MR. BOLLES: Yes, it did.

MR. PHILLIPS: Would you tell us what happened to Mr. Butler after this was published?

MR. BOLLES: It took a long while, but Mr. Butler finally resigned.

MR. PHILLIPS: Will you please go on. Were there any other racing commissioners who became involved?

MR. BOLLES: Yes. I received information that a racing commissioner by the name of Buell Tade—who was no longer on the commission, I believe has been off for some years—had been the buddy of the Funks on the commission and that they had bought thousands of glasses from him. Drinking glasses.

MR. PHILLIPS: Was there also another commissioner by the name of Marth?

MR. BOLLES: His name is Al Marth, of Phoenix. He has been a commissioner for some time. Mr. Marth went to a meeting of the American Greyhound Track Operators Association in Ireland, at state expense, and it was alleged to me that one of his principal duties there was to seek the admission of the Funks into the track operators association; that they had been consistently barred from membership or not admitted to membership, and that he was going to try and get them in. He did not succeed.

Next the committee heard a tape-recorded conversation between Racing Commissioner Al Marth and Albert Funk, Bradley's cousin. Their talk revealed a cozy relationship between the regulator and the regulated. The Pepper Committee listened, then Counsel Joseph Phillips summed up what they heard.

MR. PHILLIPS: The thrust of the conversation with Mr. Marth, the racing commissioner, is that he is advising Mr. Funk, in advance of the hearing, what questions the commission is going to put to him; is that correct?

MR. BOLLES: That is correct.

MR. PHILLIPS: In other words, Mr. Marth is telling the racing applicant what the questions are going to be; that these questions are not in any way going to embarrass them; they are going to give him the questions in advance so he can appropriately answer them and the commission can put on a good show so they grant the license and still not be criticized; is that correct?

MR. BOLLES: That was basically what was said.

The committee was interested in George Johnson and quickly shifted its focus to his wiretapping.

MR. PHILLIPS: Can you tell us about the discussion with George Johnson?

MR. BOLLES: Johnson, basically, told us the things he told you and this committee yesterday; that he caused a wiretap to be placed on my personal telephone at home; that he used a banker to get into my private bank account; that he had used a telephone company employee to get out my records of telephone calls I had made over quite a period of time. One thing that I want to insert here: it was stated yesterday that these were long-distance telephone records. The records which Mr. Johnson delivered to us were interzone telephone calls, where you might, in Phoenix, call from north Phoenix to south Phoenix. That would be an interzone call. To my knowledge, these are only recorded on the logs of the telephone company, because there is no operator interference. These interzone telephone calls were recorded and I looked at the log they had made, and also with little notations out to the side as to who I had called. I recognized those numbers and those persons as being identical, not only with things I knew were associated number and name, but calls I had, in fact, made. He also told me he had checked into my credit rating, into my personal life, and—

MR. PHILLIPS: Is your credit rating and your personal life as impeccable as Congressman Steiger's seems to be?

MR. BOLLES: I hope so. I am an AA credit rating.

MR. PHILLIPS: Please continue.

MR. BOLLES: That was the gist of it. He played for us certain tapes on that occasion, very briefly, and then simply handed a whole pile of this information he had gleaned, his own personal notes and memorandums to himself, and telephone records of a large number of individuals.

MR. PHILLIPS: Did he say who had employed him to do this?

MR. BOLLES: On that occasion, I do not think he did.

MR. PHILLIPS: Did he ultimately tell you who had employed him to do it?

MR. BOLLES: Yes, he did.

MR. PHILLIPS: Would you tell us who that is?

MR. BOLLES: He said it was the Funks and the Emprise.

Congressman Claude Pepper had a few salient questions:

CHAIRMAN PEPPER: There have been a good many insinuations about motivation in this case. It has been intimated by the Emprise

group, the Funk group, that your paper was prejudiced against them, had
never printed anything favorable to
racing in that area, and that you were
out to get them, as you would say in
the language of the trade. Will you just
state, as you are testifying under oath,
was this inquiry initiated, and has it
been carried on by the people who
were interested in the newsworthiness
and in the merits of the manner in
which this operation was conducted,
or has it been directed by the owners
or the proprietors or the managers of
your paper with an ulterior motive
against these people?

MR. BOLLES: Under oath, there was never an attempt to get the Funks, or Emprise,
or anybody else. We were trying to
bring the conditions at the racetrack—and in my opinion, outlandish
relationships with the racing commissioners—to public light, and we have
done so. I think this has resulted in
the final awareness by the racing commission that they have a responsibility
to act in the public interest, and by
the legislature that even though they
passed a watered-down bill, that at
least they had to do something.

CHAIRMAN PEPPER: And there have been no orders issued
in the past by the proprietors of your
paper that you fellows who do the
work have got to get these people?

MR. BOLLES: Absolutely not.

Counsel Phillips praised the reporter, saying to the Committee and staff dealing with Mr. Bolles that "he has been ex-

ceptionally cooperative and I found him to be a man with a high degree of honor, integrity, and caution."

The Pepper Committee's final report concluded that Emprise and the Funks used "innuendo and false accusations" against Bolles and Congressman Steiger, and found no evidence of conspiracy against the Emprise-Funk racing monopoly.

Early in 1977 there occurred an odd and sad footnote to the whole affair. Congressman Steiger, who had fought long and hard against Emprise, asked outgoing President Gerald Ford to pardon the corporation for its 1972 felony conviction. Steiger was about to leave public office, having given up his House seat to wage a losing battle for the U.S. Senate against Dennis DeConcini.

Steiger later explained his seemingly baffling change of mind: "There was no mystery about it; they [Emprise] had me by the balls." Ongoing lawsuits by Emprise against the congressman left him owing sixty thousand dollars in legal fees, and he envisioned no relief. "They [Emprise] contacted me, and I told them I'd write the pardon letter if they'd lay off the lawsuits. Besides, nobody really cared in Arizona who ran the racing industry. I know it wasn't very savory, but that's the fact."

Steiger didn't sell out entirely. "I called Jerry [Ford]," he said, "who I knew from Congress, right after I wrote the damned letter, and told him to ignore it. I may have been in bed with Jeremy Jacobs for a second, but I wasn't getting under the sheets."

11

''A Matter of
Jurisdiction''

All of my discovery papers went to the defense lawyers. If Dunlap and Robison won release, it would come through the judicial system, with the attorneys pulling the necessary strings. I viewed my function as similar to a hod carrier's, bringing bricks to the mason who builds a case. Without the mason, the hod carrier has only a pile of bricks.

"Mr. Savoy," I said, visiting his office on January 12, 1979, "have you had a chance to look at the material I sent over?"

"Not all of it," Savoy said, "but enough to make me think you're on to something. Unfortunately, until the Arizona Supreme Court rules on our appeal, we can't move with this information. We're forbidden from introducing newly discovered evidence prior to a ruling on our pending motions. As you know, an appeal in the supreme court stays all other proceedings. I grant you, often it seems unfair, and maybe it is, but that's how the system works."

"Do you have any idea when the supreme court will rule?"

"No way we can predict that, or hurry it along. Our chances for a reversal are slim to none, I'm afraid. You should keep digging, learn everything you can for the appeal, which we'll base on points not covered during the trial. Your press conference helped a lot."

"Maybe. But none of the reporters seemed fired up by what they heard."

"Lake, rest assured, members of the supreme court read the story in the *Progress*. And it could have an impact. Like everyone else, they're influenced by the media."

I gave Savoy my impressions of the Funk-Emprise-Bolles battle that began in 1969, spilled into the 1972 Pepper Committee hearings, had hardly settled when the *Republic* pulled Bolles off the story in 1973, and then could have flared again shortly before the bombing with Bradley Funk finding out his ex-wife had talked to the reporter about preparations for her incendiary lawsuit.

A dozen times I'd read Funk's hearing testimony, full of bullet-dodging ramblings and excessive preoccupation with Bolles and "the conspiracy." Then, in 1976, shortly before the bombing, up popped Funk's recurring nightmare. Perhaps this time Funk feared the reporter had honed his expository pen scalpel-sharp—not to peel away layers covering a questionable business arrangement but to publicly eviscerate Funk's personal secrets. If Funk knew that Bolles nosed around his ex-wife's lawsuit, what must have gone on in his head?

Betty Funk Richardson told Detective Marcus Aurelius about Bolles showing up at a child support hearing: "He just sat there and glared at Brad, and I love him for it. I think Don's been kicked around and around and made to look ridiculous for years. And finally when they couldn't shake him, they tried to destroy him. I hope Don becomes a Jesus Christ . . . and you all rally around the poor guy and recognize what he's been fighting alone."

Attorney General Robert Corbin, who took over the Bolles case in 1978 when Bruce Babbitt became governor, twice described Bradley Funk as a "contingency suspect" in the murder. Whatever that means, the Phoenix police interviewed Funk for less than one minute, suggesting they get together later with the racetrack magnate "to talk." But that talk never took place.

Why not? I asked Savoy. What kind of police investigation was this?

I'd never accepted the alleged motive for the murder, that Kemper Marley ordered the hit because a newspaper story cost him a post on the racing commission. But since that first night reading the discovery, I'd learned Marley had lost his bid for the position *before* the Bolles article. The weak motive had turned into no motive.

I felt discouraged and shackled with the defense apparently unable to use the new information. Dammit, I fumed to myself, Robison and Dunlap should be out on bail, awaiting a new trial.

But sitting there in Savoy's office, I couldn't even be sure they would be retried. Prosecutors had gone to great lengths to convict them on the flimsiest evidence—simply Adamson's testimony—and it was nose-on-the-face clear that the only "solution" to the case the powers that be wanted was the one they had now. I wondered what else they feared would be found, and assured Savoy as I left his office that I'd continue to look.

"Absolutely," he said. "As a private investigator you're not hampered by a state bar or canon of ethics that restricts lawyers from dealing with the press during a pending criminal action. Stay with it. You're filling our quiver with arrows for a new trial after the appeal is denied."

On January 20 I sat opposite Max Dunlap in the drab little room at Arizona State Prison and updated him on my activities, including news that the Playboy Foundation had agreed to contribute financially to the investigation. I had been visiting Max and Jim frequently, at least once a week, knowing how anxious they were for progress reports (and Max for word from home), and to provide what moral support I could.

Max had grown progressively upbeat with each new revelation, his biggest surge of optimism coming on the heels of the press conference. Robison, the more skeptical one, saw the state determined to continue its coverup and ultimately bury the case with him and Max. "You haven't uncovered a smoking gun," he said more than once. "No," I said, "but Neal Roberts's beforehand knowledge of the killing comes fairly close."

"Close won't count," he said, and again talked about how he'd rather die than endure what he called "torture."

I always talked to Max first, and this day puzzlement was written on his open-book face. "I still can't understand," he said, "why with all these shocking things you've uncovered, we can't get a new trial."

"I think we will," I said. Actually, I *hoped* we would. But, death row reeked of enough doom and despair without my adding any. "I met with Savoy recently, and we went over this. We can't use the new information until after the supreme court rules."

Max looked puzzled. "Can't be used?"

"Not now. Not in front of the court."

"Then we're sitting here because of a technicality?"

"Sort of."

"I don't understand that law."

How could I explain it to Max Dunlap, who believed every wrong would be righted because this was America? I didn't have the heart to chip away at his naive hopes.

Still, I agreed with him. Why such a law? I supposed for the sanity and convenience of judges. A rising crime rate meant a heavier appeals load, and chaos would result if defense lawyers constantly added material to their appeals.

But what about unjustly convicted prisoners? Not only were they victims of justice miscarried in the courtroom, they were also then forced to suffer in the name of judicial order and decorum.

I tried to reassure Max. "The evidence isn't totally worthless even now," I said. "I'm feeding it to Don Devereux at the *Daily Progress*, which is firmly in our corner. Judges read newspapers. They know something is up. Maybe more important, Bill Helmer from *Playboy* is coming to Arizona soon. I hope he can interview you and Jim. Refocusing a national spotlight on your case can't do anything but help. We've dug up good information. I expect to find more."

Max asked, as always, about his family, whom I tried to visit at least once a week. Each word of their loving, encouraging messages made his eyes twinkle. But then they began to fill with tears as he said, "My daughters, bless their hearts, have had to hang their heads in school ever since this whole mess started. Lately, thanks to you, Lake, they've been able to look up a little. I tell you, those kids have paid the heaviest price. They went from being the 'Dunlap children' to 'kids of a killer.' "

It was true. One of Max's daughters told me that as she stood in a supermarket checkout line a shopper pointed at her and said, "That's one of the Dunlap girls. Her father murdered Don Bolles."

After lunch in my cemetery, I visited Robison.

"Jim, what do you think about talking with a senior editor from *Playboy?*"

"They want me for a centerfold?"

"You're feisty today."

"Helps me forget the pain."

"The editor's name is Bill Helmer. He's familiar with everything we have, and he thinks the magazine may be ready to run with it. Helmer's a friend of mine. Will you talk to him?"

"Yeah."

Silence. The only sound was the clang of a distant cell door.

Finally, "You're doing a fine job, Lake. That press conference was superb." More silence. "But I can't see it doing any good. The supreme court's not going to overturn this conviction, and your new evidence won't make a rat's ass difference either. Max, the eternal optimist, thinks all this will work out okay, but I don't. The name of this game is Cover Your Ass, and it starts right at the top. Schafer doesn't give a shit. The same with Sellers. They won't even go over your stuff."

"Well, I can't look at it that way. I've got—"

"I know your position. Good for you. But I'm telling it straight. It's the same way with the *Arizona Republic*: Cover Your Ass. You showed they didn't tell the truth about Bolles and the *Gallup Independent,* but did you read any correction in Phoenix? Sellers and Schafer got this whole case wrong, but they don't dare admit it. What would it do to their careers if they fessed up to blowing the biggest case of their lives and admitted putting the wrong guys on death row?"

Robison was describing the attitude of many prosecutors. I never heard one admit he was wrong, even when the true killer stepped forward and proved an innocent man sat on death row. The same held true with some police officers. Jon Sellers, presumably an intelligent man, must have known he erred when he granted immunity like a street corner hawker handing out free cigarette samples.

I could sense Sellers's way of thinking—take the easy way, appease public opinion, buy convictions with immunity—behind Schafer's telling the jury: "Give us these convictions and more arrests will follow."

Schafer had meant Kemper Marley. But now it was 1979. In the year and a quarter since Dunlap and Robison had been convicted, whenever questions were raised or protests jarred the comfortable case-almost-closed complacency of prosecutors and police, the same tired line was heard: more arrests will follow.

Yet no one busied himself beating the bushes for suspects or leads. Nor could police and prosecutors play what they still smugly considered their ace in the hole: Robison and Dunlap snitching on Marley to save their own lives. Schafer and Sellers must have been confident that the condemned men, faced with the reality of execution, would roll over on the rich man. Only it hadn't yet happened that way, and the continuing lack of outrage from the Arizona media over those immunity arrangements was enabling the prosecution to succeed, as Robison put it, in the Cover Your Ass game.

Unlike Robison, I didn't feel this case was hopeless. I *couldn't.* If I believed myself foredoomed to failure, I would have been guilty of taking money under false pretenses. Several times in past cases, after studying the evidence, I had refused to work an investigation because I believed it would do no good.

"Nothing," I said to Robison, "can make up for the time you've lost. But there's a qualitative difference between getting you out sometime and your being executed."

Robison gave me a dead-level serious look and said, "I've got something in my head that *will* make a difference. I'm working on it now, and when I get it perfected, I'll need your help. I don't mean to be mysterious, but I just can't discuss it today."

What did he mean? My mind wrestled with a dozen possibilities. I considered them all the way back to Phoenix.

The Arizona Supreme Court roadblocked the introduction of new evidence on the Bolles case, but I had another route to follow. With Robison and Dunlap held in suspended animation by the state judicial system, I was going to stir up action with the feds. If I convinced the U.S. attorney to impanel a grand jury with subpoena power, a key player like Neal Roberts would be forced into either the truth or perjury. His "loud and clear" remark and reporting three cars stolen on the day of the murder were only two of many areas a grand jury could fruitfully explore.

I called Assistant U.S. Attorney Morton Sitver. After my press conference, he had told newspapers he would listen to me.

It was not what he told me now. "I'm not the one to listen, Mr. Headley," Sitver said. "I'm the assistant U.S. attorney. You need to talk to my boss Michael Hawkins."

"Can you transfer me?"

"You're better off hanging up and dialing back."

Better off? Meaning he didn't want to be involved? "Mr. Hawkins," I said, "I'd like to meet with you and discuss the Bolles bombing. I have information and documents that your office should find quite interesting."

"I believe the state is handling the matter," Hawkins said in a voice that didn't convey a flicker of interest.

"The FBI has been involved," I argued. "And other U.S. agents. I just want you to talk with me and look at what I have."

"I don't think a meeting would be appropriate."

I hate the word *appropriate*. It can cover a thousand unvoiced motives.

"Mr. Hawkins, two men have been condemned to the gas chamber. Strong evidence suggests they're innocent. Even if you weren't a U.S. attorney but only a citizen, I'd think it 'appropri-ate' for you to check out this possible tragedy in the making."

"It's a matter of jurisdiction, Mr. Headley."

"You work for the Justice Department. The FBI, also an arm of the Justice Department, has already been involved. To me that indicates you have jurisdiction."

"I don't want to debate with you, Mr. Headley. I tell you what: Send your material over to me, and I'll look at it."

I provided Hawkins a detailed report of my key findings, plus corroborating official documents, and requested that he impanel a federal grand jury to investigate the Bolles killing. I distributed copies of my cover letter to the press and electronic media in a deliberate effort to keep everything aboveboard—no secret deals, no backroom bargaining out of public earshot—and hoped dis-closure would pressure Hawkins to launch an independent in-vestigation. Also, if (as it turned out) he did nothing, I didn't want this federal prosecutor excusing his inaction by claiming a lack of knowledge.

After talking with Hawkins, I hit the streets to work more prosaic tasks: actual investigation rather than dealing with lawyers (Sa-voy), prisoners (Robison and Dunlap), and prosecutors (Sitver, Hawkins). None of them could or would help.

I started by looking at the assertions of Barry Goldwater and Neal Roberts. The two men denied knowing each other, yet from the start of my investigation I'd been hearing their names lumped together. Feeling that anything which shook Neal Rob-erts's story was good for Robison and Dunlap, I undertook a search for Antje Roberts, Neal's ex-wife.

The local credit bureau listed her employer as Goldwater's Department Store in Scottsdale—a touch of irony, I thought—and the assistant manager there told me she worked in cosmetics.

Using a description provided by Claude Keller ("a dead ringer for Lauren Bacall"), I spotted her in the notions section. "Are you Antje Roberts?" I knew she was and handed her my card.

"I recognize you," she said. "I read the papers."

"I'd like to ask you some questions."

She reached under the counter, took a card from her purse, and coolly said, "This is my lawyer. Get in touch with him. If he says it's all right, I'll talk to you."

Fat chance, I thought. He'll just dish out another crock of legalese.

Putting on my best little-boy face with a but-why-can't-you-come-out-and-play? expression, I said, "For right now, could I ask you *one* question?"

She couldn't repress a smile. "Okay. One question."

"You were married to Neal Roberts for a long time. Does he know Barry Goldwater?"

"Yes. Very well."

"Did you ever see them together?" I asked, pushing my luck.

"You said one question. I answered it. Now call my lawyer."

I searched for Gail Owens, Adamson's girlfriend, who had admitted under a grant of immunity from Jon Sellers that she'd scouted out Bolles's haunts and where he parked his car, so Adamson could choose a site for the killing. She'd also admitted to Sellers that she accompanied Adamson when he purchased the dynamite.

Sellers had given her immunity for conspiracy. I figured that, from her own admission—driving around looking for Bolles's car—she could have been charged with aiding and abetting murder.

No one had been closer to Adamson than Gail Owens, who truly might have merited some kind of plea deal *after* she revealed everything she knew about the killing. In addition, no one was more capable than Gail of unraveling the lies Adamson told.

I urged the Phoenix police, and U.S. Attorney Hawkins, to subject Gail Owens to very close questioning, but my recommendations were ignored. I also struck out when I attempted to find her.

I did locate her father, however, a well-to-do businessman who told me Gail was out of the country on an extended vacation. "I don't think she'd talk to you anyway," he said. "My daughter wants to put all of that behind her."

I was sure she did.

I learned that for many years Neal Roberts had dated a woman named Kay Kroot. Using an old reliable source, the telephone book, I found her number and called.

"I'd like to talk to you about Neal Roberts," I said.

"I don't think that would be in my best interest," she said.

Otherwise Kay Kroot was friendly, and we chatted about Phoenix, her favorite restaurants, the book she was currently reading. Whenever I maneuvered the subject back to Neal Roberts, she laughed and steered the conversation away from him.

The next day I sent her flowers, which I followed up with a phone call and dinner invitation.

"You just want to talk about Neal," she said.

"Not 'just' him. I think we'd have a good time."

Her turndown didn't help my ego.

I sent more flowers. Repeated the invitation to dinner. Was turned down again.

Terri Lee ribbed me about not being much of a Don Juan. My counter was that maybe, because of her, my heart wasn't in it.

"Well, get your priorities straight," Terri Lee said. "You need to talk to that woman. Be more persistent."

I'd been persistent, I thought, but to keep from looking like a dud in Terri Lee's eyes, I turned up the charm level on Kay Kroot.

More flowers. More phone calls. And finally she agreed—not to dinner, but to talk with me at her place.

Kay—in her mid-forties, petite, attractive—had been the other woman in Neal Roberts's life for a long time. "People who knew about our relationship called us Mutt and Jeff," she said. "He's tall and I'm so short. But, I don't suppose that's the kind of information you're looking for."

"I'm trying to get a better picture of Neal."

"I'll tell you the same things I told that detective. Sellers, I think his name was."

Not having seen any report in the discovery concerning an interview with Kay Kroot, I made a mental note to go through it again. And to complain loudly if, as I suspected, it wasn't there.

"Neal's ordeal with his parents," Kay said, "had a profound impact on his life. His father killed his mother, you know, and then committed suicide. Neal came home from school and found them dead."

"Tell me about you and Neal."

"I was more of a mother figure to him than a girlfriend. I wasn't comfortable with being his buddy, his confidante. He drank a lot, and told me many things, mainly about his parents, that he probably didn't even talk to his wife about."

"Did he ever mention Barry Goldwater?"

"Often. And intimately. As if Goldwater were one of his best friends."

"Did you ever see them together?"

"Once. Neal and Senator Goldwater appeared on a television talk show together here in Phoenix, and Neal took me along to watch. He introduced Goldwater to me as an old friend, and from the way they acted, that certainly appeared to be true."

This proved, if nothing else, that Roberts and Goldwater had lied when they denied knowing each other.

The day after my visit with Kay Kroot, I viewed the tape of the TV talk show she'd told me about. Sure enough, Roberts and Goldwater bantered back and forth on camera like old buddies.

Another comb through the mass of discovery failed to produce the Sellers interview with Kay Kroot. What I did find, however, having somehow overlooked earlier, was a police interview with Antje Roberts. Antje described meeting Neal at a restaurant where he produced an envelope that, according to him, contained twenty-five thousand dollars in cash "from the junior senator from Arizona." The money, Antje said Neal told her, was for *John Harvey Adamson's defense.*

The junior senator from Arizona was, of course, Barry Goldwater. But why in the world—assuming Antje had her facts straight—would Goldwater contribute to the defense fund of sleazy John Adamson?

I remembered Vlassis talking about the Navajo reservation, Goldwater's keen interest in the vast natural resources upon which the Indians sat, Roberts's reputed plan to replace George Vlassis as the tribe's general counsel, and Adamson's own charges that Roberts had retained him to "create havoc" and discredit Peter MacDonald.

Most significant, Bolles, in the last months of his life, had spent a great deal of his time investigating the reservation's tangled affairs.

12

Goldwater

In mid-February 1979, Terri Lee and I had dinner with Don and Naomi Devereux. I'd been seeing a lot of Terri, socially as well as professionally—movies, candlelight dinners, late-night sessions coordinating the mass of investigative material into a coherent, workable whole. This evening Devereux thought a relaxed, roundtable exchange of ideas on what we knew individually and collectively about the case would help.

But first we ate, and I continued to be pleased with how well Terri and Naomi hit it off. They got along great on a personal level—talking about clothes, fun places, the Devereux children—and as members of an investigative team, they meshed like movements in a Swiss watch.

From working with Don on migrant labor articles, plus investigating the Bolles case, Naomi was a research whiz. She had volunteered to show Terri how to research court records, a task she did for Don and I needed Terri to do for me.

Terri had located the Pepper Committee transcripts, and then continued with interviews, court record checks, and newspaper files to learn everything she could about Bolles's old nemesis Bradley Funk.

The Funk family, Terri explained after we'd eaten, traced its roots in Arizona almost to the turn of the century—a long time in the last contiguous state admitted to the Union (1912). The Funks, ranked among the Arizona elite, used profits from a booming jewelry business to build Arizona's first dog-racing track in the mid-1940s, and the gambling business proved a bonanza. They parlayed one track into half a dozen, the only six in the state, which the family co-owned with Emprise. However, the state audit Bolles referred to at the Pepper Committee hearing revealed that the Funks owed Emprise a lot of money and had pledged their fifty percent interest in the tracks to Emprise as collateral.

In the late 1960s Bolles began publishing articles about the Funks' friendly relationship with racing commissioners, who were supposed to regulate the pari-mutuel industry. After he wrote about his phone being tapped, and other serious privacy violations, the Funks had filed their lawsuit, claiming Bolles, Steiger, and the *Arizona Republic* were trying to "ruin" them.

Terri suspected Emprise had its hand in this lawsuit. Attorneys call it the "chilling effect"—turning profit-conscious publishers cold to the idea of running exposés from fear of costly legal action. Often, the claimant, after making sure the publisher has expended a great deal of money in pretrial preparation, drops the lawsuit. Regardless, even if the *Arizona Republic* had won— and it probably would have since the Pepper Committee said the Funks and Emprise were the ones employing false accusations—the victory would have been Pyrrhic.

In reality, the "chilling effect" won out. The *Republic*'s secret out-of-court settlement with the Funks reportedly promised not to run any more articles about the dog-track scandal. On his own, Bolles continued to probe pari-mutuel racing in Arizona and Emprise, but he never wrote another story on either subject.

"How about Brad Funk personally?" I asked Terri.

"Before the murder he was a very heavy drinker. A loud, abusive drunk. After the bombing, but before Bolles died, Funk checked into an alcohol rehabilitation center near San Diego, called Beverly Manor. I suspect the reason had more to do with removing himself from the jurisdiction of Arizona authorities than with fighting his drinking problem."

I needed to nose around Beverly Manor and see what I could learn. Too many people had left Phoenix right after the bombing: the one-legged gambler, Hank Landry, who overheard Roberts's "loud and clear" remark, vanished into thin air; Adamson flew to Havasu; Funk went to Beverly Manor.

"Did Funk know Adamson?"

"The police think he did. They looked into Adamson's past and found witnesses who claimed to have seen a drunken Bradley Funk being helped into his car by Adamson."

"How about Funk and Neal Roberts?"

"Regular drinking buddies at the Ivanhoe."

"And Adamson hung out there every day," I added. "He used it as his office. That's not a big bar. It would be virtually impossible for him not to know Funk."

"Right," Terri said. "Nobody denies Adamson and Roberts were good friends."

"Anything else on Funk?"

"Little things. Maybe important, maybe not. He went to Phoenix North High School with Max Dunlap. His family is understandably close with Kemper Marley, also a member of that tiny elite circle that largely controls affairs in this state."

Terri Lee was our team's resident expert on Bradley Funk; and Don Devereux knew more than any of us about Barry Goldwater.

"Goldwater," said Devereux, "his brother Bob, and former Republican State Chairman Harry Rosenzweig have been *the* movers and shakers in Arizona for the past thirty years. Barry is the national political force. Bob is the money guy, a successful businessman. Rosenzweig takes care of the nitty-gritty political details."

"Tell us about Goldwater and organized crime."

"What helped launch his national career was a five-thousand-dollar campaign contribution from racketeer Willie Bioff. This was back in the forties when five thousand dollars bought something. Barry was also a friend of Gus Greenbaum, who worked for Meyer Lansky. The Goldwater family had a close relationship with Moe Dalitz, who came to Phoenix from the Midwest and paved the way for all the major hoodlums that followed. With backing from Lansky, Dalitz began wheeling and dealing in Las Vegas, and one of the results seems to have been the installation of a Goldwater Department Store at the Desert Inn."

I took notes while Devereux talked. Bolles, with the breath remaining for only a few words, had included the Mafia in his triumvirate, along with Adamson and Emprise.

"Robert Goldwater," Devereux continued, "later went into a chain-restaurant business with a close associate of Peter 'Horse-face' Licavoli, a friend of Dalitz's. Give credit to IRE for the good things we accomplished," Devereux said directly to me. "True, we probably fumbled the ball by ignoring the murder itself, but some solid investigative work got done."

Probably so, but I became agitated every time I thought of their "continuing Bolles's work" when they didn't know what that work was. Worse, they in effect allowed the wrong people to be convicted because their "seeking of vengeance" for the murder didn't include finding out who committed it.

"Greenbaum," Devereux said, obviously warmed up to his subject, "operated the Flamingo and Riviera hotel-casinos for the Mafia, where Barry and Bob Goldwater stayed at no charge. There's quite a list of things we learned. Barry Goldwater personally intervened in an attempt to obtain better prison conditions and a more moderate sentence for a syndicate member named Clarence Newman. Newman was Bob Goldwater's bookmaker. Barry Goldwater and Harry Rosenzweig took a vacation with Willie Bioff just a month before Bioff was blown up by a bomb. Bioff, by the way, started out in crime at age nine, telling johns he could fix them up with his *younger* sister. Like Bioff, Gus Greenbaum and his wife, Bess, were murdered, their throats slit in their Phoenix home, and Barry Goldwater attended Greenbaum's funeral. The Valley National Bank of Phoenix, of which Bob Goldwater was a director, loaned money to finance the Flamingo. Greenbaum's ties to the mob were very strong. He worked with Al Capone, Bugsy Siegel, and Meyer Lansky."

Devereux talked about organized crime with an ease and surety that reminded me of Don Bolles's testimony about the

Funks. He discussed Moe Dalitz, about whom Robert Goldwater said, "I am not at all ashamed to have maintained an acquaintance with Mr. Dalitz. While I know nothing of your reporters' allegations with respect to Mr. Dalitz, I do know that during the time that I have known him, he has been a public-spirited citizen."

Dalitz, a bootlegger, bookmaker, and syndicate boss, was instrumental in borrowing $93,700,000 to build Rancho La Costa Country Club, the Teamsters-financed 5,600-acre resort in Carlsbad, California. According to the FBI, La Costa gave "red carpet" treatment to Mafia visitors. "Public-spirited" Dalitz was a key figure in the murderous Purple Gang, befriended Jimmy Hoffa, and obtained dozens of loans from Teamsters pension funds. Dalitz admitted to Nevada gambling authorities that his friends had included Mickey Cohen, Frank Costello, Lucky Luciano, Anthony "Big Tuna" Accardo, and John Roselli.

Gene Butler, former husband of Barry Goldwater's daughter Joanne, said the name of Dalitz was often brought up in family conversations. Butler said Joanne was treated "like royalty" when she visited La Costa, which never billed her for her accommodations.

Interestingly, the Goldwaters also frequented the Balboa Bay Club in Newport Beach, whose members included several of the Funks. Former U.S. Congressman Sam Steiger revealed that while he was investigating Arizona dog-racing interests, both Harry Rosenzweig and Barry Goldwater asked him to "go easy on the Funks" because they were old "family friends." At the same time, 1970, Barry Goldwater wrote a letter to one of the Funks assuring that he would pass on any information he received regarding a Justice Department probe of Emprise.

The IRE charged that for years Rosenzweig, Goldwater's mentor, "nurtured prostitution and gambling" in Phoenix. Rosenzweig, the 1975 Phoenix Man of the Year, denied influence in Arizona bookmaking but admitted that "maybe twice" he recommended prostitutes to friends.

I'd been in close contact with Jerry Kammer, a graduate of Notre Dame who was soon to publish a book called *The Second*

Long Walk. In this book Kammer gave a lot more background on Adamson and Roberts "creating havoc," detailed the century-old Hopi-Navajo land dispute, and related a mysterious incident I'd also been putting together.

"The Goldwater-MacDonald story became bizarre in February 1977 with sworn testimony of John Harvey Adamson," Kammer wrote. "Adamson testified that he had discussed the idea of planting a bomb in MacDonald's offices with Neal Roberts, a Phoenix attorney, and Joe Patrick."

Kammer continued, "Adamson recalled asking Roberts what Patrick did on the reservation. 'Mr. Roberts said Mr. Patrick was a spy on the reservation—that he was a spy for Senator Goldwater and reported directly to Senator Goldwater what happened on the Indian reservation, especially in regard to Peter MacDonald,' Adamson said. Adamson's testimony became even more unsettling as he recalled that he, Roberts, and Patrick also discussed planting a bomb 'in a car one Indian drives back and forth to Phoenix, where he stays at the Granada Royale Hotel.' He said the plan was to rig the bomb in such a way that it could not explode. Later it was learned that the 'other Indian' who drove back and forth to Phoenix was Tony Lincoln, who was director of the Bureau of Indian Affairs on the Navajo reservation. Explaining the rationale for planting a bomb that could not explode, Adamson said, 'They wanted some havoc to be raised on the reservation.' He said the ultimate goal was to discredit MacDonald and bring about 'martial law on the reservation.'

"It was a terrifyingly rational scenario. Lincoln, a Goldwater protégé, did not get along with MacDonald. If a bomb were found on Lincoln's car, MacDonald could be blamed. Then, if federal officials stepped in to impose martial law (as they had considered doing during the Wounded Knee takeover in 1973), MacDonald would be pushed aside and Lincoln, the highest federal officer on the reservation, could assume control of the Navajo government."

· · ·

Don Devereux, no matter how keyed in to our Bolles investigation, never let the plight of farm workers wander far from his mind. This night, largely reserved for talking about the Funks and Goldwaters, he recounted the IRE team discovering that Robert Goldwater had for more than a decade profited brutally from the labor of illegal Mexican immigrants.

Robert Goldwater was president of Goldmar, Inc., whose wholly owned subsidiary was the three-thousand-acre Arrowhead Ranch, northwest of Phoenix. IRE learned that in 1977 Mexican workers at Arrowhead labored from sunrise to sunset for an average of five dollars per day, a wage bled down even further by Social Security deductions and food prices charged by overseers. The workers lived in orange crates amid their own excrement surrounded by black plastic sheets hung from trees so they couldn't be seen by passersby. Each of these super-exploited toilers had paid a hundred dollars and more to "coyotes," who smuggled them to Arrowhead Ranch where they labored in 110-degree heat.

Gene Butler, Barry Goldwater's former son-in-law, had told IRE there was no doubt the senator knew about the employment of the illegal Mexican workers, and Butler remembered Robert Goldwater saying that Arrowhead would have to go out of business if the border patrol became more vigilant.

Not much chance of that happening. "The border patrol are my friends," an Arrowhead foreman had asserted. "If there is ever a report, the border patrol calls me, and I tell my workers to hide."

Said a public health nurse who visited Arrowhead Ranch: "It was a horrible situation. The conditions in which these men lived . . . no sanitary facilities, no shelter, crowded together . . . make them prime targets for disease and infection. Communicable diseases like tuberculosis, lice, scabies, impetigo, influenza, etc., would spread through a camp like this very rapidly."

Men weren't the only Mexicans the IRE team saw struggling for survival at Arrowhead. A pregnant woman and her family of five lived in a packing crate. The reporters found a six-month-old baby lying on a blanket, flies swarming around his dirty face. Another baby was seen eating soup whose main ingredient appeared to be half-dead insects.

Of course, the Social Security deductions were a scam to take back what little the workers were paid. All but one of the Social Security numbers began with the digits 000, which the Social Security administration does not use.

How could this go on? The head of the U.S. border patrol office in Phoenix, Raymond F. Feld, said that he and only four other agents were totally responsible for patrolling a thirty-six-thousand-square-mile area extending from south of Phoenix to Idaho.

Several days after the dinner conference, I found myself in a Phoenix restaurant having coffee with Joe Patrick, the reputed Goldwater spy. A slender, distinguished-looking man in his early sixties, he dressed in cowboy clothes and generated the demeanor of a slick PR man. The business card he handed me looked like this:

HORSE TRADER

JOE PATRICK

WARS STARTED	WHISKEY SMUGGLED
WOMEN PROCURED	ABORTIONS ARRANGED
ORGIES ORGANIZED	BARS EMPTIED
ADVICE ON HOW TO GO IN DEBT	BRANDS ALTERED
EX-MAYOR, WAKE ISLAND	MERCENARY
HAS BEEN FIGHTER PILOT	WILL STILL TRY

Remember, any war is better than no war at all.

Joe Patrick ranked as possibly Barry Goldwater's best friend, the senator's "wing man" in the Air National Guard, and a former Phoenix television personality. He and Goldwater fished and hunted together, shared confidences, worried about each other's family, and generally were just comfortable in a friendship that had lasted for decades.

Patrick wanted to confine the interview to telling me what a great guy Barry Goldwater was, but I had other interests. Before meeting with him, I'd obtained copies from the Navajos of Patrick's daily logs, which he had to give to tribal authorities to justify his pay. These logs confirmed that Patrick had several meetings with Don Bolles.

The most recent meeting, Patrick admitted, occurred just two weeks before the bombing. I asked him what they talked about.

"Bolles asked questions," Patrick said, "about the attempted bombing of the Indian Health Services Building."

"The one Adamson was involved in," I said.

"Yes."

"What else did Bolles want to know?"

"He asked about the plane that crashed carrying those Navajo councilmen. He found it suspicious. He seemed to be looking for connections between the Health Services Building and the airplane crash."

I wondered about that, too. Adamson had confessed to planting the bomb at the Health Services Building. He had confessed conspiracy to commit bombing on the reservation. Did he also have something to do with that tragic plane crash?

The interview with Patrick ended. If it accomplished nothing else, it uncovered a possible motive—fear of Bolles sniffing out potential homicides—more compelling than the one used to convict Robison and Dunlap.

Finding motives for the killing of Don Bolles, as a matter of fact, did not rank as a difficult task. It was turning out that with a smorgasbord to choose from, the prosecution had latched onto just about the only one that made no sense.

13

Robison's Way

I made one of my regular visits on March 1, 1979, to Max and Jim at the Arizona State Prison. I spent the morning explaining to Max new developments in the investigation, answering questions about his family, and taking personal messages to deliver to his wife and children. Every new piece of information delighted this optimist, raising in his mind hopes that vindication was near, and I found myself walking a fine line of trying not to temper his enthusiasm—which kept him going—while reminding him that courts weren't usually known for their speed.

As had been true for some weeks, I looked forward more to the afternoon discussion with Jim Robison, who I knew possessed more information than he'd told me. He had, after all, been very close to John Adamson. I sensed from the first time we met that I would have to invest a lot of trust-building time in this man before he opened up to me. Well, more than three months of cultivating that trust had been time enough. Sitting in the cemetery that day, munching a sandwich from my brown bag lunch, I had decided to confront Robison, tell him I needed to be steered in a direction. But when I faced him in that tiny interview room, I found out he'd made the decision to steer himself.

"Lake," he said when we sat down, "I've decided to take control of my life. I feel the appeal is hopeless, and they're gonna execute me. It will be a long time coming, but it will happen. So, I'm gonna take the time I have left and compress it. Make it shorter. Lessen this torture."

Robison didn't want me to interrupt. It was his play, so I didn't say a word.

Steady, serious, determined, but most of all relieved that he had made a decision he felt capable of carrying through, he got right to the point.

"I've decided to starve myself to death," he said matter-of-factly. "I got the idea from that IRA guy Bobby Sands. I've been in my program two weeks already. No solid food. Nothing that will sustain life. I figure I can last another seventy-five to ninety days. It's indicative of the disregard they have for us here: no one's made anything of my not having eaten for fourteen days."

"Why are you doing this, Jim?"

"First, I want to know that you won't interfere. In fact, I'm going to ask your help."

"It's your business. You tell me your life is unacceptable. Who am I to say you're wrong? But will you explain why?"

"Yes. It's to take control of my life in the only way left open to me. If I slash my wrists or try to hang myself, they'll probably catch me before I succeed and stop me from trying again. All I'd accomplish would be to hurt myself. Funny, huh? They'd save my life to take it away at their convenience. My way I have *some* time left, but not *much*. I want you to tape record what I *think*. I don't want my thoughts lost forever. To help somebody else would be fine—so much the better if that results. But believe me, Lake, I'm doing this mostly for me. This is a miserable existence, as you can see, and you're probably tired of hearing me complain. My way is better than theirs. I've told you time and again, the judge didn't mention torture in my sentence, and that's what this is."

I didn't doubt his sincerity, and sensed steel behind the soft-spoken words.

Nor did I argue. He had answers to anything I could say. Jim considered me a hopelessly misguided romantic, thinking I could beat the system.

"What do you want me to do?" I asked.

"When they bother to notice, they'll try to force-feed me. I want you to stop them."

"How can I do that?"

"Put up a fight. Get a court order."

"I'll try," I said, and stopped before adding that I didn't think it would work.

"I'm concerned about Max," Robison said. "What I do with my life is my business, but I have no right to hurt him. There are things I've figured out, other things that I know, and I need to share them with you."

I'd been waiting for this moment for Robison to point me in a direction, and it didn't surprise me that he did it more for Max Dunlap than for himself.

"Remember this name: Ralph Clark. He runs a bar near downtown Phoenix. He's a friend of mine. Find Clark. Tell him who you are. Say I sent you."

I jotted the name down and waited.

"This filthy hole isn't a good place for thinking," Robison continued, "but I haven't had anything else to do. It's clear to me how they managed to put Max and me here. Don't forget, the Arizona legislature set a precedent when it appropriated one hundred thousand dollars to investigate Don Bolles's murder. Those legislators wanted to see results. And there was all that pressure, from the media and the public, to solve the case quickly. The police had John Adamson, and when Neal Roberts came along with his theory, Jon Sellers grabbed it hook, line, and sinker. *Not* because he bought Roberts's story, since Sellers had to know this homicide led to some very high places that he was better off not searching. Christ, look at what you've discovered just from reading the police's own investigation."

I agreed. Even extreme incompetence couldn't explain interviewing Bradley Funk for less than one minute. Or granting immunity to Neal Roberts, Mr. Loud and Clear. Or three stolen vehicles on the day of the murder. Or so many other things overlooked, all red flags that would have alerted the most dumb-witted investigator to the fact that he was walking the wrong road.

"Sellers," Robison said, "orchestrated Roberts's theory. Remember, Roberts didn't name me. He fingered Dunlap, Kemper Marley, and somebody named Jimmy. That Jimmy, I think, was Jimmy Frattiano, but he could hardly say that, could he? I got plugged into the killing because I knew Adamson."

"Also they were pretty sure you wouldn't have an alibi," I said innocuously, to keep him talking.

"Right. But I had an alibi. They just ran roughshod over it. Anyway, they plugged me in, hoping for corroboration of Adamson, and corroboration is a strange aspect of the law. Because of the Adamson Act, his testimony was sufficient to convict Max and me, but not Kemper Marley. If he said Max or me told him that Kemper Marley told us to kill Bolles, that's hearsay. To convict Marley, they needed Max or me to corroborate Adamson. We wouldn't tell that lie for them."

"How many times were you offered a deal?"

"Dozens. My attorney told the jury about them. Getting me here didn't end the offers. I was told I could walk off death row in a heartbeat if I'd corroborate Adamson. They said: 'Be smart. Look at the deal Adamson got. We'll give you the same thing, only better. We realize you're older than Adamson, and twenty years might not seem too attractive to you. But when this blows over, we're sure even the twenty years could be negotiated.' "

"You blame Sellers the most for this?"

"Hell no. Sellers only does what his instincts say are expected of him."

"But you just said that Sellers orchestrated Roberts's theory."

"That's what I think. But I don't *know*. Anyway, it doesn't matter. I believe Sellers has good instincts, except when it comes to understanding people like Max and me. See, Jon Sellers had worked twenty years with snitches and criminals, slime like John Adamson, and he naturally assumed smart Mr. Robison and frightened Mr. Dunlap wouldn't take the pressure of prison; they'd fold up and grab any deal offered. Hell, hardened crimi-

nals crack, Robison and Dunlap should be easy. Lake, the prosecution had run out of alternatives. They told Bruce Babbitt and
the press, 'This deal with Adamson is going to work; we'll get
Marley and clear this whole thing up.' But their plan collapsed
because Max and I refused to lie for them. Still, they have to
keep trying. They've got almost three years and a lot of taxpayer
money invested in this, and it's not possible for them to admit
to the public, 'Hey, we were wrong all along.' Christ, no cop or
prosecutor would do that."

"You told me on an earlier visit that you didn't think they
wanted to execute you. But that's changed? Now they want to
do it?"

"Right. There's no statute of limitations on murder. The only
way the prosecution can claim the Bolles murder has been
cleared up is for Max and me to lie, which we won't do, *or* for
us to die. Then they can say, 'Well, Marley was the brains, we
know it, we solved the case, but there's nothing we can do to
get Marley.' "

"Don't you think your suicide will play into the prosecution's
hands?"

"Goddammit!" Robison flared, "you don't understand. Max
and I will never lie, so the only people suffering through this
are us. And Kemper Marley, who can't be safe from a murder charge until we're gone. Now, I respect Max's right to do
what he wants, but I'm going to follow my own lights. Another
thing: I don't want you ever calling this a suicide. *I* don't consider it suicide. I think we all begin to die the moment we're
born. What I'm doing is compressing the time I have left because the reality of existence is worse than dying. My home for
twenty-four hours a day is a windowless, vermin-infested la-
trine."

Much as I wanted to throw Robison a lifeline, I respected his
wishes and didn't try. He was an adult, intelligent and thoughtful, and I believed his life was his own to do with as he wanted.
However, since he'd requested my assistance, I asked him to put
into writing his exact intentions. What ensued is the following
statement:

This is March first, approximately 2:00. My name is James Robison and the statements I will be making are strictly my own and had no influence from anyone else. I've come to the decisions and the planning that I intend to carry out strictly on my own, and I have developed and devised a plan that can be best entitled Operation Termination, or anything along those lines.

What I intend to do and fully intend to carry out is stop the intake of food until such time as my life-support systems fail. I am of sound body and of sound mind. I'm not some kind of a nut. I'm doing this with total purpose. I am not considering this as suicide, because to me suicide is a stupid senseless act and has no purpose except to the perpetrator.

What basically I'm doing is that rather than live like an animal in a subhuman environment such as I am in at this time, I choose to take what time is left to me here on Earth and compress it into a smaller time for me. My purposes for doing this are many.

First, benefit to myself, naturally, because it will put me beyond the reach of the people that have subjugated me to this type of treatment. . . . To my best calculations, this plan should culminate in a period of seventy-five to ninety-five days. Today's the fourteenth day that I have not had a bit of food, and it's a sad commentary, also, on the system, that no one in the system is even aware of this. But, as my physical condition deteriorates, it will be something that somewhere down the road the establishment will have to recognize.

The only one qualified to argue whether I'm doing right or wrong, I feel, is myself, because without going through what I've gone through and seeing what I've seen and coming to the conclusions that I've come to, there's absolutely no one on Earth qualified to argue the right of what I'm doing or my right to do it. I cannot anticipate what interference might be placed in the way of my plan, but the basic plan is something that I fully intend, 100%, to carry through to termination. . . . Because the plan is mine and I will implement it, I've chosen Lake Headley to represent me as far as anyone or any statements that I might make in regard to the information that I have. I will not talk to any newspaper people, any media people, or anyone else without first talking to Lake and . . . discussing it and getting his advice on who I should talk to or if I should talk to anyone else. At first, I don't expect anyone to really take me too serious, but as I approach the termination date and approach a demise, I fully expect or anticipate that I will be taken seriously before I'm finished.

When I rose to leave that afternoon, Robison said, "I'm carrying this all the way. I'd never throw a saddle on this horse if I didn't intend to ride it to the end."

What Robison embarked on didn't change the purpose of my job: obtaining justice for him and Max. Nor had the means of achieving that goal changed—informing the public about the facts of the case.

The prosecution's version of events had gone unchallenged too long.

Playboy's Bill Helmer came to Arizona. Together with David Derickson, Robison's attorney, I arranged to get Helmer into the prison for an interview, not an easy feat.

I also contacted Molly Ivins, the Denver, Colorado, bureau chief of *The New York Times*. Molly said she'd be happy to come down to Arizona and study the evidence.

I was delighted, too, to learn at a meeting with Dunlap Committee members that they had contacted Mike Wallace of "60 Minutes." Wallace had expressed interest in coming to Phoenix to look over what we'd discovered.

Playboy. The New York Times. "60 Minutes." With these names rolling across Carolyn Robinson's desk at the Arizona State Prison, I confidently hoped that from there they'd gain the attention of everyone in the Arizona establishment. I wanted to make this cliquish crowd uncomfortable enough to question the value of their coverup in the Bolles murder.

Robison had told me to look up a bar owner named Ralph Clark, but before I could carry through with that lead, I got diverted onto the trail of a person who would become the prime witness in our investigation.

14

JoDon

Don Devereux and I sat in the Westward Ho Coffee Shop. We met, or talked on the phone, every day, and often went from these confabs to conduct interviews or research.

"Last night," Devereux said, "as I thumbed through my old IRE notes, I came across the name Michael JoDon."

"What's JoDon about?"

"I can't recall exactly; I've misplaced my notes on him. All I have is a name, a phone number, and a reference to Monte Kobey. Kobey was, I think, related by marriage to Bradley Funk and was indicted with Ned Warren for land fraud."

The mention of Ned Warren captured my attention.

Sent to Arizona in the late 1960s by New York City underworld bosses, Warren worked his way up to a fifty-year prison sentence in 1978 for land fraud. When he called himself The Godfather of Land Fraud, he didn't exaggerate. He bilked tens of millions of dollars from thousands of investors. Warren and his cohorts engineered gold and diamond swindles (flecks of gold were shotgunned into the walls of a depleted mine); oil, gas, and coal scams; the sale of arthritis and cancer cures (the arthritis remedy was a simple cactus juice and water concoction); and of course the staple: "a dream tract of land" that turned out to be an arid desert nightmare, the cruelest sort of fraud directed mainly at people who had worked a lifetime to save enough to buy a retirement home.

Not surprisingly, Don Bolles was among the first in the nation to investigate and expose Arizona land fraud operations.

My interest was piqued, however, by more than Ned Warren. There were those Mafia connections, and of course the name Bradley Funk always made my ears prick up.

"Did you ever meet with JoDon?" I asked.

"Yeah. He told me he dated Kara Kobey, Monte's daughter, and he overheard part of a conversation about the Bolles murder. I didn't have time to pursue it then. But when I found the name in my notes, I thought you might want to."

"What do you know about JoDon?"

"Practically nothing. He was an informant for the Scottsdale Police Department, and they had some sort of falling out."

"Let's call that number now."

We carried Styrofoam cups of coffee to my suite. More would be ordered up if locating JoDon outlasted four cups. So obsessed had I become with trying to find ways to free Dunlap and Robison that every waking hour was devoted to the case—including fun times with Terri Lee—and at night, visions of death chambers and exploding cars would blast me out of sleep.

Even threatening phone calls, which I probably would have taken more seriously in less hectic times, got ignored. I'd received four already, the last only two days before. "Get out of town tonight, asshole," rasped a menacing voice. And added, just so I understood: "Fuckin' asshole, you don't leave tonight, you'll end up like fuckin' Bolles."

My four threats from nameless, faceless callers amounted to a trickle compared to the flak Devereux was encountering on the street. Constantly being told his life was in danger, the journalist could believe it after that pickup truck tried to run him down in the alley. But neither of us was going to back off. We'd probably have to get into a new line of work if we did, and in any case be always haunted by the knowledge that we didn't have what it took.

"May I speak to Michael JoDon, please," I asked when a voice answered the ringing phone.

"This is his father. Can I help you?"

"Mr. JoDon, my name's Lake Headley. The Dunlap defense committee has retained me to investigate the Bolles homicide. We're trying to accumulate enough evidence for new trials. I'm sitting here now with Don Devereux of the *Scottsdale Progress*. Mr. Devereux spoke with your son about a year ago and tells me Michael has information on the Bolles killing. I'd like to talk with him."

"I'm sorry. He's not here. My son is a fugitive."

"From what? Why is he a fugitive?"

"He's wanted for sale of hashish to an undercover police-woman. They framed Michael, Mr. Headley, because he knows too much about the murder of Don Bolles. He realized he can't get a fair trial, and he left the state. Actually, he's afraid for his life."

"I assure you, Mr. JoDon, I'm not a police officer and I have no interest in jailing your son. I only want to talk to him about the Bolles killing."

"He knows a lot about that. But I don't know if he will talk to you. And he's a long way away."

A long way? Distance didn't matter. If he knew "a lot" about this murder, I'd travel around the world to see him.

"Can you get in touch with Michael?" I asked.

"To tell the truth, I have no idea where he is. He calls me once a week, but says it's better that I don't know his where-abouts."

"When is he due to call again?"

"Day after tomorrow."

"Mr. JoDon, please do me a big favor. Give your son a mes-sage. Ask him to call me collect at the Westward Ho Hotel."

"I'll give him the message. I can't promise he'll call.'

"Urge him. Tell him maybe we can help each other." I felt I might be able to assist JoDon with that fugitive warrant.

"Fine. I will. I sure hope you can help him. Michael doesn't deserve to be in this jam."

Michael JoDon called two days later. I told him who I was, what I did, and that I wanted to talk to him.

"Talk." He sounded young. "It's your dime."

"Do you remember Don Devereux?"

"Yeah. The reporter."

"Well, he's sitting with me right now. We'd like to talk to you about Don Bolles."

"You understand, I'm sure, that I'm a fugitive. I have to be careful who I talk with. I was scheduled to appear in superior court on a phony sale-of-hashish charge, and I didn't show."

"Tell me about the beef."

"After I started making noise about the Bolles killing, the Scottsdale police framed me. It was less than a gram of hash—twenty dollars' worth—I gave to this undercover policewoman who a friend brought over to my house. What you need to know is that I've been a confidential informant for numerous police agencies. Made a lot of cases for them. I was a damn good C.I. But when I gave Bob Powers information on the Bolles case, they all turned against me."

"Who is Powers?"

"A sergeant in the Scottsdale police department detective bureau. He works intelligence and narcotics. I'd been feeding him information for years, and I thought we were tight. I walked in and out of the detective bureau just like I was a cop. I hung out with him. Met his wife."

"What happened to that relationship?"

"It soured after I told him about Bolles."

"How long after the Bolles homicide did you give him your information?"

"It wasn't *after*. I told Powers that Bolles was going to be killed *before* Bolles was killed."

NEW ORLEANS, LOUISIANA. APRIL 15

I stood in front of Pat O'Brien's on St. Peter Street waiting for JoDon. It had taken several telephone conversations to persuade him to meet me. I'd given him my physical description, and he said he'd be here, 10 P.M. sharp.

The French Quarter wasn't an unpleasant place to wait. Tourists wandered the car-free streets and the best of American jazz filled the air. Echoes of Brando's "Stel-l-l-la" bounced through my memory.

JoDon came five minutes late. Behind him two burly young men stopped several yards down the sidewalk. I pegged them as bodyguards. Amateur bodyguards at that, they tried so conspicuously to look inconspicuous.

After we introduced ourselves, I said, "I'll need to talk with you alone. I want to tape record."

"I'm alone," JoDon said.

"No, you're not," I said, nodding toward his tag-team shadows. "Tell your muscle to go munch on some beignets or take in a strip show. You won't need them for a while."

JoDon sized me up and made a decision. "Okay. Where to?"

"I have a room at the Monteleone. Let's walk."

Surrounded by the delectable sounds and smells of the Quarter, we made small talk as we walked slowly toward the hotel. JoDon kept checking over his shoulder and didn't seem too comfortable that I was beside him. How could he be sure I wasn't a cop who'd tricked him?

"Relax," I said. "There are lots of people around. It's Easter Sunday, for chrissakes."

"Sure," he said, giving me a suspicious glance. "I just feel a little too vulnerable without Justin and Emil along. They're two good ol' Cajun boys I pay to watch my back when they're in from their jobs on the offshore oil rigs."

Besides what I saw—a nice-looking, clean-cut man still in his early twenties, slender, with curly brown hair, wearing jeans and a short-sleeve shirt—I knew quite a bit about young Michael JoDon thanks to Naomi Devereux's research.

JoDon's connections with the Scottsdale police department began in 1972, and he soon acquired the reputation of an extremely accurate and valuable informant. Early on he helped Scottsdale narcotics detectives seize $1.2 million in illegal drugs, and he followed this success with several more. JoDon had always wanted to be a cop, and working as an informant seemed likely to pave the way. Actually, he probably hurt his own cause. Generally, a good informant is worth more than a dozen detectives and a roomful of computers. The information JoDon fed the police was so accurate that Scottsdale loaned him to other law enforcement agencies: the Phoenix police department, the Arizona department of public safety (state police), the DEA, ATF, and FBI. He was sent as far away as Overland Park, Kansas, where he was instrumental in what was, at the time, the largest drug bust in Kansas history. JoDon won several official commendations for his work. The government paid him well, considering it a good investment. His information was always "the best." That is, until he came around with his disclosures about Don Bolles.

The tape recorder sat on a table between JoDon and me. I pressed Record and said, "Mike, tell me what you know about the Bolles case and how you came to know it."

"I was born in Scottsdale, went to school there. While I was in high school, I started dating Kara Kobey, Monte Kobey's daughter. Monte leases parking lots in Phoenix. He used to be in real estate until he got indicted with Ned Warren. Anyway, I dated Kara off and on in high school and after. Frequently her dad was at the house with friends when I went to pick her up. Monte looked on me as just another kid who hung around with his daughter. To him, I could have been a lamp, a piece of furniture, a sort of permanent fixture he didn't pay a lot of attention to. The first week in May—1976—I was at Kara's house, and her dad was with some of his friends. I heard them talking about Don Bolles. How they were going to kill Don Bolles. I'd never heard of Bolles, and I asked Kara who he was and why they wanted to murder him. She told me he was an *Arizona Republic* reporter, and she didn't know why they were after him, but maybe it had something to do with Ned Warren."

"Did you take this conversation seriously?"

"Probably not right at first. But Kara kept talking about it."

"Who were the other people at Kobey's house?"

Don Bolles's Datsun after bomb exploded. WIDE WORLD PHOTOS

Don Bolles. WIDE WORLD PHOTOS

Max Dunlap *(top)* and James Robison. WIDE WORLD PHOTOS

Adamson, wearing bullet-proof vest,
being escorted from jail to courthouse. WIDE WORLD PHOTOS

William Schafer delivers opening statement at trial
of Robison and Dunlap. WIDE WORLD PHOTOS

Gail Owens

Robert Corbin

Bradley Funk

Neal Roberts

Jon Sellers

The day the Arizona Supreme Court overturned the convictions:
(from left, back row) Lake Headley, Naomi Devereux, Don Devereux;
(in front) Terri Lee Yoder (later, Terri Lee Headley).

"I didn't know any of them. Kara called them her father's business associates. I think she knew but didn't want to tell me."

"Did they say how they planned to kill Bolles?"

"I heard them say, 'Blow him away,' which can mean a lot of things. Kara told me also that she heard her dad talking with Ned Warren, who she called Uncle Ned, about killing Bolles."

"What did you do after you heard this discussion about murder?"

"Keep in mind that I was an informant. I considered myself a police officer. Well, I thought I had great information and that I'd be viewed as a hero, so I went to Sergeant Bob Powers. I remember the date. May tenth. I told Powers what I had. When I didn't hear anything, I went to him two more times."

"When were these two other times?"

"Both in May."

"What did Powers say?"

"He didn't say much. Mostly listened to my information. After Bolles was killed, I was really shook up, as you can imagine. I'd told Powers it was going to happen, and it did. I got more scared when no one came around to see me."

"What did you do?"

"A couple of weeks later, I went to the Arizona attorney general's office and talked to a Mr. Wolf."

"Who is Mr. Wolf?"

"An investigator for the attorney general. I told him what I'd overheard at Monte Kobey's house and about telling Powers. Wolf thanked me, said he'd look into it, and I never heard from him again."

"Did you ever get in touch with the feds?"

"Yes. I went to the FBI. They acted the same as Wolf: 'Okay. Thanks a lot. We'll look into it.' And that's the last I heard from the FBI."

"Did you talk to anybody else?"

"Yeah. When the authorities wouldn't do anything, I went to the press. I talked to some of those reporters who came to Arizona."

"The IRE team?"

"Yeah. They weren't interested either."

I turned off the tape recorder and stared at JoDon. A dozen thoughts zoomed in and out of my head, vying for attention. Clearly, one question was paramount: Was JoDon telling the truth?

"Will you tell the authorities what you told me?"

"I already did. But, yes, I'll tell them again, with one provision. I want immunity for that phony hash bust. I didn't ask for anything before. I'm not asking for much now."

The arrest didn't make sense to me, unless something else was factored in. JoDon was a prize informant. The cops don't bust people like JoDon for a twenty-dollar sale of hashish.

"I'll see what I can do about getting you immunity," I said. Ought to be a piece of cake, I thought. A twenty-dollar drug sale? They passed out immunity for murder like handbills on the street, and at that often obtaining false information in return. Good information—and deep in my heart I felt JoDon told the truth—should swing the deal.

Arizona Attorney General Bob Corbin, Assistant Attorney General William Schafer, Don Devereux, and I sat in Corbin's office. We had just listened to JoDon's tape-recorded statement, and each one of us had typed transcripts of the interview.

"In exchange for his testimony," I said, "JoDon wants immunity for that twenty-dollar drug bust."

Corbin and Schafer looked at each other.

"It's up to Schafer," Corbin said.

A classic case of passing the buck. Like spectators at a tennis match, Devereux and I swung our eyes to the man who prosecuted Robison and Dunlap.

"What JoDon says on this recording," Schafer said, "is too vague."

Too vague? It seemed clear enough to me. JoDon said he'd overheard the murder being discussed *a month before* Don Bolles was killed. Unless one believed in psychic powers, that those people JoDon overheard were divining the future murder of Don

Bolles, this deserved top-priority attention. I looked hard at Schafer, never letting myself forget that he'd worked hand in glove with Jon Sellers to put Dunlap and Robison on death row.

"Mr. Headley," Schafer said, almost choking on the *mister*, "we just can't out of hand give immunity to drug dealers."

"Assistant Attorney General Schafer," I said, almost choking on the *assistant attorney general*, "you didn't have any trouble with that immunity given to Neal Roberts."

The previously chilly atmosphere in Corbin's office turned downright frigid. Corbin and Schafer didn't like me, feelings that on a totally impersonal basis I reciprocated. They tolerated Devereux, who as a reporter could cause them some harm, and I imagined they'd bow and scrape to Jonathan Marshall, a newspaper owner. If we met again, I'd ask Marshall to come along.

I briefly argued about the "too vague" dismissal of JoDon's statement, but saw Schafer wasn't going to budge.

"Bring him in here," Schafer said.

"JoDon's not coming back without immunity," I said. "And I don't think you'll extradite him for twenty dollars. How about if I get you another tape?"

"We're always willing to listen," Schafer said.

Listening wasn't good enough. Listening didn't accomplish anything. Schafer could listen right up to the moment news bulletins announced Dunlap and Robison's execution at the state prison. "In the meantime," I said, "you might ask Powers and Wolf why they did nothing with the information JoDon gave them."

Wolf and Powers were contacted, brushing off their inaction by saying they "didn't think it had any value." When I learned of the "no value" remarks, I got even hotter. JoDon had reported a murder plot, and the murder happened. Powers tacked on an additional excuse: the case belonged to the Phoenix police department, not Scottsdale's. This didn't wash with me at all. Many years before, as a Las Vegas sheriff's detective, when I had knowledge of crimes being handled by another jurisdiction, departmental policy and common sense dictated that I share the information.

Frustration mounted. Robison was continuing to starve himself and had lost forty pounds. He'd had a dizzy spell and injured himself in a fall in his cell. I didn't doubt he'd carry through to the finish. Pleas wouldn't stop him. The only hope, I thought, was information so encouraging that he could see an alternate outcome to death. The JoDon information, I thought, together with everything else, might change Robison's mind.

But not if Schafer sandbagged. I doubted that confessions from Monte Kobey and Bradley Funk eyewitnessed by five nuns could change Schafer's mind. He stood to lose too much. Who would want to be remembered as the man who prosecuted the wrong defendants in a case as major as the Bolles murder? To obtain justice, I believed, we'd probably have to go under, around, and over William Schafer III.

Before flying back to New Orleans, another round-trip expense that further dug into my meager savings, I played the JoDon tape for Phoenix detectives assigned to the Bolles investigation, Lonzo McCracken and Mike Butler. They weren't any more impressed than Schafer had been.

At the New Orleans Hilton I obtained a second, more detailed, tape from JoDon. Then, fearing I might lose this most valuable witness, I flew him to Albuquerque, New Mexico, and left him in the care of Bill Hume, who had worked on the IRE team. Putting him in this safe house won me a measure of trust from the jittery JoDon.

I returned to Phoenix and arranged another meeting in Corbin's office.

Present along with Schafer, Corbin, Devereux, and myself were Jon Sellers (now retired from the Phoenix police force and, outrageously I believed, working for the attorney general's office on the Bolles case), publisher Jonathan Marshall, and Marshall's attorney. This time we had brought some clout.

We listened to JoDon's taped account of the conversation he'd heard at Monte Kobey's house, and how no one in law enforcement seemed interested when he told them. JoDon's statement jibed exactly with the first tape, but the presence of Marshall and his lawyer meant we couldn't be shoved aside so easily.

"I'll bring JoDon in," I said, "but first he needs immunity on the drug beef."

"He'll have to pass a polygraph test," Corbin said.

"That's fine," I said. I thought of Robison and Dunlap. "What more can you guys want? Neal Roberts wasn't asked to take any lie detector test. Tell me you'll give JoDon immunity if he passes the polygraph, and let's get this circus on the road where it belongs."

Corbin looked at Schafer.

"Get it done," Corbin said in a level voice.

I called my son Lake III in Las Vegas and asked him to meet me in Albuquerque. Lake, twenty-three, was a big strapping young man, smart, who worked on a construction crew. He'd helped me on other cases, and for the Bolles investigation he brought two essentials I needed: he'd do exactly what I told him and I could trust him implicitly.

Lake and I transferred JoDon to Phoenix, and I put them up in another hotel. They were the same age, and I figured they'd get along with each other. Most important, Lake would be with him every second, insuring that the understandably nervous JoDon (I'd received a phone call threatening *his* life) wouldn't bolt.

I took five sworn affidavits from JoDon, all attesting to what he'd first told me in New Orleans. He breezed through a polygraph examination and was questioned intensively while in a hypnotic trance. The conclusion: JoDon was telling the absolute truth.

Devereux arranged for attorney Victor Aranow to work out the immunity agreement with William Schafer. When Aranow called Schafer, he found himself talking to Corbin instead. "I'm ready," Aranow said, "to surrender Michael JoDon at any time after we draw up the immunity agreement."

"We can't do that," Corbin said, "until Schafer gets back."

"From where?"

"Israel. He's gone to Israel, and won't be back for two weeks."

"Screw this!" I said when Aranow related his conversation with Corbin. "This is the most important murder case they'll ever handle, and they just keep stalling, playing with it, toying with us. I say screw them."

Angry didn't begin to describe how I felt. One of JoDon's sworn affidavits had contained the following startling revelations:

> Shortly after the Don Bolles homicide I had occasion to have a lengthy conversation with [my friend] Mike Decker. In this conversation Mike Decker related information to which he was privy due to his mother Joan Decker's position as legal secretary to Phoenix attorney Marvin Johnson.
>
> Decker told me he knew that Neal Roberts had gotten money from H. Monte M. Kobey for the murder of Don Bolles. Decker further related that Roberts had given money, several thousand dollars, to Gail Owens on more than one occasion.

I received a second telephone death threat against JoDon and jotted down the names of the few people who knew about the entrance of our star witness into the case.

I couldn't expect JoDon to hang around and be a sitting target for two more weeks until Schafer got back from a vacation or whatever he was doing in Israel. The best way to handle this— I'd known it from the beginning but made the mistake of trying to play by established rules—was to go public with everything.

I told Aranow I was going to call a press conference, and I told myself to get loaded for bear.

15

The Second Press Conference

Devereux's diligent digging discovered another potentially important witness whose testimony, I thought, should frost the cake at the upcoming press conference: Keith Nation, a forty-seven-year-old gambler and gadfly. A tile roofer by trade, he looked more like a retired jockey. Nation said that for years he had supported himself by gambling at the Funk/Emprise dog tracks, and during that time he had come to know the tracks' operations and employees inside out.

From Keith Nation I obtained a sworn, signed, and notarized affidavit—a statement made under oath which could result in a perjury indictment if found to be untrue. Although lacking in specifics (no matter how hard I tried, Nation refused to be pinned down "at this time" on his source), he swore to the following:

In January of 1976, I became aware of a phony divestiture scheme involving the Funk family.

This scheme entailed some manner of clandestine track trading arrangement in conjunction with a subsequent State of Arizona divestiture requirement.

I also learned from a reliable source that thirty to forty-five days prior to the June 1976 bombing of Don Bolles,

Bradley Funk and Albert Funk reportedly expressed great concern about Bolles's apparent awareness of this scheme.

From this same source I also learned that in a private conversation, Bradley and Albert Funk said in effect that something had to be done about Bolles, that he was going to get them this time.

Except for the desk clerk at the Clarendon whom Bolles spoke to briefly when Adamson failed to show for his appointment, and a phone call the reporter received from Adamson (who cancelled the meeting), it seems likely Nation was the last person Bolles talked to before the bombing. They had seen each other about 11 A.M. at the legislature, where Nation was following the track divestiture hearings.

"Tell me about your conversation that day at the State House," I said to Nation.

"You've got to understand, Bolles and I knew the score. We talked about how the Funks would go through a lot of legal mumbo jumbo and divest on paper, only with no actual change. Bolles was angry, but he'd resigned himself. 'What can be done about it?' he asked. 'Emprise runs the state.' "

"Did you tell this to the police?"

"Yes, I talked with Phoenix intelligence squad detectives several times."

"Did you tell them about the Funks?"

"The same things I told you."

"What did they do?"

"Well, the attorney general took over the investigation, and no one from that office ever contacted me."

The Phoenix Press Club also served as the site for the second news conference, held at 2 P.M. on May 2, 1979. Some thirty media people were present, representing local newspapers, radio stations, and the three network TV affiliates, plus reporters from San Diego, Los Angeles, New York, and the Navajo reservation.

Dunlap Committee members and most of Max's immediate family also came.

This time I'd had Dunlap and Robison authorize the press conference to avoid possible complaints from their lawyers, who still wanted to stick strictly with the appeals process and not make waves with a lot of publicity over an "unpopular cause."

Most important among the media gathering, I felt, was Molly Ivins of *The New York Times*, a paper that carried worldwide clout.

Molly had come down a few days earlier, making good on my invitation in March (at the suggestion of Bill Helmer), and I learned she was no stranger to the Bolles case or Arizona: she had researched and written a story about uranium pollution on the Navajo reservation.

"Can you get me in to see Dunlap and Robison?" she had asked on the phone.

"Yes."

After Molly arrived in Phoenix, I drove her to the Arizona State Prison.

Robison told *The New York Times* reporter about phone calls he had received from Adamson, shortly after the bombing. Even after helping commit the murder for which he would later frame Robison, Adamson couldn't resist boasting about his exploits.

Inside the cramped quarters, with voices reverberating off the prison glass, Molly's tape recorder picked up a garbled interview, so I gave her the backup tape I had made. The next day she went out and bought the same Sony model I used.

First *Playboy*, in the person of Bill Helmer, had entered the prison gates. In response to the Committee's contact and my follow-up efforts, "60 Minutes" would do a feature on corruption in Arizona, casting an unwelcome light on the state. And now *The New York Times*. I noticed the guards had been a little more polite when an out-of-state journalist was at my side, and I hoped maybe the supreme court justices considering the appeal might get some ideas also.

When we returned to Phoenix, Molly, a quiet, resolute woman who carefully read without comment all the material I showed her, dug in her heels and interviewed Neal Roberts. Mr. Immunity-for-a-theory demanded that she keep everything he said off-the-record except for one statement: "I never passed any money to anyone."

Although I tried, I couldn't find out what Roberts had said about those three stolen cars, the "loud and clear" remark, or his relationship with Barry Goldwater; Molly took his off-the-record stipulation seriously. In fact, "reading" Molly was impossible for me. I knew how important it was for her to judge objectively the evidence we'd uncovered, but all I could determine from our talks was her thorough, businesslike approach to reporting.

"Good afternoon, members of the press," I said, standing behind a podium on a slightly raised dais. "I have invited you here to see and learn about new information uncovered in the Bolles investigation. The two key people we want to talk about are Keith Nation and Michael JoDon. You'll learn from Keith Nation's sworn affidavit that Don Bolles, right up until the time the bomb exploded underneath him, maintained a keen interest in the Funk/Emprise dog-racing empire. Mr. Nation was one of the last people to speak with Bolles, and their conversation centered on the Funks and Emprise.

"I also want to bring to your attention the sworn affidavits of Michael JoDon, a police informant with a long record of truth telling, not just to Arizona police authorities, but to police in Kansas, the FBI, and the DEA. Federal, state, and local law enforcement agencies have attested to JoDon's reliability and veracity. I'd appreciate in particular your noting how JoDon swears that three times *before* the bombing he overheard talk about a plot to kill Don Bolles. JoDon apprised Scottsdale Police Sergeant Robert Powers of the situation. Powers did nothing. After Bolles was assassinated, JoDon made additional attempts to convey his knowledge of the murder plan to law-enforcement agencies. Still no action. Then the Scottsdale police framed him in a bogus twenty-dollar hashish deal. Now

Michael JoDon seeks immunity in exchange for his testimony in this most important matter. So far he has not received immunity, though I'm sure most of you know that for some in this case immunity has not been difficult to obtain. Regardless, JoDon's sworn statements are here for you to take with you and study. All the information we've accumulated has already been turned over to the attorney general's office but, sad to say, I've detected little enthusiasm from that august law enforcement agency."

In my next remarks I brought the audience up-to-date on the highlights of the investigation since the first press conference in December 1978: Terri Lee's research on Emprise; Jim Robison's starvation program—now in its seventy-sixth day—which had recently been joined by Max Dunlap and several other inmates; Antje Roberts and her admission that Neal and Goldwater were close friends; Kay Kroot, also tying Roberts to Goldwater on that TV talk show; and the taking of an extended vacation by the immunized Gail Owens, Adamson's former girlfriend. Then I opened the floor for questions.

"Aren't you being paid by the Dunlap Committee?" asked Pat Sabo of the *Phoenix Gazette*.

Here we go again, I thought, my heart sinking. "Yes," I said. "I'm receiving compensation from the committee." I didn't add that I was losing a lot of money on the arrangement. "What matters, it seems to me, is the importance of the information I'm gathering."

Next an *Arizona Republic* reporter stepped up: "Isn't it true you yourself are the object of an investigation for working as a private investigator without a valid Arizona license?"

"That's right. Resources which could better be spent solving the Bolles homicide are being wasted investigating me. The fact is, I'm doing work on the Bolles case for two national magazines, one of them *Playboy*."

"How can you claim objectivity if your paramount interest is getting a good story?"

"I'm giving what you call a 'good story' to *you*. My concern is to prevent the execution of two innocent men. The evidence

I'm asking you to study indicates we have an ongoing miscarriage of justice, one that needs desperately to be remedied."

"What," asked the *Republic* reporter, "does the attorney general's office plan to do with your 'information'?"

"The attorney general says he will try to determine the validity of JoDon's statements; but judging from past performances, I doubt we'll see much action."

"Have you given this material to the Phoenix police department?"

"Yes. To Detective Michael Butler."

"What is the attitude of the Phoenix police?"

"Not as enthusiastic as I'd like them to be. As I've pointed out, JoDon has been an extremely reliable informant for several years. However, at this point, I believe the critical issue is what *you*, members of the media, not the Arizona law enforcement agencies, consider important."

"I've just looked at JoDon's affidavits," said a Phoenix radio newsman, "and he doesn't seem to say anything really new."

What was this guy reading? *Nothing new?*

"What JoDon reveals is not only new but significant. Almost a month before the bombing, JoDon told Sergeant Powers that Bolles was *going to be killed.* Powers took no action that might have prevented this murder; on the contrary, he later withheld what he knew from defense counsel during the trial of Robison and Dunlap. What JoDon swears to shouldn't be viewed as an end, but as a starting point for more investigation. I urge the authorities to do this."

"Evidently you presented these affidavits to the police and failed to impress them. Why is that? And why should *we* be impressed?"

"Not just evidently. All this information *has been* presented to the attorney general and to the police. And their enthusiasm, or lack thereof, smacks of the continuing tunnel vision that led to the conviction of two innocent men."

"Doesn't a statement like that indicate you're playing God?"

Déjà vu. A mixture of anger and frustration sickened me, but I needed to control myself. "I'm not *playing* anything. I'm giving you critical evidence which was withheld from the press and the defense."

"Back to the question of your being a private investigator. That's what you are, let's face it, and you're breaking Arizona law."

"Why are you people dwelling on what amounts to a technicality? Why aren't you concerned about your fallen brother, Don Bolles? Instead you want me to confess to a crime, and I've committed no crime. I'm working for *Playboy* magazine, and nothing is stopping you from checking with them. I've been sought out for many years by literally scores of newspapers to provide them information. I've recently signed a book contract to write my autobiography."

If I thought this would satisfy them, I was wrong.

"Autobiography? Or your version of the Bolles killing?"

"I signed the book contract long before I was contacted to investigate this case."

"Mr. Headley, why would the Dunlap Committee, ostensibly interested in freeing Max Dunlap, hire a writer? They hired a detective, didn't they?"

"Because of a hostile press, abundantly evident here today, the committee realized that any material I uncovered would be useless if it couldn't be gotten to the media. It was felt I could accomplish this."

"Since you may be indicted, don't you think we should take that fact into consideration when judging your so-called new information?"

"If someone came in here and yelled, 'Fire!', would you question his qualifications? I'm only asking you to look at the evidence I have. Evaluate it. If you think it's garbage, write it up that way; but study it first."

"What will you do if the attorney general indicts you?"

Clearly they were more interested in gunning me down than focusing on the plight of Robison and Dunlap. They didn't care a whit about injustice or the condemned men. I faced a stone wall, and I was nearing the breaking point when Devereux stood up.

"What's all this got to do with anything?" he asked in a loud voice directed at his peers. The TV cameras swung around to catch his image. "We should concentrate on what Mr. Headley says, not his potential problems."

This flew right over the heads of most in attendance.

"Aren't you attaching too much credibility to statements provided by JoDon, who is, after all, a fugitive?"

"No. JoDon is *their* informant, not mine. For years they took him at his word. Why is this the exception? And remember, JoDon is a fugitive because of what he knows, not because of a minor drug charge."

"About your possible indictment for practicing without a license . . ."

Geesus. No questions at all about the Neal Roberts/Barry Goldwater relationship, or the grim fact that Jim Robison was starving himself to death. The bigger story, in most minds, was my possible indictment.

This second press conference, more hostile than the first, finally wound down. Interspersing my remarks with pleas for them to read what I'd provided, I hammered away at the new findings, especially JoDon's sworn statements. But the more I gave them, the more angry they became. They didn't like the messenger *or* the message. These purportedly inquiring minds didn't want to know or study the new evidence; instead they chose to remain dogged to the finish in hot pursuit of the saga of my license and the credibility of JoDon.

At last it ended, and night seemed to descend on my mind, so dark were my thoughts.

I invited Devereux, Terri Lee, members of the committee, Molly Ivins, and the Dunlap family to the Westward Ho for sandwiches, soft drinks, and a postmortem. I was wrung out, and getting from my car to the hotel lobby exhausted me further: Phoenix in May is hotter than hell, or even Las Vegas.

Some of the guests were upbeat—at least the press had taken the affidavits—but all I wanted to do was find a quiet corner and lick my wounds. I collapsed in an easy chair and sipped an icy soda, away from the rest.

Molly Ivins came over and sat on the floor next to me. "Lake," she said, "you must be worn out. I couldn't believe that press conference. I covered Watergate for the *Times* and was at almost every news conference Nixon called. The hostility there wasn't nearly as bad as this. What's the difference whether you have a private investigator's license? They acted like their minds were made up and they didn't want to be confused by facts. I've been a journalist for a long time, but the way those reporters acted today makes me ashamed of my profession."

I looked at Molly, and tears shone in her eyes.

Molly Ivins wrote several major articles about the Bolles case, the first dealing with the May 2 press conference.

REPORTER'S MURDER GETS NEW ATTENTION

Defense Committee Trying to Gain 2d Trial for Convicted Man— Affidavits Are Disclosed

By MOLLY IVINS
Special to The New York Times

PHOENIX, ARIZ., May 3— Pressure to reopen the Don Bolles murder case is building here. A defense committee of more than 300 people, convinced there has been an injustice, has raised enough commotion to disturb even some of those who were responsible for convictions in the reporter's death.

The defense committee is acting in behalf of Max Dunlap, one of two men sentenced to die for the murder. Mr. Dunlap is a builder and earth mover with no previous criminal record. He was president of his high school class and has hundreds of friends who are trying to win a new trial for him.

Their belief in his innocence is so strong, in fact, that some of them have mortgaged their homes to help finance the effort to free him. They have raised over $30,000, taken out newspaper advertisements asking for a new trial and hired a private detective to look for new evidence.

In the latest development in the case an affidavit was made public yesterday in which a police informer says he told the Scottsdale police of the plan to murder Mr. Bolles three or four weeks before it happened.

Record of Calls Is Unlikely

The police were unable to confirm that fact. Yesterday, Walter Nimitz, chief of police in Scottsdale, said departmental procedures make it extremely unlikely that there was any record of such a call. The officer to whom the informer says he placed his calls is now employed by another law enforcement agency and could not be reached for comment because he was on vacation. However, a police source says the officer states that he was called after Mr. Bolles was murdered, not before.

It was the defense committee detective, Lake Headley, who tracked down Michael JoDon in New Orleans. Mr. JoDon, once an informer for several law enforcement agencies, had been indicted on charges of selling $20 worth of marijuana to an undercover police agent and fled the state.

He has been trying to bargain for immunity in exchange for his testimony on the Bolles case. Roger Golston, the acting County Attorney for Maricopa County, said yesterday that the authorities are negotiating with the idea of dropping the charges against Mr. JoDon, provided he meets certain conditions. One condition is that he surrender, another is that his story check out.

Echo of Earlier Allegations

But members of the Dunlap Defense Committee, suspicious of those in official positions, decided to go ahead and present Mr. JoDon's testimony yesterday at the press conference here.

Mr. JoDon's affidavits echoed charges made at the murder trial that a lawyer named Neal Roberts, since disbarred, arranged the murder of Don Bolles, a reporter for The Arizona Republic. The affidavits quote two sources as saying Mr. Roberts acted at the behest of a man indirectly tied to the Emprise Corporation of Buffalo, N.Y., which had been investigated by Mr. Bolles.

The man named by Mr. JoDon as Mr. Roberts's contact vigorously denied the allegations.

Mr. Roberts's name first arose in the case because he chartered a plane to fly John Harvey Adamson, the man who confessed Mr. Bolles's killing, out of Phoenix the day of the bombing.

In exchange for a pledge of immunity on charges of accessory after the fact, a transcript of the meeting shows Mr. Roberts gave the police what he called "pure speculation" about the case. Mr. Roberts's speculations, backed by the word of his friend Mr. Adamson, became the basis of the prosecution's case.

The Prosecution's Argument

The prosecutors said that Mr. Adamson had killed Mr. Bolles with the assistance of a plumber friend, Jim Robison, and that Mr. Dunlap had paid him. Mr. Dunlap, they said, was acting at the behest of Kemper Marley, a wealthy rancher and liquor dealer who was said to be angry about some articles written by Mr. Bolles that cost Mr. Marley a position on the State Racing Commission.

Mr. Dunlap and Mr. Robison were sentenced to death, and Mr.

Adamson, who confessed and co-operated with the prosecutors, got 20 years, which he is serving in an Illinois prison.

Mr. Marley was never charged. Prosecutors, who are not willing to talk on the record, say they nonetheless remain convinced that the Marley theory is correct. They also say they are troubled by the information involving Neal Roberts.

Mr. Robison is in Arizona State Prison and has been refusing to eat since mid-February, contending that he will starve himself because he was framed and he despairs of ever being released. He elaborated in a recent interview on the argument that his lawyer put forward at his trial.

Mr. Robison now says he got two or three phone calls from Mr. Adamson in the days immediately after the bombing, while Mr. Bolles lay dying in a Phoenix hospital. Mr. Adamson told him, he says, that $10,000 was coming from the coast, $6,000 for Mr. Adamson and $4,000 for Mr. Roberts. Mr. Adamson wanted Mr. Robison to pick up and deliver his share, but Mr. Robison refused, he says, adding, "So they got Max Dunlap to do it." Mr. Robison also says he believes Mr. Dunlap, too, is entirely innocent.

Mr. Dunlap's story is that a mysterious stranger appeared at his house one morning with an envelope full of money and told him Mr. Roberts wanted the money delivered to an office downtown. Mr. Dunlap said he did deliver the money as a favor for his old friend, with whom he had gone to high school.

Mr. Roberts, asked about Mr. Robison's and Mr. Dunlap's comments, granted a long interview but insisted that all but one sentence be off the record. On the record he said: "I never passed any money to anyone."

Mr. Adamson was not available for comment.

The Molly Ivins article, the first stemming from our investigation other than Don Devereux's pieces in the *Progress*, put Arizona authorities on notice that they couldn't confine scandals to their cozy corner of the country, that the whole nation might start watching.

Molly Ivins did keep watching. It was just the kind of pressure—not pleas for justice to the attorney general's office, police, and the Phoenix media—that represented Max's and Jim's best hope.

16

The Barrel Bar sat in a rundown section near downtown Phoenix, a high-crime, low-employment area that most middle-class Phoenicians avoided. Jim Robison had suggested I look up the tavern's owner, Ralph Clark, a friend of his, but until now, mid-May, I'd been too busy with Michael JoDon, Keith Nation, and the press conference.

Some checking had revealed that Ralph Clark had come from Chicago; and his brother had been identified by the Chicago crime commission as a Southside Mafia rackets boss.

"Is Ralph here?" I asked the bartender, who looked like an ex-heavyweight prize fighter.

"Who are you?"

I handed him my card.

"Just a minute. I'll see if he wants to talk to you." He came out from behind the bar and disappeared down a corridor in the back. I assumed it led to an office. The bartender returned a minute later, followed by a rough-looking, heavyset man in his forties.

"I'm Ralph," he said in a gravelly voice, shaking my hand and motioning toward a booth away from the action.

"Do you see Jimmy?" he asked when we were seated and the bartender had brought us Cokes.

"At least once a week."

"How's he getting along?"

"He's not eating, you know."

"Yeah. I read that in the paper. It's too bad. I like Jim. I've known him a long time. He's a helluva guy."

"Jim told me to come and see you. He said you might be able to help us."

"Well, I might. I got this cop who maybe would talk to you."

Clark was vague. I suspected he had it all mapped out, otherwise he wouldn't waste time with me. Everything about Ralph Clark suggested secrecy and organization.

"I'd like to see the cop," I said. "Can you set up a meet?"

"Maybe. I can't be too upfront about all this, you understand? I got plenty of heat myself."

"I'm sorry to hear that."

"You know about heat. I heard you been catching some yourself, trying to help Jim and the other guy."

"Max Dunlap."

"Does Jim need any money? I could send some up by you, but nobody could know where it came from."

"He suspected you'd offer. He said, 'Tell Ralph thanks but no; I don't have anything to spend it on.' He doesn't smoke, and he isn't eating."

"Give him my regards."

"I will."

"Yeah. I'll talk to the cop and try to put you two together."

I sensed that wouldn't be a problem. I had no inkling what the cop wanted to talk about, and I didn't ask.

Robison was in a wheelchair when I saw him. Very thin and drawn. In the joint everyone's complexion fades to a prison pallor, but Robison's had worsened and become chalky with a sickly tinge of gray. The prison authorities hadn't tried to intervene in his refusal to eat, calling his actions a "hunger strike."

"It's typical that they'd misunderstand," he said. "This isn't

a hunger strike. I'm not making any demands. I'm starving myself to death."

It irritated Jim that Max and others had joined him in what
they *did* call a hunger strike. He doubted they'd stay with it long
because they lacked his own serious intent, and he felt their
attempt at solidarity had somehow diminished the impact of his
own actions.

We shook hands. His was bony. I learned later that even his
shoe size had shrunk.

"How do you feel?" I asked.

"I'm weak, but not as weak as they think I am. I've continued
to exercise, and that helps. If I'd just been lying around, I probably wouldn't have the strength to get out of bed. That'll come,
but it's not here yet."

"Is there anything I can do?"

"You're doin' it. Workin' as hard as you can. If you find something that radically changes the perspective, I can stop this program. Lake, I don't want to die. I just refuse to live under these
circumstances."

"Speaking of investigation, I saw Ralph Clark."

"Nice guy, isn't he?"

"He was friendly."

"Did he say anything that helped?"

"He said he has a cop who might meet me. I'll follow through
on it."

"Be sure to. Clark's all right. He's been around Phoenix for
a while, and he has his fingers in a lot of pies. But be careful
with him. Ralph's got his own problems. Keep his name out of
the newspaper."

While I was there, I visited with Max. Increasingly I saw only
Jim—Max, truly, had nothing that could help the investigation.
He himself had said, "I appreciate your seeing me, but probably
I'm better off with you on the street looking for information."

Max, still the optimist, thought the press conference had gone
well, especially with the *New York Times* coverage, and asked

questions about his appeal (nothing happening, waiting for a ruling from the Arizona Supreme Court).

After entering the prison at Florence, Max had discovered a special talent for drawing, and today he proudly showed me his most recent work: a large picture of his wife and kids. Over the months the contractor-turned-artist had produced a sizable collection of sketches, experimented with style, and refined his technique. But he never varied his one and only subject, his family: pictures of Barbara, of each child, combinations of Barbara and the children. The five-foot-tall group portrait of his loved ones was Max's pièce de résistance.

Three nights later I stood in front of a booth at the Barrel Bar looking down at Phoenix Police Detective Harry Hawkins, a husky man in his forties. Ralph Clark had given me his name, pointed him out to me.

"You Hawkins?"

"Yeah."

"I'm Lake Headley. I'm working on the Don Bolles case."

"I know who you are and what you're doing. Sit down, Mr. Headley."

"Call me Lake. Ralph said you wanted to talk to me."

"I never thought Dunlap and Robison got a fair shake. When I read in the paper what you're doing, I figured there was something I should tell you."

"You know I want to hear it."

Hawkins looked nervous. His eyes searched the bar, as if fearing one of us had been followed. "I decided you're serious from reports in the media. Damned if I know how you found out some of those things, but you got balls. I suppose I could have gone to the defense lawyers at the time of the trial, but they've got Arizona connections. Know what I mean?"

Yes, I did.

"I've checked you out," Hawkins said. "It looks like you're the guy I should talk to. There wasn't anybody else before," the veteran police detective added with a sigh.

I sensed Hawkins was about to reveal something significant, but I couldn't have imagined its immense, long-range impact on the investigation. Nor could I. have known that the outwardly passionless, hard-boiled Hawkins harbored a haunted conscience he needed to unburden. There could be no other reason: what he told me, guaranteed to torpedo his career, came out like long-pent-up water rushing through a dam break.

"At the time of the Bolles murder, I worked in the detective bureau assigned to the organized crime section. You worked intelligence, so you know we get a lot of unsubstantiated information. Rumors from the street, that sort of thing.

"Well, for years we'd been putting together a file on the Funk family. Their connection with Emprise. Also, in general, what went on at those race tracks. As you can imagine, that file contained some heavy shit.

"I guess the brass got nervous, or something. One day, toward the last of September 1976—I don't remember the exact date, but it's written on my calendar—I got a call from Sergeant Weaver. That's Jack Weaver, our resident expert on organized crime. He's lectured all over the country, knows the family trees of the Bonannos and Horseface Licavoli, all that stuff.

"Anyway, Weaver told me to meet him in the intelligence office. So I did. And Lieutenant Sparks, the intelligence commander, was also there.

"Weaver said, 'Harry, there's a lot of material in that Funk file that might be subpoenaed when the case goes to court. Take this key and open the door over there. Inside that room you'll see a table. On that table you'll find a file numbered Eight-Five-One.' "

Hawkins described how Weaver had given him step-by-step instructions fit for a child. Clearly, Weaver wanted no mistakes.

"He told me: 'We want you to go through File Eight-Five-One and take out every piece of paper that connects the Funks to organized crime, Emprise, or John Adamson. Take out anything that might damage the Funks in this community. After you've read the file and removed the material—I don't care how long it takes—I want you to bring me what you took out. Then

I want you to renumber the file pages and recopy them so no one can tell that anything has been removed. You got that?'

"I said, 'Sure.' Weaver then said, 'After you've done all this, type up new index cards on the contents of the file. I want you to start right away, and not stop until the job is done. This is important, Harry. Take out everything that's not public information.'

"So that's what I did. I gave the material to Weaver, and it's bothered me ever since. I hope this information does you some good."

Does some good? It was like receiving a road map to Atlantis. I looked at Hawkins, and he started to stand up. He'd said his piece.

"I need time to digest this," I said, not wanting contact between us broken. "How can I get back to you?"

"Set it up through Ralph. Let him know when you want to see me, and I'll be there. But I don't want to talk to attorneys or anyone else except you. I'm probably in for a lot of heat. Regardless, I've given you the information. Run with it if you can."

I'd found a monster: *the systematic destruction of a key intelligence file,* an act in itself denying a fair trial to Dunlap and Robison!

As I walked out of the bar, it struck me that my life might be in danger. Not from the Funks, Neal Roberts, or the Mafia, but from the police. I drove straight to Don Devereux's home, told him what I'd learned, and urged him to follow up if something happened to me. When it came to knowing about Harry Hawkins, two beat one.

Despite repeated efforts to meet with Hawkins again, he avoided me for more than two weeks. Finally, with help from Ralph Clark, the cop and I sat together in the same booth at the Barrel Bar. He looked even more uptight than before.

A warning signal—APPROACH WITH CAUTION—flashed in my brain. I had to guard against scaring Hawkins away, and besides, I didn't want to get him into a jam. I soon learned, however, that the line of communication had been scrambled since our first contact.

"This will be the last time I talk to you," Hawkins said. "It's possible the brass are on to us. Last week they had a big conference at the department. Captain Kimmell told me personally to keep a tight lid on the document-purging incident and warned me not to tell anyone about it. I'll bet that fucking Lieutenant Sparks is trying to pin the whole thing on me, and he's got some help. Calvin Lash—he's a sergeant—told me not to talk to Weaver about anything, not even personal business. You can see what a mess this is. Here I got one sergeant, Lash, ordering me not to speak to another sergeant, Weaver, who's my boss. I can't risk being seen with you. That would put my ass in a sling for sure."

"How high do you think this goes?"

"Right to the top. Strong, the assistant chief, told everybody at the meeting not to talk about purging the file. Afterward, some of us talked about why Eight-Five-One got altered, and the older guys pretty much agree that the documents taken out of it would rebut the state's theory of the Don Bolles murder case. So you see why I have to be careful. Lash told me there'd be a directive right out of Chief Wetzel's office to screen every file for references to Adamson, Emprise, and the Funk family. I wasn't permitted to assist in the search."

"Why not?"

"Beats me. I guess they don't trust me anymore. Maybe they found out I talked to you."

"I'm sorry you've got all these problems. But as long as you're here, can I ask you a few questions?"

"Go ahead, shoot."

"What did you do with all that material you took out of the Funk file, Eight-Five-One?"

"I gave it to Sergeant Weaver."

"What did he do with it?"

"I don't know. I never asked, and he never said. I always suspected he destroyed it."

"Do you think our getting together prompted that conference the other day?"

"I have no idea. They call meetings; I go. It seems pretty

coincidental, though. I do know they're down on me, and I don't like it."

"What can you do about it?"

"That's what I've been wondering. Do you think you could get me in to see Robison?"

The question came out of the blue. I could see enormous positives if Hawkins met Robison (perhaps even solving the Bolles case), and plenty of negatives.

The bad news: Hawkins was a cop, and this could be a trap.

The good news: Robison's friend, Ralph Clark, evidently vouched for Hawkins.

I didn't know if Robison would agree to see the intelligence detective, and if he did, how we'd pull it off against a likely phalanx of objections: from Robison's lawyer, the attorney general's office, the police department in general, and Hawkins's superiors in particular.

Dealing with not only a cop but a member of an elite unit put me in a tough spot. What if the police brass had thrown Hawkins at me as bait, and he aimed to obtain a confession from Robison? Or, through Robison, to get at Kemper Marley?

On the other hand, a meeting with Robison would allow me continuing contact with Hawkins, maybe a chance to obtain affidavits from him, something clearly impossible as matters stood. Best of all, Hawkins might bring another detective in as corroboration.

"Why do you want to see Jim?" I asked.

"There are things I know about this case that have never been discussed. Robison was Adamson's pal. If Robison and I got together and talked, we might combine our information and figure out who was behind the Bolles murder. It's a tall order, but I'd like to try and arrange it."

"I'll give it a shot. I need to see if Robison will go for it."

I hoped it would work out. I thought Jim would agree, based on Ralph Clark's endorsement of Hawkins, but I had serious doubts about others who would probably try to insinuate themselves into the situation.

Two days later I laid the pros and cons out for Robison, saying I didn't believe—assuming a worst-case scenario—that Hawkins could trick him. Jim was, after all, innocent.

Robison agreed, but with one stipulation: my presence. I thought Hawkins would buy that.

I called Carolyn Robinson—part of a dreary drill we went through every time I wanted to visit the penitentiary—and she set in motion the needed bureaucratic machinery.

So—two key players wanted to meet, but the sabotage from others started immediately. I talked it over with Tom Henze, Robison's new lawyer (replacing Derickson, who would shortly accept a superior court judgeship).

Henze didn't oppose a Robison/Hawkins meeting, but insisted he'd have to be there too. The police said okay, but they demanded that a homicide detective be present. The attorney general's office said okay, but William Schafer III had to sit in.

"Jesus Christ," I said to Terri Lee, "pretty soon we'll need a stadium."

Alas, the meeting fell through because of the many conflicting demands of the "interested" parties, and the door closed forever between Hawkins and me. I never saw him again.

A few months later, however, I interviewed Sergeant Jack Weaver. A retired street-smart cop with more than twenty years on the force, Weaver specialized in organized crime, and he knew his business.

"Don Bolles wasn't as lily white as people think," Weaver opened.

"What does that mean, Jack?" I said, irritated that he seemed about to malign someone I'd viewed all along as a hero.

"I tell you, Lake, a lot of people hated Don Bolles, and they were glad to see him dead. He was always poking his nose into places it didn't belong."

Well, if that was all he had on Bolles, my admiration for the late reporter was safe. "I'm interested in what happened to File Eight-Five-One," I said. "I have information from a good source that it got purged."

"Your source is right, to a degree."

"What do you mean?"

"That file didn't get cleaned out once, but *three times.* I couldn't talk about it while I was still on the force. Now I'm retired, and they're trying to blame me for the purging. I'm not going to let them dump that on me. I didn't initiate those purge orders; they came from Lieutenant Sparks, and higher up than him. You can tell those attorneys for Robison and Dunlap that I'll testify to this." He paused. "There's something else I'll testify to. I haven't told anybody this, but a couple of months after the Bolles bombing, I took an intelligence report to Sergeant Mc-Kenzie and suggested it go in the Bolles bombing file. Mac said, 'No chance. There's nothing going into that file concerning Adamson, the Funk family, or Emprise.' "

Not only were the files purged, they were closed! Nothing could be developed by the police on what obviously were three key players.

"What happened to the material taken from the file? I guess you destroyed it?"

"No. I couldn't stomach what Sparks had ordered me to do, and I knew it surely would come up again. So when Harry Hawkins handed me the material, I locked it in my desk drawer, which only I have a key to. I kept it there until they forced me to retire."

"Did you take the papers with you?"

"No. They outsmarted me. The day I cleaned out my desk, two detectives were present to take possession of all official documents."

"Where do you think the documents went, Jack?"

"Right to Chief Wetzel. Those papers had such a high priority, I don't think Wetzel would have trusted them with anyone."

"Did you read what got purged from Eight-Five-One?"

"Sure I did, but remember, this was almost three years ago, and I've read hundreds of reports since then. I can give you a general idea what they said: information about the Funk family's connection with Adamson; the different deals the Funks had with Emprise; and organized crime individuals who had been associated with the Funks, or been observed meeting with Funk family members."

Jack Weaver had been forced into retirement over the controversy generated by purged File #851.

Harry Hawkins's reward for whistle blowing, I was shortly to learn: assignment to a foot patrol in the most dangerous and crime-ridden section of Phoenix.

17

New Mexico
Dynamite

"I've started to eat," Jim Robison told me when I visited him one day in early June.

"Good. I'm glad you've given up that starvation routine. I think you and Max are going to get out of here."

I was indeed pleased, and told Jim the unvarnished truth. The JoDon, Nation, and Hawkins information, piled atop so much else, plus many official documents disputing the prosecution's version (such as "loud and clear"), all combined to form a veritable Everest of evidence against which I didn't think the state's case could stand.

"I agree our chances look better," Robison said. "The Hawkins stuff is powerful. It was good of Ralph to help, and I don't think it's hopeless anymore."

This very strong man acted embarrassed and almost sheepish, like an alcoholic who stays off the sauce for several months, then relapses. Falling off the starvation wagon, however, marked definite progress.

"How long did you go?" I asked.

"I don't know. Maybe a hundred days."

I counted it in my head. It was a hundred and five. Jim, pale, shaky, and weak, had lost at least eighty pounds. Wisely, he had resumed his food intake cautiously: orange juice, oatmeal, only soft foods.

Although Jim's body bore the scars of his slow journey into the valley of death, his eyes twinkled with the rebirth of faith, a Lazarus rising from the grave. "I just don't see," I said, not wanting to darken his mood, "how the press and prosecution can ignore Hawkins's information."

"Maybe so. But one thing will never change. Lake, as I've told you over and over, these people adhere to only one principle: Cover Your Ass. They'll never admit they did a lousy job, that they flat-out did wrong. Just yesterday, one of the hacks came around and said, 'Why are you going through this? Give 'em what they want, and they'll bring a limousine around to take you away from here.'"

"They *still* want you to finger Marley?"

"Sure. Marley. That's all it's ever been."

I thought about Kemper Marley on my drive back to Phoenix. Clearly there had to be a mastermind, a money man, behind the scenes, and Marley had been earmarked for the role. Why? And why did the state and the press continue to cling desperately to the original discredited version of the murder, even though the case against Marley, resting on Adamson's word alone, had disintegrated when the alleged motive proved to be no motive, when a Bolles article or evidence of a Bolles investigation *did not* cost him a post on the racing commission?

My own best hunch was that both the Phoenix police and the Phoenix newspapers, part and parcel of the Establishment's soul, had tried to put it on Marley because he was a loner, because he was not a member of the Establishment. Yet *somebody* had called for the reporter's murder, and clearly the Establishment was wallowing in guilt—probably over the murder and surely over the coverup—and hoping that by ignoring bad news like the purging of File #851 the nightmare would somehow go away. The papers saw the Bolles case as a downtown *High Noon* bombing bad for the image of Phoenix. Thus—keep it closed. If it reopened in full swing now, it would be worse than the first time around.

Too bad. I wasn't going away, and neither were Devereux,

Marshall, Naomi, Terri Lee, nor *Playboy* and *The New York Times.* It was getting to be like Watergate: there was always more. And as with Watergate, the more that came out, the more the established powers tried to stonewall.

Terri Lee and I had been working together virtually every free hour she had (she was attending college and holding down the bartender job) and we had grown closer and closer. I couldn't believe my luck: a young, beautiful woman who didn't seem a whit perplexed by what had turned into a serious romance with a guy pushing fifty.

Also, it was a pain to separate each night and then regroup early the next morning to plot the day's activities. But my concern went much deeper than saving time and gas. I'd fallen in love and wanted to be with her all the time, but hesitated to suggest a different arrangement. Don't be an old fool, I told myself, cursing our age difference. It wouldn't be fair to her. So, when I returned from visiting Robison, I wasn't prepared for what Terri Lee said over brunch.

"I found a place," she said, "that we can rent on Camelback. A one-bedroom, unfurnished apartment. I can fix it up really nice, and there's lots of light for my plants."

We can rent on Camelback?

"I'll take care of all the details. Of course, I want you to look it over first, see if you like it."

The apartment was in a one-story, adobe brick complex, directly across the street from the high school Terri had attended.

"Like it?" she asked.

"Love it." I really did, though I would have eagerly settled into the Bates Motel if she'd been part of the package.

CHICAGO, ILLINOIS. JULY 10, 1979

Don Devereux's research had uncovered another previously withheld police report, dated June 20, 1976, and written by Phoenix police officer Terry Rhiel. The report described the activities of William Rocco "(Rocky)" D'Ambrosio, Frank Mossuto, Dan Basil, and a man with the last name of Perry. Here's what Rhiel wrote in that vital police report the prosecution didn't bother to include in the discovery:·

On 6-19-76 at 2300 hours, I contacted Officer Ron Dean, Scottsdale P.D., reference an informant of his who had some information on the Bolles case. This informant is reliable and confidential to Dean. Upon my arrival at Scottsdale P.D., I was introduced to this informant and was told by him that his name was not to be used in any capacity as his life would be endangered. Officer Dean could vouch for his ability and knowledge of the people involved.

This informant has known all participants for various lengths of time; from D'Ambrosio for years, to Perry for several months. The informant is in and out of town, and two months ago (unable to pin down further) the informant was running odd jobs for Rocky out of the Scottsdale Towers. He described Rocky as being the main man at the Scottsdale Tower bar, but Frank is always with him. Frank allegedly has no criminal record so his name is on the liquor license. Both Frank and Rocky work for Mike Robinson w/m 60, who owns Scottsdale Towers. According to the informant, Robinson has strong Mafia connections to Chicago and Rocky and Frank do not make a move without Robinson knowing about it. Robinson is wealthy and has political ties to *Goldwater*.

Robinson also has an ex-partner, and still good friend, named Lee Goines w/m 50 (not positive on last name). Goines is allegedly a member of the *Dixie Mafia* and owns an investment company in the valley. The only known connection at this time is that Goines and Robinson know what the other is doing.

At this time, two months ago, Rocky's mother, or mother-in-law's car broke down in Grants, N.M., and he asked the informant to go pick it up. Frank then said that since he was going to N.M., how about picking up some dynamite? The informant went to Grants, then Gallup. While in Gallup, he contacted Dan Basil, who was tending bar at The Village Lounge, and asked him about some dynamite. Basil put him in touch with Perry. Perry told him he'd get him a case for $500 (which according to the informant is about $300 more than the going rate). The informant told him O.K. and returned to Phoenix. (This trip was two days.)

After returning to Phoenix, the informant contacted Rocky and Frank and told them the deal. Both agreed and Frank told him to get #8 or #9 dynamite as it worked better. The informant had meanwhile told them he would set the deal up but wouldn't transport it. They agreed and Frank handed him five $100 bills. The informant was in Phoenix three days, then returned to Gallup and paid Perry. The informant later heard that a week later someone picked the dynamite up. Since that time, the informant has been bouncing back and forth between Gallup and Phoenix. He has been mostly in Gallup because Rocky and Frank don't want him around the city.

Right after he paid Perry, and was back in Phoenix, he heard Rocky and Frank talking in the office. They kept mentioning "reporter," but he did not hear a name. They also asked him a couple of times if he wanted to make "five grand," and he told them no way.

When asked about Adamson, the informant stated that he (Adamson) wasn't smart enough to do a deal like Bolles. In his opinion Rocky wasn't either, it would have to come from Robinson. He stated Adamson and a guy named "Dan" used to run "Bluebird Towing" out around the dog track. Both subjects knew Rocky from there and also from the Roman Gate, on E. Camelback. Rocky used to have part of the Roman Gate, along with John Hobson and the Verive brothers, Carl and John (last name uncertain). Hobson, Rocky and Adamson were fairly tight before Rocky went to prison and they still keep in touch. The informant said Hobson has been involved in some "heavy" deals, but refused to elaborate further at this time.

Unbelievably, the police hadn't bothered to follow up on Rhiel's report. Devereux, once put on the scent, had traced D'Ambrosio to Chicago, and obtained a phone number.

I called and set up a lunch meeting with D'Ambrosio at the Drake Hotel. Devereux wanted to go with me, but he already carried two jobs, with the migrant worker's union and the *Scottsdale Daily Progress*.

D'Ambrosio looked the part: solid, built like a slab of concrete, dark complexion—a tough guy with a gravel voice.

"How do you like being back in Chicago?" I began.

"I prefer Arizona. But I got too much heat down there."

I didn't ask him for what. "They're giving me trouble, too," I said, attempting to put myself in with him, to show I wasn't a cop. I mentioned the issue of my p.i. license, and my status as persona non grata in certain high Arizona circles.

"You didn't come all the way to Chicago to discuss heat. What do you want to ask me?"

"Don Devereux with the *Scottsdale Progress* has found information that in 1976 you bought dynamite in Gallup, New Mexico. Is that true?"

"I never bought any dynamite anyplace. I don't know what the hell you're talking about."

"According to Devereux's information, you sent a guy to New Mexico in April of '76 to pick up a broken-down car. On the way back, he made arrangements to obtain dynamite from a man named Perry."

"Well, the first part's right. I had a car picked up. But the guy didn't stop in Gallup, I don't know nobody named Perry, and I sure never bought no dynamite."

"You know somebody named Frank Mossuto?"

"Yeah. He's a friend of mine."

"What's Mossuto doing now?"

"Selling used cars in San Diego."

"You know John Adamson, right?"

"You're talking about the Bolles killing, and I had nothing to do with that. But, yeah, I know who Adamson is. He came in the Scottsdale Towers a few times. I thought he was a piece of shit. I didn't want nothing to do with him. They got the right guy with Adamson in the Bolles thing, but from what I hear—and I got good connections—Dunlap and Robison didn't have nothing to do with it."

I viewed myself as a baseball player stepping up to the plate, with three strikes allowed. I had swung and missed at D'Ambrosio, but Devereux and I later drove to Gallup and located Perry, a black man who worked in a junkyard (also, as a small-time fence). Perry denied knowing anything about buying or selling dynamite. "That's illegal, isn't it?" he asked.

Strike two.

I flew to San Diego and tracked down Frank Mossuto through the state licensing bureau (California requires a license to sell used cars).

I left a message at his car lot, and he returned my call, probably thinking I was a customer. "Mr. Headley, this is Frank Mossuto."

"Mr. Mossuto, I need to talk to you."

"What about?"

"I'm working on the Don Bolles case, and I'd like—"

Mossuto's voice exploded in my ear. "I don't want to talk about the Bolles case. Not now, not ever."

He hung up.

Strike three.

I'd obtained virtually nothing from D'Ambrosio, Perry, and Mossuto, and lacking prosecutorial authority—the means to call them to testify in front of a grand jury—my chances of getting more information were nil. Yet here again was a clear instance of certain people knowing Bolles was slated to die, and there had been no police follow-up.

Had these three been players? Certainly someone had filled the roles of Robison (the detonator of the bomb), Dunlap (the middleman between the money man and those executing the hit), and the mastermind himself (the role falsely assigned to Kemper Marley).

Meanwhile, with police and prosecutors reporting no progress in their "ongoing" investigation into the Bolles murder, the issue of my practicing as a private investigator without a license was edging its way from back burner to front. If convicted, as I expected would happen, I faced six months in jail and a one-thousand-dollar fine. Far down the line, at some distant point, in an appeals court, I knew I likely would win, but wasting time fighting this battle would mean that my activity in the Bolles investigation would grind to a halt.

Don Devereux rescued me from the state by introducing me to retired Phoenix police detective Tom Atchinson, who had the required year's residency to obtain a license. By Arizona law, I wouldn't need a p.i. license if I worked for someone who already had one. The situation was analogous to owning a tavern: an owner must be licensed, but not his employees.

Despite affidavits from Bill Helmer and Molly Ivins verifying my position as a journalist, I was headed, in hostile Arizona, for a conviction, until the Atchinson opportunity presented itself. I paid for his p.i. license, and he hired Terri Lee and me.

The state still could have split hairs and prosecuted for the time I had worked unlicensed, but that would have been too draconian, even for Arizona. The authorities said they wanted me to function legally in their state, and I had now complied. More significant, I suspected, was an underlying fear that if I were brought to court, and Bruce Babbitt, Robert Corbin, William Schafer, and Jon Sellers were called as witnesses, my defense counsel, George Vlassis, would attempt to turn *my trial* into a retrial of the Bolles murder, with all the predictable attendant publicity. If that's indeed what Babbitt and the others feared, they had reason.

Eventually, the previously retired Tom Atchinson actually discovered a new career as a private investigator. He did pretty well, I hear, which makes me happy. He put himself on the line for us.

18

''Contamination''

My paid relationship with the Dunlap Committee ended on June 30, 1979. It seemed clear to me that enough evidence had been gathered to guarantee acquittals somewhere down the line, and I didn't want to continue to draw a salary draining money from people who already had sacrificed a great deal for Max.

I had no intention, however, of abandoning the investigation until Robison and Dunlap were cleared, and I promised to make myself available, with or without the committee, to pursue any new leads.

Body and soul were kept together financially by working for Vlassis's busy law firm, especially on cases involving the Navajo reservation, and for a young, dedicated attorney in Flagstaff named Michael Stuhff. His clientele also consisted largely of Native Americans, and many of this compassionate lawyer's legal services were pro bono.

In the years that followed, Stuhff became one of my most valued friends, and we collaborated on several cases, including the U.S. Senate's impeachment of Judge Harry Claiborne, and the court-martial of Marine Sergeant Clayton Lonetree.

Terri Lee and I continued to work hand in hand. Through Stuhff, she began teaching Navajos the ins and outs of legal research, and I conducted paralegal classes—how to conduct investigations, take statements, process evidence, etc. We felt it important that these Native Americans be well versed on procedures needed to protect their people's oft-trampled rights.

The Tribal Council paid expenses for six young Navajos at a time to travel to Phoenix, stay in a motel, and attend the courses we held in our East Camelback apartment.

These were good times for Terri Lee and me. We were engrossed in satisfying endeavors and enjoyed almost everything together: going to movies and watching TV, romantic dinners, tending what grew into a mininursery of plants, and long late-night rides into the eternal desert. She and Willie Nelson sang "On the Road Again" as soft white light streamed through the moonroof, bathing our souls in what Rod McKuen called gentle.

But Robison and Dunlap, rotting on hellish death row, were never far from my thoughts, and on some nights, when my mood bordered on the murderous, I took drives alone, my mind clouded no matter how clear the starry skies as I pondered their fate.

What the hell took the supreme court so long?

Little things upset me. I had read about two of those justices attending a Paradise Valley social bash, enjoying cocktails and a sumptuous menu. I tried to tell myself, Lake, judges have a right to relax, too, but still I worked myself into a rage over their wasting time at lavish parties instead of rectifying the Dunlap/Robison horror.

July turned into August. September came and went. October, lost. Still no word from the men draped in the robes of justice.

And what in hell were the police and prosecution doing?

It was like a broken record: "The case is an ongoing investigation. We expect more arrests."

Ongoing? Sure: it was going on, and on, and on. Like a transmission locked in neutral, the motor ran but the machine did not move.

From the start the state had adopted "ongoing investigation/more arrests" as an unofficial motto.

OCTOBER 31, 1977

In his summation to the Robison/Dunlap trial jury, William Schafer III said, "We do not have all the conspirators yet, but we will have." Schafer virtually pled with the jury to return guilty verdicts on Robison and Dunlap, hinting that these two, when faced with the gas chamber, would cave in, as Adamson had.

NOVEMBER 1, 1977

Schafer vowed, "We haven't got all the conspirators yet, but we will."

NOVEMBER 7, 1977

Jon Sellers: "Investigation on this case goes on all the time. It slowed down a bit recently because of the trial, but we were still documenting information. Now, we'll probably sit down with Mr. Schafer and sift through the information. We'll probably resume the investigation one hundred percent. I'm glad this part of it is over."

Phoenix Police Chief Lawrence Wetzel: "Now that the trial is at an end, there will be a review to determine what directions further investigation should take."

Attorney General Bruce Babbitt: "Mr. Schafer, myself, and the police believe there were others involved. The file remains open. It will be the subject of a continuing, intensive investigation by the Phoenix police and this office. That investigation will not cease until everything humanly possible has been done to bring to justice everybody involved in this outrageous and depraved act."

APRIL 5, 1979

Phoenix Police Captain Jerry Kimmell: "Two detectives, Mike Butler and Ed Flores, will continue to investigate the Bolles murder. It will continue to be their number-one priority, with both men authorized to work on the case up to one hundred percent of their time."

JUNE 3, 1979

Phoenix Police Organized Crime Bureau Detective Mike Butler: "It's still an open investigation."

OCTOBER 3, 1979

Attorney General Robert Corbin: "We're not certain about organized crime participation. There are always things being said that are being investigated."

Police, government officials, politicians. One after another took turns jumping up on the soapbox, but no matter how many words tumbled out of their mouths, it consistently boiled down to the same pat phrases: The case is still being investigated; more indictments are expected.

Well, the state might not be turning up anything in its "ongoing investigation," but our little team, operating with a fraction of the state's resources and manpower, was uncovering a whole string of leads. The latest came when Don Devereux discovered the existence of Terrell Bounds, a state employee who had been stationed in the information booth at the State Capitol on the day of the Bolles bombing. Ms. Bounds said she fielded a telephone call at approximately 10 A.M. (the bomb exploded at 11:34) from a woman caller who mentioned a bomb threat on an unidentified reporter's car. The caller claimed to be the secretary of County Sheriff Paul Blubaum, but a later police investigation ruled this out.

Terrell Bounds wrote the time of the call on her log as *10 A.M.*
She referred the caller to the Capitol press room and remembered being "shocked" upon returning from lunch that afternoon to learn Bolles had been bombed.

Who made this call to Terrell Bounds? The police showed
little interest and never found out. Worse, when Devereux tried
to find out, Detective Michael Butler instructed Bounds not to
cooperate.

The *Progress* wanted to learn if Ms. Bounds could identify
the caller through its extensive collection of voice tapes related
to the Bolles case. Butler said Bounds should instead listen to
police-controlled voice tapes, but *never* managed to get around
to playing them for her.

The police not only "purged" information and refused to
follow up on leads, they squashed attempts made by other people trying to get at the truth. I had called Ted Krum of the
Rodeway Inn at Lake Havasu to check on John Adamson's stay
there immediately after the bombing. The reservation and plane
fare for Adamson had been paid by Neal Roberts. But Krum
refused to talk to me, saying Jon Sellers left instructions to obtain clearance from him before discussing the case with anyone.

Even Molly Ivins got stonewalled. She tracked Eileen Roberts—Neal's secretary during the crucial days leading up to and
right after the bombing—to Boston. Eileen Roberts had overheard Neal Roberts discuss raising money for Adamson's defense, and a Roberts conversation about how "Bolles got what
he deserved."

Trying to find out who Roberts had talked with, Molly scheduled an appointment with Eileen Roberts, but the witness cancelled the meeting.

"I had told Eileen," Molly Ivins said, "that I wanted to show
her some pictures she might or might not recognize.

"Eileen told me that, apparently for years now, she has had
an agreement with William Schafer that when anyone ap-
proaches her about anything connected with the Bolles case, she
gets in touch with him.

"She had done so after I had called and set up the appointment. And she said that Schafer had advised her not to talk to me.

"One reason Schafer had given Eileen Roberts was that she might be a witness in a future trial. And there was some implication that her testimony in a future trial would be tainted by talking to a newspaper person, which I find absurd."

Future trial? My heart briefly fluttered with hope when I mistakenly thought Schafer might be referring to Robison and Dunlap. But, no. Evidently, he still clung to the fantasy of dragging Kemper Marley to the dock.

Schafer confirmed that he had advised Eileen Roberts to steer clear of the *New York Times* reporter. He said he wanted to protect possible evidence from "contamination," which he claimed could come from contact with people untrained in law enforcement procedures.

Ridiculous. It was the very people "trained in law enforcement procedures" who had engineered the muck and mire the police and prosecution were now trying to extract themselves from by warning off witnesses like Terrell Bounds, Ted Krum, and Eileen Roberts.

Devereux called William Schafer, saying that since the assistant attorney general didn't want Molly Ivins showing pictures to Eileen Roberts, he presumed Schafer would run them by her.

Devereux reported Schafer's response in the *Scottsdale Progress:* "Schafer ... is unaware of any intention by the state of Arizona to run its own photo lineup before Eileen Roberts in an attempt to identify the people in question."

Perhaps most shocking of all, Detective Mike Butler asked the *Progress* and Tim Ryan of KPNX-TV news to stop showing photos to potential witnesses. Ryan and the *Progress* complied, based on Butler's promise that the police would do the job. Of course, they never did.

Capitalizing on the media-government trench warfare over who could best serve truth and justice for the sake of Don Bolles, Governor Bruce Babbitt launched a radio campaign in his bid for reelection. The former attorney general's voice flooded airwaves with boastful reminders of how he had played a major role in solving that blot on fair Phoenix, the Bolles murder.

I had to hear this to believe it. Babbitt's radio ads actually urged the Arizona electorate to keep him as governor because of his work convicting Robison and Dunlap!

The supreme court justices took a month's "recess" without deciding on the appeal, the start of their vacations coinciding with a visit I paid Robison and Dunlap. The contrast hit me hard: for one group, fun-filled romps on open sandy beaches or following the bouncing ball over dewy lush greens in early morning rounds of golf, dining on gourmet meals, and freedom to go anywhere anytime; for my clients, one hour a day of supervised exercise inside the bleak prison yard, watching still another six-legged creature scavenge through filthy stone cubicles, choking down the same old slop, and only one exit—the gas chamber.

I didn't return to the apartment and Terri Lee when I left the prison that late afternoon. I don't remember where I went. I must have driven aimlessly for many hours, my thoughts dark, fading to black.

I found myself early the next morning behind the Clarendon Hotel, right alongside the parking space where more than three years ago six sticks of dynamite had reduced a new Datsun to a contorted heap of scrap metal.

I got out of my car and looked at the spot. The parking lot was as quiet as my cemetery in Florence—all of Phoenix, the air itself, sat as eerily still as the deceptive calm before a hurricane.

My mind flashed back through all that had happened to Robison and Dunlap, to Phoenix, yes, and especially to Don Bolles.

As I focused on the reporter himself, I suddenly fantasized that he stood next to me in the filtered golden light of dawn.

"Bolles," I said softly, "for Christ's sake, give me some help."

19

The Downey
Connection

DOWNEY, CALIFORNIA. NOVEMBER 17, 1979

I swam in a sewer. What brought me from Phoenix to this community just south of Los Angeles was the critical August 17, 1976, police report written by Jon Sellers, which, incredibly, *had not found its way to the defense until recently, more than three years after Bolles died.*

On 8/17/76, investigator flew to Downey, CA after receiving a telephone call from Det. Gary Morrow of the Downey Police Department. Det. Morrow related to investigator that he was in touch with a Bill Wright who allegedly was in an alcoholic hospital with Bradley Funk shortly after the Bolles incident. He related to investigator that Mr. Wright was giving him information concerning statements that Bradley Funk allegedly made to him during their stay at the hospital.

On 8/17/76 at approximately 1:30 P.M., investigator interviewed William D. Wright, c/m, D.O.B. September 21, 1921, present address of 8276 Telegraph, Downey, CA, no phone. Mr. Wright related that he is a retired truck driver.

A tape recording of the conversation held with Mr. Wright was made and the tape was retained for future reference. For a complete verbatim account of what was said, please refer to the tape. The following is the highlights of the conversation held with Mr. Wright.

He said that on June 7, 1976, he was admitted to the Beverly Manor Hospital located at 401 South Tustin in the city of Orange. He said that the hospital is a private hospital for alcohol and drug-related problems. He said that on June 7, 1976, he was in the detox center and was present when Bradley Funk came into the hospital on June 8, 1976. . . . He said that at the time he did not know this was Bradley Funk but that he and this person were ultimately assigned the same room, Room #211, and spent approx. 25 days together in this room. . . . He said that Funk became very nervous following Bolles's death and bought the paper every day and received numerous clippings from Arizona concerning the Bolles investigation. He related that Funk told him that he felt his family was going to be blamed for the bombing. He said that Funk stated that in his opinion, some dog owners were the ones that killed Bolles. He also stated that there were going to be some big people hurt as a result of this and named Steiger and Goldwater. Wright said that Funk mentioned some land deals and that he at some time during the conversation believes he mentioned Max Dunlap's name. Wright was unable to be specific as to the conversation or how it took place. He did maintain, however, that at no time did Funk implicate himself or his family in the bombing of Bolles and simply stated that they were going to get the blame for it.

Wright stated that he remembers Funk telling him that he believed Bolles was blown up by a controlled device and remembers him telling him that the explosives or something were purchased in San Diego. He further stated that one time during their stay together, when they were on pass, Funk took him to a hobby shop when he was buying some material for a model boat that he was putting together and at this time Funk pointed out to him a remote control device, stating that it was something like the one that was used to blow Bolles up. He said that Funk only pointed to the device through the case and did not handle or examine the device. Wright described the device as being brown but later changed the color to black and was shown a photograph of the remote-control device which investigators suspect is similar to the type that was used. At this time, Wright said that the device that Funk showed him was similar to the one that investigator had a photograph of.

Sellers had concluded that a follow-up interview with William Wright wasn't necessary.

I concluded differently.

Through a contact I had at the California Department of Motor Vehicles, I attempted to run Wright down using his date of birth and former address, obtained from Sellers's report. But the DMV had no information on his current whereabouts.

Knowing he was a retired trucker, I contacted Teamsters Local 896 in Los Angeles and talked to Frank Martinez, a union steward. Years earlier Martinez had helped me with an investigation I conducted for the Teamsters. The Justice Department had charged them with shaking down packing houses by refusing to move meat unless paid a bribe. I was able to show that the Justice Department informants lied to obtain lenient sentences for themselves, and charges were dropped.

Through Martinez I obtained Wright's current address. I didn't want to just show up on his doorstep, unannounced, but I couldn't call and make an appointment because he had an unlisted phone. So I went to a contact at the telephone company—who charged a hundred dollars per number—and got Wright's listing.

I don't like this procedure, but the police use it, and they don't have to pay. One time I had coffee with a pair of cops in Las Vegas. "What you doing, Lake?" one asked. "Not much," I said. "Let's find out," the second cop said. "We'll run his tolls." He was joking, but he could have done it, even though by law a court order is required. A former CIA agent once told me he could get unlisted phone numbers anywhere in the world.

I flew to Los Angeles, rented a car, and drove to the Downey police station, where William Wright had agreed to meet me.

Wright, thin and balding, introduced me to Detective Gary Morrow, who seemed protective of the truck driver. Morrow expressed disenchantment with the Phoenix police's handling of this witness and remarked that Wright's anxiety stemmed from the Mob connotations in the Bolles bombing.

"Mr. Wright," I said, "I read Jon Sellers's report of his interview with you."

"I'm glad someone's interested. I don't think Sellers liked what he heard from me. He never came back."

"Well, we're shooting for a new trial, and I want to talk to you. I can't answer for Sellers."

"It surprised me," said Detective Morrow, "that we didn't hear back from Phoenix. I thought they would check out what Bill told them."

"You were never subpoenaed to the trial?" I asked Wright.

"All I had was that one talk with Sellers."

"When did you meet Bradley Funk?"

"On June 8, 1976, the day after I checked into the hospital."

"Who admitted you to Beverly Manor?"

"I admitted myself."

"No. I mean what person at the hospital did the paperwork?" I wanted to go see this individual, who might also have admitted Funk.

"I don't remember. He was a young, big guy."

"And you met Bradley Funk on your second day at the hospital?"

"Correct."

"What kind of shape was he in?"

"He seemed okay to me. Frankly, I wondered why he was even there."

That Funk checked into a detox center before Bolles died,

thus removing himself from the scene of the investigation, struck me as a coincidence not dissimilar to Neal Roberts having had three cars stolen on the day of the bombing.

"Did Funk mention John Adamson to you?"

"Yes. He said Adamson was just a 'stooge' in the murder conspiracy."

Some of what Wright told me had been contained in the Sellers police report, but not the truck driver's opinion that Funk didn't need alcohol rehabilitation, nor that Funk had called Adamson a "stooge."

On what did Funk base this judgment? He claimed he met Adamson only once, at the Stockyards Restaurant, describing the killer as "a slimy-looking guy with mirrored glasses." Adamson, for his part, claimed he had *never* met Funk.

"Did Funk tell you he knew Adamson?"

"He said he saw him numerous times at the dog tracks."

"Did Funk ever mention Don Bolles?"

"That's mostly all he talked about."

"What did he say?"

"Not much until Bolles died. Then he told me he knew his family would be blamed, but he said he believed some dog owners were responsible."

"Dog owners?"

"That's what he said."

"Did he name any of these dog owners?"

"Like I told Sellers, the only names I remember were Steiger and Goldwater. Brad said some big people were going to be hurt."

Adamson owned dogs. But most dog owners revered Bolles, saw him as a champion in their fight for better purses from the Funk-Emprise racing monopoly. Dog owners wouldn't want Bolles dead.

"What else did Funk talk to you about?"

"He mentioned some land deals being exposed because of this killing."

"Can you be more specific?"

"No. Just that land deals would be exposed."

I wondered if this connected with JoDon's revelation about Monte Kobey, who had been indicted with The Godfather of Land Fraud, Ned Warren.

"Did Funk say anything about how Bolles was killed?"

"Yes. He told me he was blown up by a bomb triggered by a remote-control device."

"In Sellers's police report, he quotes you as saying that Funk told you the explosives or something—'or something,' that's the way he words it—were purchased in San Diego. What did you mean by 'or something'?"

"I think Brad told me the explosives had been bought in San Diego. But I can't be one hundred percent sure. I know something was purchased there."

If Adamson did buy the dynamite in San Diego, it contradicted his trial testimony, which stated that he had stolen it from a bunker on the property of a rancher named Stan Tanner. However, Adamson and Gail Owens *had visited* San Diego, where they purchased the remote-control device, which she paid for and stored in her home. During this same visit, Adamson had met with the underworld figure known as San Diego Ralph.

Later I refreshed my memory by reviewing the January 4, 1977, sworn statement made by John Adamson to Assistant Attorney General William J. Schafer III:

SCHAFER: What was actually stored in Gail Owens's clothes closet?

ADAMSON: The device.

SCHAFER: The radio control device?

ADAMSON: Yes. And I believe some of the dynamite.

SCHAFER: If there was dynamite there, then you're saying she only had two [sic] things in her apartment, the device itself and the dynamite and the container they were both in.

ADAMSON: Right.

SCHAFER: And if I understood you right yesterday—or correct me if I'm wrong—at the time you put that stuff in there, she knew what it was for?

ADAMSON: Yes.

SCHAFER: Because you told her; is that correct?

ADAMSON: Yes, sir.

SCHAFER: Did she know it was for Don Bolles at that time?

ADAMSON: Yes.

SCHAFER: Because you had used the name.

ADAMSON: (Nods head.)

SCHAFER: And she knew it was there to eventually kill Don Bolles.

ADAMSON: Yes.

Immunity for Gail Owens had been almost as outrageous as immunity for Neal Roberts.

"Did Funk," I asked Wright, "tell you how he knew the explosives 'or something' were purchased in San Diego?"

"No. But he sure seemed positive."

"Tell me about the visit to that hobby shop. When did it take place?"

"Around June fifteenth. The hobby shop is just a few blocks from the detox center, and we went there to get supplies for a model boat he was building. Out of a clear blue sky, he pointed to a remote-control device and said, 'That's like the one used to blow up Bolles.' "

How could Funk know this? I later reviewed every newspaper article I could find dated before June 15, 1976, and indeed Funk could have discovered the bomb was detonated by remote control, since the news appeared as early as June 10. But what of the statement that Adamson purchased the dynamite, "or something," in San Diego?

I had been led to Wright by Sellers's report, which the detective described as "highlights" of his interview. These highlights had not been available to defense counsel during the trial, and the complete taped interview still wasn't.

Highlights, I thought. Here was a key witness in the biggest murder investigation in Arizona history, conducted by a detective with twenty years of experience. I couldn't help flashing back to homicides I worked while a police officer in Las Vegas, and imagining how my boss, Chief of Detectives Captain Bill O'Reilly, would have reacted had I presented a report called "Highlights." I could almost hear O'Reilly roar, "Highlights, my ass! I want either the complete conversation on my desk in the morning, or your badge."

"Lake," said Detective Morrow, "you've got a copy of Sellers's written report. Did he mention those cards I gave him?"

"Yes, he did." I handed Sellers's report to Morrow, pointing out the paragraph in question:

> At this time, Det. Morrow turned over to investigator two business cards, one with the name of Bradley J. Funk imprinted on the front with a handwritten telephone number on the back as follows: Area code 602/273-7181. The second card was identified by the letters ANC Towing imprinted on the front with handwritten phone number on the back: Area code 602/248-8243. This card had been torn up by Mr. Wright and dropped on the ground which he [Morrow] ultimately retrieved. Mr. Wright was asked about this ANC Towing card and stated that he could not remember anything about the phone number or why he threw it away.

Through Terri Lee, I had attempted to run down ANC Towing. She had back-checked business licenses for ten years, but could find nothing listed under ANC. I suspected the "A" stood for Adamson, who we knew operated a shady towing business. He wasn't the sort to bother with a business license.

Terri Lee had gone to the 1976 *CrissCross Directory*, found nothing, and then to the phone company itself, but it kept records only for six months.

A dead end. So that "A" in ANC remained a mystery.

"Sellers's report," I said to Morrow, "doesn't indicate why you had those cards. How did you get them?"

"From Bill Wright. He came to me about his relationship

with Funk—that's why I called Phoenix—and handed me the cards Bradley Funk had given him."

"Why," I asked Wright, "would Funk give you an ANC Towing card?"

"You need to remember, this was three years ago. I really can't recall."

Right. But Sellers's taped interview, conducted just two months after Bolles died, should contain the answer. A top priority was obtaining that interview.

"Mr. Wright, I'd like you to show me Beverly Manor, and also the hobby shop."

"Sure. I'm ready now if you are."

The two—hospital and hobby shop—were quite close to each other, definitely within walking distance. Wright and I entered the hobby shop and he showed me the display case that had contained the remote-control device Funk had pointed out. Then I drove Wright to his home and headed to the airport.

Upon my return, I called on Murray Miller, a Phoenix criminal defense attorney whom the Dunlap Committee had recently retained to help convene an evidentiary hearing—separate from the appeal, designed to provide a forum for the mass of new facts we had uncovered since the trial, information now widely disseminated in the press but technically not being considered by the Arizona Supreme Court.

Murray Miller's entrance into the case encouraged me. I believed some of the others were too willing to wait for the outcome of the appeal, in effect tying our hands until the supreme court ruled. Miller also thought we might be stymied, but had decided to open up a second front anyway—get things moving, force some action. Of course, I wholeheartedly supported his activism.

Miller, not part of Phoenix's good-old-boy network, proved himself willing to make waves. He listened to my appraisal of the Wright interview and declared without hesitation, "Let's go back there. I want to hear this with my own ears."

He and I hopped a flight to Los Angeles and drove to Downey, where Bill Wright repeated the story of his relationship with Bradley Funk at Beverly Manor Hospital.

Miller shot off a letter to Attorney General Corbin and Assistant Attorney General Schafer:

It has recently come to my attention that your office is in possession, custody, or control of a tape recording made by the Phoenix Police Department, of a conversation with William Wright, recorded in the state of California, in the month of August 1976.

A three-page synopsis of the police officer's version of what this witness said was submitted to Judge Thompson in your Petition for Determination of Discoverability filed with the Court, July 24, 1979.

We respectfully request that you permit us to listen to this tape recording immediately and if a transcript of this recording was made, that we be permitted to inspect it forthwith.

We further request an immediate written response as to whether or not this tape recording, and/or a verbatim transcript, was ever furnished Judge Thompson prior to trial, or at any subsequent time.

If the tape recording and/or a verbatim transcript of the tape recording was furnished to Judge Thompson, please inform us of the date this was done.

A copy of this letter is being forwarded to Judge Thompson so that the Court file may reflect its contents.

It didn't take long for Schafer to reply. Herewith his answer, in its entirety.

Dear Mr. Miller:

In view of the actions of the trial court, I do not deem it appropriate for us to answer the questions you posed in your letter of November 27.

What actions of the trial court? Perhaps this referred to Judge Howard Thompson's earlier wringing of hands when Miller sought to obtain the contents of File #851. Thompson finally had ruled that he had no jurisdiction and laid the matter in the lap of the Arizona Supreme Court. This buck passing yielded no results (the supreme court hadn't yet ruled), and maybe Corbin/ Schafer felt Thompson would decide the same way if confronted with the withheld Wright tapes.

Miller was determined to find out. Faced with the attorney general's refusal to cooperate, he filed a December 6, 1979, lawsuit, worded in the strongest possible way, in the Superior Court of the State of Arizona, Maricopa County:

> Defendant Dunlap respectfully submits this Supplemental Memorandum and requests the Court for an immediate Evidentiary Hearing for the following reasons:
>
> The material recently discovered by the Defendant, Dunlap, indicates that there may have been a massive cover-up by the Government of material, significant, and vital evidence, which enabled the Government to obtain a conviction of this defendant in deprivation of his constitutional right to a fair trial. . . .
>
> NONDISCLOSURE OF SECRET TAPE RECORDING
>
> The prosecutors have had in their possession and control a secret tape recording made by the chief homicide investigator, Jon Sellers. Detective Sellers flew to Downey, California, on August 17, 1976, and taped a lengthy interview with a key witness named William Wright. A sterilized version of this interview appears in the Court files, which were certified to the Supreme Court of Appeal, and is attached as Exhibit 1.
>
> A mere glance into this exhibit indicates that as early as August 1976, the Phoenix Police were aware of a witness who told them that during the same month that Don Bolles was murdered, the witness was taken to a hobby shop in California by Bradley Funk and was shown a

remote-control device that was similar to the one used to
blow Bolles up. Detective Sellers verified this by showing
Mr. Wright a photograph of the remote control device,

> "which investigators suspect is similar to the type that
> was used. At this time, Wright said the device that Funk
> showed him was similar to the one that investigator had
> a photograph of."

This report was never given to defense counsel prior
to trial. Even more incredible is the fact that the full,
complete, and unedited interview of William Wright, as
tape recorded by homicide investigator Sellers, was never
shown to defense counsel, and to the best of our knowledge was never given to the trial Court.

A sincere attempt was made to learn the contents of
this secret recording and to determine whether or not the
State ever submitted it to the trial Court. This knowledge
is crucial to defense counsel and is a prerequisite to requesting Post Conviction Relief on the basis of newly discovered evidence.

To this end, a letter was addressed to the Attorney
General, dated November 27, 1979, requesting this specific information. A copy of this letter is attached as Ex-
hibit 2.

An informative response was received from Attorney
General on December 3, 1979, in which they stated (Ex-
hibit 3):

> "In view of the actions of the trial court, I do not deem
> it appropriate for us to answer the questions you posed
> in your letter of November 27."

Our ex-president notwithstanding, a clearer case of
"Stonewalling" is difficult to imagine. . . .

No Court, nor any defense counsel, can accept a police officer's summarized version of what a witness stated,

when in fact, a verbatim tape recording of the witness's testimony has existed from the very beginning. If in fact they never submitted this secret tape recording to Court or counsel, this is clearly prosecutorial suppression of evidence.

The time for "Stonewalling" has long since past. Two men are held in death row. We are entitled to answers, and therefore requesting an Evidentiary Hearing.

While Murray Miller pressed forward on the legal front, I raised cain in and with the press. Jonathan Marshall continued the *Scottsdale Daily Progress*'s barrage against the official explanation of the Bolles homicide; the *Los Angeles Times* reported the ongoing struggle; even the *Arizona Republic* became less cocky in its commitment to the guilt of Robison and Dunlap, quoting chunks of Miller's allegations of withheld evidence.

Finally, the police department announced it "couldn't find" the Sellers interview of William Wright.

Couldn't find? "It's lost," said a police spokesperson.

"Ludicrous," Terri Lee said.

"I'd bet the farm," I said, "that it isn't lost at all. It's been purged, just like File Eight-Five-One."

I wondered aloud why Sellers hadn't been disciplined, both for presenting only "highlights," and also for "losing" the tapes.

But the scandal had to extend far beyond Sellers. He had superiors who were supposed to steer him back onto the track whenever he veered off. Who were these people, and did they act with deliberate malice?

20

Convictions Overturned!

"Lake, have you heard?" It was February 25, 1980, about 2 P.M., and the voice on the other end of the line belonged to Max's wife, Barbara.

"Heard what?" I feared something might have happened to one of the Dunlap children, an auto accident perhaps.

"Oh, Lake, I'm so happy. It came over the radio, and Murray Miller just confirmed. The supreme court overturned the convictions. There will be new trials."

"Hooray! That's great news, Barbara."

"The kids and Max's mother are coming over. Will you and Terri drop by?"

"We're on our way."

I hung up and stared at Terri.

"Well?" she asked. "Where are we going?"

My face was wreathed in a smile as bright as the Arizona sun, the dawn after a long night of storm and near-tragedy.

"Come on, Lake, don't tease me with that cat-who-ate-the-canary grin."

"Is your camera loaded? You're about to have a once-in-a-lifetime photo opportunity."

"For Pete's sake, tell me what happened."

"The supreme court overturned the convictions."

"All right!" she shrieked with joy.

"There will be new trials," I said.

"Where Schafer gets laughed out of court."

"You bet!"

I tried to call Devereux, another who owned a big role in this triumph, but couldn't reach him. He would find out soon enough. So would all of Arizona.

Terri and I chattered happily on the fifty-block ride to Max's house. "Do you know the reason the supreme court used to overturn?" she asked.

"Barbara didn't say. Maybe those justices read the *Progress*. It took long enough," I said, suddenly bitter, thinking of the more than two years Max and Jim spent eying the door to the gas chamber. But today wasn't the time for negatives.

"Savor the moment, Terri Lee," I said. "This is a big one. Not many turn out like this." I reached over and pulled her closer.

At Max's home I glowed all over. Six of the seven Dunlap children were there, including the fourteen-year-old twin boys, and I figured the missing daughter, Susan, twenty-five, was probably on the way from her Flagstaff home.

The children hugged one another, and us. Here I knew were memories to treasure a lifetime: the heartfelt "if it hadn't been for you" and "you're a wonderful man" and plenty of "God bless you, Lake."

Tears of relief and happiness flowed unashamedly at Max's home, and a lump clogged my throat. Barbara Dunlap looked like a woman just given a ticket to heaven.

The doorbell rang. "That will be Max's mother," Barbara said. "Lake, she wants to see you. Why don't you answer the door?"

When I did, seventy-seven-year-old Elizabeth Dunlap gave me a big hug. "This is a wonderful day," she said through tears. "The happiest day of my life."

Terri Lee and I stayed perhaps forty-five minutes. Shortly afterward I reached Devereux, who took my earlier negative feeling a step further: "I don't see why everyone's so happy; this should have happened a long time ago."

"Do you know the details of the court's decision?" I asked.

"It was unanimous. Five to zero. They ruled that the defendants' constitutional rights were violated when Adamson was allowed to plead the Fifth Amendment and not answer certain questions during the trial."

"Well, that's one hook they could use. I can think of a hundred others, right at the top of the list being that Max and Jim are innocent. So what's this about new trials?"

"It's not clear if they'll be tried separately or together. First there's a period allowed for rehearing or continuance motions. Then the trial or trials must be scheduled within sixty days, or the charges dropped."

"I say they'll drop the charges. I'd love new trials, and Dunlap and Robison would, too. They want their names cleared in a court of law."

"I know they do."

"Has Schafer made any comment?"

"Yeah. Can you believe that guy? He said the decisions didn't surprise him. He claimed that at the supreme court stage it's a fifty-fifty shot this will happen."

"He said *fifty-fifty*?"

"Exact quote."

"Jesus Christ. More like one in a thousand, I'd say. But," I said, joking, "maybe with him it is fifty-fifty, if he handles all his homicides like he did this one. What did he say about new trials?"

"He's going for them."

"Good. He'll get blown away in a retrial."

There were plenty of kudos to go around in the heady days following the overturn of the convictions. David Fraser, a bellwether of the Dunlap Committee, at first much maligned and alone in questioning and attacking the trial court verdict, issued a statement to the press:

"We accomplished the three things we set out to do to this point:

"We changed the atmosphere of the community regarding the Bolles murder and the complicity in it of Max Dunlap. The *Scottsdale Daily Progress* was a key to that effort.

"We raised the money for a first-class private investigator in Lake Headley.

"We kept enough money coming in to retain Murray Miller, a first-class attorney and criminal lawyer. In the new trial, he will demonstrate very clearly that Max Dunlap is innocent."

And Jim Robison, too. Robison lacked only the wonderful friends Dunlap had.

David Fraser could also have singled out his own committee as a substantial force toward ending the nightmare. Without the unwavering support of Max's supporters, he and Jim would have been doomed.

Jonathan Marshall, his heart certainly bursting with pride, wrote an editorial he had long waited to pen:

> The Arizona Supreme Court unanimously ruled Monday to overturn the convictions of Max Dunlap and James Robison for the murder of reporter Don Bolles on June 2, 1976. The two men have been on death row since their sentencing in January 1978.
>
> Robison and Dunlap steadfastly have maintained their innocence. They and their friends have charged that others were involved in the case and that the true story has not been revealed. . . .
>
> This time the community will not be calling for revenge, and the trial should be conducted more calmly and objectively. Whether it is held again in Phoenix and whether the two are tried separately remains to be seen. . . .
>
> If justice is to be obtained and if the truth about the killing is to be known, it is essential that all information now should be revealed. This should be done even if it embarrasses the prosecution and prominent members of the community.

Marshall had risked a lot with his long, lonely, courageous stand. A Phoenix weekly, *New Times,* pointed out, "It hasn't been easy for Marshall and his small *Scottsdale Progress*— circulation, 21,000—to go after the biggest story in Arizona and one of the biggest in the country. For a while over the last couple of years, he had police protection. He was advised not to travel the same road home every night. He was warned to be careful; to leave 'well enough alone,' to watch out because he was 'getting too close to some very big people.' "

Molly Ivins also had to feel a deserved sense of accomplishment as she wrote the lead paragraph of her *New York Times* article: "In a unanimous decision, the Arizona Supreme Court yesterday reversed the convictions of two men in the 1976 murder of Don Bolles, the Phoenix newspaper reporter fatally wounded when a bomb blew up his car."

How about Robison and Dunlap themselves? I drove to the Arizona State Prison the day after the verdict.

"Say, fuck this!" Robison growled. "I shouldn't have been here in the first place. But don't get me wrong. I'm grateful to you and Devereux. If you two hadn't done all that digging, and he hadn't kept grinding out all those stories, Max and I never would have seen a reversal."

Max said enthusiastically: "What a turnaround! I'm looking forward to the new trial. I don't want them dismissing these charges. Jim and I deserve to be vindicated."

I agreed. And it could and should happen *twice.* It wasn't fair to either Robison or Dunlap to be tried together. They had *never met* before their arrests for "conspir[ing] to kill Bolles."

Let Schafer, Sellers, Babbitt, and the rest eat a double portion of crow. Could Schafer really be serious about new trials? In my head I made a partial list of the many witnesses who would be called, a few of whom would be vindicated, others embarrassed, and some destroyed:

John Adamson
Bradley Funk

Betty Funk Richardson
Ned Warren
H. Monte M. Kobey
Neal Roberts
Antje Roberts
Eileen Roberts
Gail Owens
Kay Kroot
Barry Goldwater
Michael JoDon
Keith Nation
James McVay
Lawrence Wetzel
Jon Sellers
Michael Butler
Harry Hawkins
Jack Weaver
William Wright
Hank Landry
John Zollinger
Terrell Bounds

... plus a conglomeration of additional police officers and prosecutors who had overlooked, hidden, and destroyed evidence vital to the defense.

Previously, the Dunlap Committee literally couldn't *buy* publicity for its cause. Now, AP, UPI, the *Boston Globe*, and papers in places like Idaho and South Carolina jumped on the bandwagon. The headline of a follow-up Molly Ivins story in *The New York Times* said it best: "A Reporter's Death Puts State on Trial."

On March 7, 1980, Murray Miller announced he would seek bail for Dunlap, a move opposed by Attorney General Corbin.

Robison didn't qualify for bail. After being arrested for the Bolles murder, he had been convicted in a separate assault case, and given a twenty-six-year sentence. I believed, and Robison swore, that he stood innocent of this crime, also. What put him away: largely the testimony of John Harvey Adamson.

On March 13, 1980, we again were reminded of the erratic nature of Arizona justice. The state—despite its generous dispensation of immunity agreements to key figures in the Bolles case—had decided Michael JoDon needed to be taught the seriousness of a twenty-dollar drug sale to an undercover agent. JoDon's first trial had ended in a hung jury, but on this date Maricopa County Superior Court Judge David L. Grounds found him guilty. Judge Grounds tentatively scheduled sentencing for April 10, with JoDon facing five years to life!

Perhaps emboldened by this outrage, Schafer and Corbin talked confidently about plans for the retrials of Max and Jim. They weren't, evidently, prepared for the bombshell their own lying snitch, John Harvey Adamson, dropped in their laps on April 9.

Adamson, in a letter to prosecutors, listed a series of "demands" he wanted met before agreeing to testify again. They included: full immunity from *any* crime he had *ever* committed; immediate release from prison; a new identity; a new wardrobe; money; protection for his ex-wife; and an education for his son.

If the prosecution didn't agree to his terms, Adamson declared, he would not testify against Robison and Dunlap.

Murray Miller saw the matter differently: "The unmitigated gall of this convicted assassin will make the attorney general's office a laughingstock across the nation." Miller suggested that "since the Waldorf Astoria is not readily available" for Adamson, prosecutors "should take advantage of spring and summer rates at the Arizona Biltmore or Camelback Inn."

What was Adamson up to? Surely he didn't want to reenter the courtroom arena as a lamb against lions. But did he actually expect the state to grovel so abjectly? Or did he purposely put an inflated price tag on his testimony to keep himself from being ripped apart on the stand and perhaps forced to name his true co-conspirators? He had referred to them once, saying, "My people don't give immunity."

Except for denying Max and Jim the chance to hear themselves publicly acquitted, it didn't matter one way or the other what this lowlife did, but watching would be fun.

21

Adamson Versus Corbin

The supreme court reversal generated movement: Max Dunlap to the less demeaning conditions of Maricopa County Jail, where he awaited his bail hearing; Jim Robison from death row to the general population at Arizona State Prison; and John Adamson from a previously undisclosed out-of-state location to Maricopa County Jail, nearer prosecutors ostensibly urging him to drop his demands.

In context, how outrageous was Adamson's position? He, at least, had put in some prison time. Neal Roberts never served a day, thanks to that trade of theory for immunity, nor had Gail Owens. Immunity-according-to-Arizona (none for JoDon on a twenty-dollar hash deal, despite the potentially critical evidence he offered) was a wondrous thing to observe.

Why shouldn't Adamson go for it?

Because, Attorney General Corbin whined, the convicted killer had *given his word* to cooperate "fully and completely."

Given his word to lie would have more accurately described the deal, and to take the Fifth. Prosecutors hadn't uttered a peep at the trial when Adamson's "full and complete" testimony included refusal to answer questions he didn't like.

I had to wonder if Schafer and Corbin, wringing their hands, were merely playacting. Did they sincerely want this case tried again? If police and prosecutors had conspired in a broad coverup to protect powerful Arizonans, as gut instinct and vanished evidence told me they had, why should they let their dirty linen be aired in public?

Certainly Murray Miller wanted it back in court. "Are we ever ready!" he proclaimed to newsmen. Miller projected the confidence of a fleet admiral backed by nuclear forces squaring off against a leaky rowboat.

Don W. Harris, the interim Maricopa County attorney originally slated to prosecute the Bolles murder before being elbowed aside by Bruce Babbitt, now came forward with an inevitable I-told-you-so. Harris said William Schafer, working under "a greedy attorney general who wanted to be a U.S. senator," had brushed aside his suggestions of Mafia involvement in the killing. He repeated earlier charges that "a judge, a civic leader, and others" (people he refused to identify) had pressured him to back off investigations into the role of organized crime in the Bolles murder.

Was the contest between Adamson and the prosecution a charade to avoid new trials? I didn't believe Adamson was playing a game, but I suspected Corbin and Schafer were. Adamson was shrewd enough to realize he faced a buzz saw if he took the stand again, and his only safeguards were gaining full immunity, guaranteed immediate release from custody, and a new identity. For these gigantic concessions, he'd bear the opprobrium of being proved a liar.

Adamson had working for him a most intriguing argument, hotly debated throughout the Phoenix legal community: that he was being subjected to double jeopardy. He had already gone to court and been sentenced for murder. Could he be prosecuted again if he refused to testify? Adamson said no, that since he had been tried and sentenced once, he had nothing to lose by his refusal to take the stand again.

On April 15, 1980, the killer appeared to be winning. Corbin went so far as to offer him new clothes, "improved" confinement, and protection for his family during the course of a new trial. But immediate release from jail was too much even for these prosecutors.

On April 18, 1980, at a preliminary bail hearing for Max,

Adamson invoked the Fifth Amendment on thirty-one of thirty-two questions asked by Murray Miller. The one answer the con man gave: "What I said at the preliminary hearing [in 1976] was true."

He should have pled self-incrimination on *thirty-two* of thirty-two, because he laid himself open to perjury with his one answer. His 1976 preliminary hearing testimony was full of lies.

The next day Adamson took the Fifth Amendment *one hundred and thirty-six* times. Superior Court Judge Robert L. Myers did not order Adamson to answer, thus saving him from contempt citations.

I couldn't help smiling when I watched Adamson's entrances into the courtroom, wearing a bulletproof vest and surrounded by four U.S. marshals. Whom did he fear? "My people [who] don't give immunity"?

Another vital police report, withheld by the prosecution during the original trial, surfaced to support this supposition. The document, provided by the California Department of Justice, concerned a certain Nicolo Angelo DiVincenzo, described as a "hit man for organized crime" who "allegedly advised that he had been hired to murder John Adamson, arrested for the bombing murder of Bolles in June of 1976.

> DiVincenzo reportedly stated that he had received the contract to hit Adamson prior to Adamson's arrest because Adamson was a direct link to Funk (believed to be one of the Funks of Funks Greyhound Racing Circuit, Inc.).
>
> DiVincenzo stated that Adamson was a direct tie to Funk and other very important persons in Arizona and that Adamson could not be trusted to live. DiVincenzo stated that he did not carry out the "contract" on Adamson in time before Adamson was arrested for Bolles's murder, but that the "Commission of 13" still insisted that DiVincenzo carry out the "contract" even though Adamson was in police custody.
>
> DiVincenzo refused to carry out this contract and fell into disfavor of the "Commission." DiVincenzo then left

Phoenix and moved to Los Angeles, stating that he had contacts here (in California) that could get him "back into the business."

Long before, in that interview with Marcus Aurelius which I read the first night I worked on the case, Betty Funk Richardson had predicted Adamson's life would be in danger, saying that he would be safer in police custody. The new identity Adamson wanted became more understandable in view of the DiVincenzo allegations. So too did his repeated taking of the Fifth:

MILLER: Your previous testimony was a batch of bold-faced lies, wasn't it?

ADAMSON: On the advice of counsel, I invoke the Fifth Amendment and refuse to answer.

MILLER: Your testimony was nothing more than un-adulterated perjury, wasn't it?

ADAMSON: On the advice of counsel, I invoke the Fifth Amendment and refuse to answer.

MILLER: And the entire story you told the prosecution was a lie, wasn't it, John?

ADAMSON: On the advice of counsel, I invoke the Fifth Amendment and refuse to answer.

Adamson wore a loud print shirt and dark glasses to the bail hearing. He seemed bored, even when he pleaded self-incrimination after being asked his motives for refusing to testify. "You figured, didn't you," said Miller, "you had the prosecution where you wanted them and that you could squeeze them a little more?"

Neal Roberts also testified at the bail hearing. He took the Fifth Amendment twenty-one times. Roberts pleaded self-incrimination to the "loud and clear" remark, to "setting up" the "easy patsy" Dunlap by having him deliver that money to Adamson's lawyer, and to questions about the three vehicles "stolen" on the day of the bombing.

"I put it to you," Miller asked at one point, "that you and

John Harvey Adamson conspired and framed Max Dunlap in the murder of Don Bolles; isn't that the truth?"

But of course Roberts wouldn't reply to the question.

Had I been on the attorney general's staff, I would have felt like a fool listening to Adamson and Roberts take the Fifth. These were *their* immunized witnesses.

Again a courtroom heard tributes to the character of Max Dunlap, this time about his eminent suitability for bail. Retired First National Bank vice president Leo Baumgartner described Max as "about the most honest and gentle man I've ever known." Retired First National Bank chairman of the board Sherman Hazeltine declared Dunlap "totally incapable of the heinous crime with which he has been charged."

Judge Myers, on April 22, 1980, ruled that Robison and Dunlap must be tried separately. He postponed "for a few days" the decision about bail.

Corbin and Schafer saw their case crumbling before their eyes. Worse for them, it was veering in uncontrollable directions.

Miller, during the bail hearing, emphasized the pressure exerted on the police shortly after the bombing to come up with a quick solution to the case. William Shover, director of community and corporate services for the *Arizona Republic* and the *Phoenix Gazette*, admitted, according to the *Arizona Republic* itself, that an "offer was made during a phone conversation he had with then–Phoenix Police Chief Lawrence Wetzel around midnight three days after Bolles was injured fatally."

The *Arizona Republic* also had to concede, in an April 25, 1980, story: "Wetzel suggested that an offer of money to Adamson might loosen his tongue," Shover said, "and an amount in the range of $50,000 to $100,000 was discussed."

The offer was made, Shover admitted, but Adamson turned it down. Shover didn't comment on the propriety of offering a large sum of money to the man who helped murder the finest reporter his newspaper ever had.

We wondered if maybe the money *had* been paid. Murray Miller petitioned the court to see Adamson's 1976 tax returns, but Judge Myers ruled against the motion, continuing a long-established tradition of proprosecution decisions. Judge Myers also said the attorney general's office did not have to reveal why it took the case away from county prosecutor Don Harris.

On April 28, 1980, with the only real witness against him pleading the Fifth Amendment, Max was ordered freed on twenty-eight thousand dollars bail. At every step, the attorney general's office had cruelly fought tooth and nail against his release.

The decision to grant bail came unexpectedly and without fanfare, not in an open court but with a written order. Max decided to surprise his family by coming home unannounced, but having been away so long (three and a half years in all), he wasn't sure this was his house when he rang the doorbell.

It didn't matter. His family had gone to a movie and left the door unlocked. They arrived home at 10 P.M. to one of the happiest surprises of their lives.

Three of Max's daughters had married since he had been arrested at gunpoint and taken away. Two of them, Susan and Sandra, proudly had had a double wedding March 23, 1978, in the Maricopa County Jail, before Max got transferred to death row at the state prison. The third married daughter, Pamela, fought to have her ceremony conducted at Florence, but authorities wouldn't permit it.

After his release, reporters, photographers, and TV cameramen swarmed all over Max's northeast Phoenix home. Holding Barbara's hand and speaking extemporaneously, he said, "Most people take it for granted just to be able to walk outside in the morning, to see the sky, to do what they want to do. It's hard to explain to someone what freedom means, unless they've been through what I have."

Terri Lee and I enjoyed all of it—the expectant time leading up to Max's release, the joy of the reunited family, the anticipation of final vindication at the upcoming trials and, yes, the sight of those police and prosecutors on the run. They had acted arrogantly and unconscionably, but now had been put to full flight.

Max kept a promise he had made to me in prison and had

me over to his house for dinner with his family. We relived the recent "war days" and enjoyed a big batch of crab legs, his favorite food.

Terri Lee and I kept ourselves busy teaching paralegal classes to Navajos and working for Vlassis on the never-ending problems of the reservation. I continued to visit Jim Robison at Florence and was pleased to see the change in his attitude. The man who had thought throwing in the towel was better than a miserable existence in death row's limbo now itched for the good courtroom fight that we all expected to win with a decisive knockout.

The complexion of the case really had altered radically. On May 8, 1980, Corbin filed first-degree murder charges against John Adamson, saying the con man's plea bargain agreement had been rendered null and void by his refusal to testify in the upcoming trials.

Adamson's lawyer, Bill Feldhacker, immediately filed a superior court motion to have the first-degree murder charges dropped. Adamson, he said, had fulfilled the requirements of his pact with the state when he originally testified against Robison and Dunlap, the result being the two death-sentence convictions. Besides, Feldhacker argued, Corbin had no right to unilaterally declare invalid a court-sanctioned plea bargain. That power resided with the court, not the attorney general.

In answer to the lawyer's contention that Corbin had overstepped his bounds, Superior Court Judge William P. French declared himself "somewhat inclined to agree."

Feldhacker accused the prosecutors of setting up "some sort of legal tribunal out there," adding: "They want everyone to think my client has breached his plea agreement, but they want to be the only ones to sit in judgment of that."

I couldn't find a side—Adamson or Corbin—to cheer for in this dispute, though I loved watching them scrap it out. The attorney general richly deserved this headache.

"Karma," Terri Lee decided. "What goes around, comes around."

The distinct possibility now existed that the *only* punishment for the Bolles murder would be the twenty-year prison term negotiated in Adamson's plea bargain. Lawyer Feldhacker proclaimed, "The attorney general's office is proceeding without authority to prosecute Mr. Adamson for a crime for which he is now serving a sentence. There is no doubt he is being subjected to double jeopardy."

But on May 29 the Arizona Supreme Court held otherwise and ruled that Adamson "entered into a plea agreement with the state which by its very terms waives the defense of double jeopardy if the agreement is violated."

This hardly ended the wrangle. Feldhacker promised an appeal to the federal courts.

William Schafer said he had no intention of using the Arizona Supreme Court decision as leverage to force Adamson to testify against Max and Jim. "If Adamson wants to testify," Schafer pronounced, "he can come to us."

"I believe Schafer," I told Terri Lee. "One of the few times I have. He doesn't want Adamson to testify. He knows the beating he'll get if he retries Jim and Max, and how all that damning evidence against powerful people is bound to come out."

"Adamson doesn't want to testify either," she said. "He's no fool, give the bastard that."

Right. And nothing since the reversal of the convictions had lessened the stench permeating Phoenix. Since Adamson no longer qualified as the prosecution's fair-haired boy, leaks to the media suddenly linked him to *four other murders*, all in 1975:

1. The bombing of federal informant Louis Bombacino in Tempe, suspiciously similar to the modus operandi employed to kill Bolles.

2. The death of accountant Edward Lazar, scheduled to testify against land-fraud godfather Ned Warren, shot five times in a Phoenix parking lot.

3. The disappearance and probable killing of Jack
   West, a Phoenix businessman. He left home saying
   he was "going to see a man about some money,"
   and never returned. Adamson reportedly owed
   West $5,000.

4. The strangling murder of Helen Marston, a wealthy
   eighty-one-year-old widow, during what police called
   an "interrupted burglary" at her Paradise Valley
   home.

Under what rock had all this speculation hidden when Adamson
was ballyhooed as a witness the people should believe? It looked
to me like he had been thrown to the wolves.

It burned me, also, how quickly the Arizona Supreme Court
got its act together when the *attorney general* wanted a ruling.
In *less than two weeks* the justices decided that Adamson had
violated his plea agreement. It took the same court *a year* of
dragging ass before they reversed the trial and then, finally, ruled
on new trials for Robison and Dunlap.

Sure enough, on May 31, 1980, all charges were "temporarily
dismissed" against Max Dunlap and, two weeks later, June 13,
1980, the fourth anniversary of Bolles's death, prosecution
against Jim Robison was also dropped "temporarily."

I had no sympathy for Adamson. As one of many people who
I believed were responsible for murdering Don Bolles, he deserved appropriate punishment. What I hated was how the prosecutors now intended to go after him with the full force of the
law, and then, with the Arizona Supreme Court having got them
off the hook of a new trial, wash their hands of the dirty affair
and never have to go after the other guilty parties. I could already hear what would eventually come down as the official line:
Well, we convicted Adamson. And we would have gotten Dunlap and Robison, if that scum Adamson hadn't refused to testify.
The only one we missed was Kemper Marley. All in all, we did
pretty good.

These prosecutorial maneuvers sickened every fair-minded

individual connected with the investigation and also prompted one of the most bizarre episodes in this thoroughly bizarre case.

Murray Miller sued, *demanding that Max Dunlap be tried for murder,* or in the alternative, that charges be permanently dropped. Miller made it clear his client wanted to be tried, though it meant risking the gas chamber. I knew of no such thing ever happening before.

Miller's petition read: "Dunlap wishes to stand trial now for the murder of Don Bolles. Dunlap spent three years and three months in custody, more than two years of which was on death row. The present order deprives Dunlap of final resolution of the charges and casts him adrift to live with public obloquy, while waiting for the gendarmes to knock at his door, never knowing if and when that will be.

"As it is," Miller pleaded, "Dunlap's death alone will end this legal purgatory, a purgatory so unfair that due process commands a different result now."

Jonathan Marshall didn't like that "temporarily dismissed" either:

> If the case does not go to trial, there is no possibility for their names to be cleared unless the state prosecutes and convicts others of the crime. Thus the cloud of guilt always will hang over them.
>
> Shortly after the murder the police came up with the theory that Dunlap arranged the murder for his friend Kemper Marley, about whom Bolles had written numerous negative articles. They did not properly pursue other viable leads, and they ignored possible leads provided by informants, California law enforcement agencies, potential witnesses and the press.
>
> It has appeared that the office of the attorney general has avoided pursuing other avenues of investigation and new evidence that has been uncovered. It also seems that law enforcement authorities have been embarrassed by the possibility that they made a mistake, and so have failed to prosecute other suspects.

One man was cruelly murdered. Two men have spent more than two years on death row. If the case is allowed to be dropped, it will be a travesty of justice. Don Bolles, his family and friends, and the people of Arizona deserve to have the truth pursued, regardless of where it leads or who it hurts.

Whether or not Attorney General Robert Corbin and his staff have the courage to do this remains to be seen.

On June 19, 1980, Terri Lee and I hosted a "graduation" party for six Navajos who had completed a week of our paralegal classes. This group of outstanding students had exhibited a keen interest in the law, and not just as it applied to the reservation. As I lit the fire in the charcoal grill on the patio behind our apartment, they fired questions at me about the hottest legal topic in Phoenix, the status of the Bolles case.

The following day, a Saturday, the young Native Americans returned home, and Terri and I holed up in the apartment to complete an investigative report for Mike Stuhff in Flagstaff.

"Have you got the report?" Stuhff asked over the phone that afternoon.

"Yeah. We're just finishing it."

"Good. I'll need it sooner than I thought. The trial hearing has been moved up to Monday."

"No problem. We'll put it on the first bus out of here tomorrow morning."

"I'll be at the Greyhound terminal when it arrives."

The case concerned a beauty shop. Terri Lee, becoming a real pro, had enjoyed going undercover and interviewing several of the state's witnesses while having her hair done.

That evening we watched the late news on TV and turned in early so we could get Stuhff's package on the 8:30 A.M. bus to Flagstaff. Terri set the alarm clock for 7, with no foreboding that before the dawn of a new day, our lives would be changed forever.

22

Inferno

"You dirty son of a bitch!" I roared. "I'll kill you!" I had awakened when they took me off the ambulance, unconscious but thrashing about, calling everyone foul names. I broke a restraining strap, punched an attendant, hard, and knocked him down. Then I passed out again.

They got stronger straps—they knew how to deal with this sort of nut—and wheeled me into the emergency room.

The alarm that June 21 never went off—no, the alarm must have gone off, because we figured that's what woke Terri up. I didn't hear it.

Terri Lee doesn't remember any of this, nor do I. But we pieced it together from what the neighbors and people at the hospital told us, and the fire department report.

She woke up to an apartment in flames. The blaze had started in the kitchen and roared down a hallway toward the bedroom where we slept. She tried to wake me up, but couldn't.

The place was filled with choking smoke.

Our apartment had two doors to the outside: one exiting from the kitchen, the other opening into a little foyer, which led to the living room.

Terri opened the living room door, then fled through the one in the kitchen. She ran to a neighbor, having an early-morning cup of coffee on his patio, and shouted at him, "Call the fire department! My apartment is on fire!"

She raced back to the kitchen door, a life to save, but the intense heat drove her away. She ran around to the front.

A man stood there, mesmerized by the flames. When Terri started through the front door, he grabbed and held her. "You can't go in there! That place is going to burn to the ground!"

"I got to!" she screamed over the roar of the fire. "My old man's in there!"

Terri jerked away from him and plunged inside. She fought her way through smoke and terrific heat to reach me, attempted to shake me awake, and that's where they found her, collapsed at the foot of the bed. She was still on fire, a human torch. Overcome by smoke, she had fallen on her left side, and her nightgown was in flames.

They found me still lying on the bed.

Terri and I were each lifted onto a gurney and carried from the apartment. Outside, the man who had tried to stop Terri Lee asked a fireman, "They're going to be all right, aren't they?"

"I don't think so," the fireman said. "Both their hearts have stopped."

It really hit the guy hard. He blamed himself. In fact, paramedics had to give him first aid. He threw up, cried, sat down, and just fell apart. He moaned, "I should have stopped her. I shouldn't have let her go in there. I knew something like this would happen."

After literally jump-starting our hearts to get them beating, they took Terri Lee and me to the nearest hospital, Phoenix Baptist. From there a Medevac helicopter flew her to Maricopa County General Hospital and its highly rated burn unit.

That afternoon, a doctor at Phoenix Baptist phoned George Vlassis and asked the name of my next of kin. He told them

Lake III, and said they might reach him through my friend Nick Behnen in Las Vegas.

"He's right here," said Behnen to the caller from Phoenix Baptist, and handed the phone to my son.

"Your father and his girlfriend have been in a fire," the doctor told Lake. "Can you come to Phoenix?"

"Sure, I'll be there tomorrow."

"You better come today, if you want to be sure of seeing your dad alive. We can't be certain how long he's going to live."

Behnen drove Lake to the airport and paid for his ticket on the next flight to Phoenix. Vlassis met the plane and brought him to the hospital.

A doctor asked Lake, "Who was this woman at the apartment? What's her relationship to your father?"

"She's his girlfriend, Terri Yoder. What do you mean, what's the relationship?"

"Well, how does he feel about her?"

"He cares a lot for her. Why?"

"Because the girl can't live. She's going to die any minute now. We don't expect her to survive the rest of the day. Your father has a fifty-fifty chance of pulling through, so we want to know that if this girl dies, or *when* she dies, how your father will react. If he regains consciousness, we don't know whether to tell him about her condition, because we don't know how the news will affect his recovery."

"I can't tell you how to handle that. I know Dad thought a lot of Terri; otherwise, he wouldn't have been living with her."

The doctor gave Lake permission to see me in the intensive care unit. I was strapped down, with IVs running into me, and a catheter running out.

Lake later said that when he came into the room he noticed handfuls of Thorazine bottles and liquid Valium ampules all around the bed, scattered on the floor, and left on trays. He knew they were keeping me pretty loaded.

My son stayed with me until I regained consciousness late that first night. When I came to, he said I crashed against the restraints, screamed obscenities—"Let me loose, you motherfuckers!"—and created a big fuss. A nurse rushed in, popped me with another needle, and I went off again to lala land.

This went on for three days.

During my early momentary slips out of the drug haze and into coherence, I tried to figure out what had happened to me and where I was. I could scarcely move or turn my body. Looking down, I saw padded leather straps at each elbow holding me to the bed; my arms were black.

I thought I'd been in a car wreck and couldn't remember it. I saw IVs in both arms, knew I'd been connected to a catheter, and didn't have any clothes on. The restraints prevented me from sitting up to examine my body, but I didn't feel any bandages or sharp pains from an incision.

I looked over at the wall beside the bed and was puzzled further by what appeared to be a jagged, silver-colored lightning bolt streaking across a bright, electric blue background. I thought, Jesus Christ, who's got me? What is this place? A military unit, the Strategic Air Command? What the fuck am I into here?

Then I faded out again.

The discoloration of my arms had been self-inflicted from constantly pulling against the restraints. Both arms were black, much darker than any bruise I'd ever seen. And on my right arm the bruising extended across the back of my hand and down my middle finger, the result of punching an attendant in the head as he unloaded me from the ambulance.

Lake visited the doctor and said, "Listen, lighten up on the drugs you're giving him. I'll be here. When he comes to, I'll reason with him."

After a big dead-end hassle with the doctors, Lake called George Vlassis, who came over to the hospital and talked to them. The dosage got reduced.

When the drugs wore off and I became lucid, I looked up at a pretty young woman wearing a little white bonnet.

"You're Mennonite, aren't you?" I asked.

"Yes. How did you know?"

"I grew up with Mennonites in my hometown. Where did you go to school?"

"Goshen College. In Goshen, Indiana."

"Well, how about that. I was born and raised in Goshen. Say, they tell me I've been spitting out some real nasty language in here. I know you dislike vulgar talk, and I want to apologize for using it."

"That's all right," she said, as her cheeks turned a deeper shade of pink. "I hear a lot around here. You were hurt so badly you didn't have any idea what you were saying. It's okay. Don't pay any attention to that, just get well."

Also, one night in intensive care, after I had calmed down enough for the restraints to be taken off my arms, I woke up—I'm generally a pretty light sleeper—and glanced down at the foot of my bed. A husky guy who resembled a crouching football player was moving slowly toward my bed.

I said, "Is there something you want, pal?"

"Just a look at you. I don't know what they told you, but I was on duty the night you were brought in. You busted that restraining strap and hit me right here on the forehead and decked me. I want to tell you, I've never been hit that hard before. I worked here eight or nine years and have had plenty of scuffles, but I've never been socked like that."

"Geesus, I'm sorry. I really am."

He stayed and talked to me for a while.

"I hope," I said, "you don't want a rematch. You can see I'm not in shape for one."

He laughed and said, "No, I don't."

When Lake left me and first saw Terri on Sunday evening, he said she looked "weird." They had her lying facedown in a sling, like a hammock, up over the bed. She had been burned on the whole left side of her back, from the bottom of her buttocks to the top of her shoulder, and down her left arm.

He asked the nurse, "How is she?"

"Not good. Any minute now. She's a goner."

The nurse pointed to a heart monitor and said, "See the line going across the screen, and that little blip in the line. That's all the heartbeat she has left. When that line flattens out, she's dead."

Lake said he wished the nurse hadn't explained this; he couldn't take his eyes off the monitor.

Terri Lee looked horrible. After they began letting her have visitors, her ex-husband heard the news (reports of the fire appeared in all the papers) and came to the hospital. When he walked into the room, he took one look at Terri's charred body and fainted. He fell against a table and gashed his head, which required stitches.

This isn't to say he lacked heart. Terri really did look awful.

After I came out from under the medication fog they moved me from intensive care onto a ward. Vlassis and Lake were waiting for me. I asked Lake, "What happened?"

"You were in a fire, Dad."

"Fire? Where?"

"Your apartment. The place was totaled."

"What about Terri? Where is she?"

"Terri's okay. They've got her in another hospital. She's not here."

"Why not?"

"She had a little burn on the cheek of her ass, and they wanted to treat her at the burn center. But you're not burned."

"How is she?"

"Fine. Doing real good. I was just over there. She told me to check on you and come back to let her know how you're getting along."

"Tell Terri to call me."

"Okay."

Terri didn't call that day.

The next day, when Lake came in, I said, "Did you get over to see Terri last night?"

"Yeah."

"Did you tell her to call me?"

"Yeah, but she was busy. They were dressing her burn. She couldn't use the phone right then."

"Well, tell her to call me today."

The third day I greeted Lake with, "Terri didn't call."

"I guess she didn't have time."

"Fuck that! What's happening here? She can't be busy all the time. I mean, I know what condition I'm in. She's gotta be in worse shape or she would have picked up the phone."

Lake had stalled as long as he could.

"Dad, she's hurt worse than I led you to believe. The doctors didn't want me to tell you, so I didn't."

"Give me the truth. How is she?"

"Not good."

He hesitated again.

"Tell me."

"Terri suffered third-degree burns over thirty percent of her body, and a bad head injury. During the Medevac ride to the county hospital, she was unconscious and hadn't been secured to the gurney. She came to briefly, jerked the trachea tube out of her throat, and was deprived of oxygen for a period of seven or eight minutes."

What I heard made me weak with guilt and a feeling of helplessness. Worse, I couldn't talk to Terri on the phone to say "I love you" or "I'm sorry." I couldn't even talk to her doctors.

On a ward with three other patients I had plenty of visitors: Max and Barbara Dunlap, Vlassis, Stuhff (he said he knew right away something was wrong when our investigative report didn't arrive on the bus), Devereux, Dunlap Committee members.

Max told me, "This is because of the Bolles case. I'm sorry. I can't tell you how sorry I am."

Barbara cried. She told me how badly their kids felt for us. The Dunlap children liked Terri; several were her age.

Jim Robison phoned me from the prison. I enjoyed hearing

his gruff voice: "What you doin' in there? I didn't know you needed a vacation that much."

Molly Ivins called, and Bill Helmer.

I had access to a phone and dialed all over the country talking to people. Trouble was, I didn't make sense. I called friends, talked to them, then couldn't remember what I had said.

My incoherence was caused by smoke inhalation. As it was explained to me, breathing in toxic fumes—mainly carbon monoxide and cyanide, released from burning carpet, wallpaper, and other synthetic materials—had caused the brain to swell. The pressure of the brain pushing against the skull made me goofy at times. The doctors prescribed medication to reduce the swelling and minimize the pain, but the slow recovery process required time and a lot of rest.

I had already used up a lot of time. After hospitalization for ten days, seven in critical condition, I was up moving around and anxious to leave. I desperately wanted to be with Terri, and for some reason thought I could talk the doctor into releasing me because Bill Helmer was coming to town.

So I made my pitch, promising no driving a car for thirty days, no working for six months, and no smoking, ever. I also agreed to take it easy and see him as an outpatient every day for the next month. I said, "Yeah, yeah, yeah," to anything he wanted, just to bullshit my way out.

"I probably shouldn't release you. But since your girl needs you, and your friend is coming to Phoenix, I will. You have to keep the promises you've made."

Lake, who had faithfully pushed visiting hours to the limit for me and Terri, stayed in Phoenix for two weeks after I got out of the hospital.

He never hesitated to chauffeur me places or run errands—requests I didn't always make at the most appropriate times. And my son kept his broad shoulders available for me to lean on, which I did often.

The day after I checked out, Lake took me to see Terri. As he pulled the car into the parking lot at Maricopa County General, Lake laughed and said, "Dad, don't get me wrong. You know I love hearing your stories. But that's the sixth time *straight* you've told me the same thing."

"Back-to-back?"

"Yeah. You finish it, and then start again without skipping a beat."

The doctors had told me that smoke inhalation had a disastrous effect on short-term memory. I could remember vividly where I was born and raised, but had trouble recalling day-old events.

And Vlassis said, "You're pretty good in the mornings. We talk and you make some sense. But by noon I'm watching you fall apart mentally."

Before I got to Terri, her chief physician, Dr. Salazar, took me aside.

"I want to prepare you," he said, "for what you're about to see."

"What's the matter? Is Terri worse?"

"No, not exactly. Physically, she has made remarkable progress. Her lungs and air passages have sloughed off dead tissue nicely; a lot of the burned, blistered skin on her back has been removed in the whirlpool, which contains Betadine solution, antiseptic, and chlorine bleach to hold down infection; and we've pumped gallons of fluids into her system to counteract dehydration."

I shifted on my feet and thought, Give me a break, Doc. I'm not up to a med school lecture.

"Basically," Salazar said, "we've stabilized Terri, and by this time should have completed the skin grafts on her back. But . . ."

I watched the furrow in his brow deepen.

"What's the delay?" I asked.

"Her mental condition. We don't know what effect the anesthesia will have on her mind."

Specialists from the Barrow's Institute, a prestigious neurological clinic in Phoenix, had been called in as consultants. They visited Terri every day. She suffered some sort of amnesia and brain damage due to oxygen deprivation during the fire and the subsequent helicopter ride to the hospital. The neurologists had a medical library full of complex theories about what had caused the brain damage, but no one knew whether, or to what degree, it would be permanent.

"Doctor Salazar," I said, "may I please see Terri?"

"Yes, of course. She's been asking for you. But I want you to understand, what you see might be what you get. On her good days, Terri has the mental age of a fourteen-year-old. On bad days, which are more frequent, her mental capacity is that of a child of five or six. Mr. Headley, you need to think about that seriously, and about who is going to take care of her. We won't release her unless you tell us she will be well cared for. Believe me, she will require a lot of attention."

Dr. Salazar turned me over to a nurse who showed me how to get suited up for entrance into the burn unit. To protect patients from infection, each visitor had to put on a long gown, face mask, shower cap, shoe covers, and rubber gloves.

When I walked into Terri's room, I knew the doctor had been right to warn me: she didn't have a good grip on anything. Taped on the wall beside her bed, at eye-level, was a sign someone had printed in big block letters on a sheet of typing paper: MY NAME IS TERRI YODER. I WAS IN A FIRE.

Whenever she awakened, Terri couldn't remember her name. She had no idea why she was here.

I followed the nurse into the room and around the foot of the bed. Terri lay on her stomach, her eyes closed.

"Ms. Yoder," the nurse said loudly, "you have a visitor."

Terri opened her eyes and tried to figure out whose face hid behind the sterile mask and cap.

"Hello, sweetheart," I said softly.

"Oh, Lake, where have you been?" She squirmed around in the bed and groaned several times as she positioned her body on the right, unburned, side. "I'm so glad you're here. A terrible thing happened."

"What, Terri?"

"You know Michelle . . ."

"Yes." Michelle had lived near our apartment.

"It's just awful. Michelle had a fire."

"No, she didn't, Terri."

"Oh, yes. She did. Michelle had a fire, and her little dog burned to death."

"Honey, you have some things confused. Michelle didn't have a fire, and she didn't have a little dog that was killed. But, Terri, *you* had a fire. And *you* were hurt very badly."

She made a painful, sighing sound, rolled her eyes back and dozed off.

Thank goodness, I thought. I took deep breaths and walked around the room. Get a grip on yourself, Lake. You've got to be strong for her. Terri looked so tiny, so wounded, so defenseless.

She opened her eyes again and said drowsily, "Lake, please give me a cigarette."

"Terri, I can't. The doctor said positively no smoking."

"Please, just one."

Lake had told me about how Terri constantly bugged everybody around her: "Please, oh God, please. Can't I have a cigarette? Look at me; what's the difference? Please, please, please. Don't take that away from me, too."

Terri had to lie on her stomach most of the time, and nurses had given up trying to keep an oxygen mask on her face. So they had placed large cylinders in each corner of the room and opened the valves, making the entire enclosure a giant oxygen tent.

"Terri," I tried to reason with her, "if we light a cigarette, these oxygen tanks will launch us into outer space. You can't have a cigarette in here; you can't have one anyplace."

Her bottom lip stuck out in a little girl pout, and I thought she was about to cry.

"Honey," I said, "you look tired, and it's about time for the nurse to come and run me out. Get a good night's rest. I'll see you in the morning."

"I love you, Lake."

"I love you, too. Sleep well."

But how could she rest or sleep? I wondered as I left the hospital. How could anybody who had half her back and left arm burned away?

Lake told me Terri constantly had tried to convince hospital personnel of two things: one, she was in much better shape than she actually was; and two, she needed more drugs. Every time they came around with morphine, she pleaded for more.

One time after the nurse gave her a shot for pain, Terri got out of her bed, walked down the hall to a bathroom, unwrapped the bandages, and took a shower. When she finished bathing, she fell and hit her head, and they found her lying on the floor. After that, they didn't listen to any talk about feeling well.

Later, the nurses told me they were absolutely amazed Terri had been able to get to the bathroom unassisted and take off the dressings by herself. She had been bound like a mummy.

The next morning Terri said, "Lake, did you bring those accident report forms?"

"What?"

"In this state, you have only twenty-four hours to file a report after you've been in an accident."

"I don't think we need to report this."

"Of course we do. I had an automobile accident and have to file a report. I don't want to lose my driver's license."

"Honey, you didn't have an auto accident. You were burned in a fire. Our apartment burned."

"Oh," she said wistfully. "Is that what happened?"

After they removed the restraints, Terri developed a habit of slipping out of bed and prowling through the corridors late at night, when the nurses thought she slept soundly in her room. Several times they caught her on the roam. Once she went to the room of a man who had been fried when he hit a high tension power line. Terri stood over his bed, quietly looking at his charcoaled body.

"One of these nurses hates me, you know."

"What do you mean?"

"She does. I know she does because she comes in here every night and hurts me. She puts stuff on me that burns."

"Terri, that's medicine. The nurse doesn't want to hurt you, but she has to put a silver nitrate solution on your back so the burn won't get infected."

"No. I know she hates me. But I got something that will hurt *her*. Look here."

She pulled out a sock filled with used hypodermic needles she had collected on one of her middle-of-the-night scavenger hunts.

"When that nurse comes in to hurt me again, I'm gonna stick her."

"Terri, you've got to stop this," I said and took the weapons stash away from her.

I went to see the chief of the burn center, hoping to achieve an objective for Terri that Lake had earlier accomplished for me.

"Look, Doctor, I don't mean to tell you how to run your business, but Terri Lee's not progressing very much. She'll lie there for the rest of her life telling you she needs more morphine. As long as you give it to her, she'll take it. If you back off the drugs a little, maybe we'll see some improvement."

"Okay," he said. "We'll try it."

That afternoon Terri's mother, Terri Raife, came to the hospital. She had arrived from Las Vegas a few days earlier. Over a cup of coffee in the hospital cafeteria, Terri Raife told me, "There's nothing I can do for her."

Had my *hearing* been impaired by the fire? This was a mother talking about her daughter. "Mrs. Raife," I said, "you know I'm not up to par yet myself. If you could stay around and help me with Terri when she gets out, I'd appreciate it."

"No," she replied firmly. "If you can't take care of her, then you'll have to put her into a home. I'm sorry, I just can't handle this."

Someone claiming to be a reporter had convinced the nurses to let him into Terri's room, but she'd been too exhausted after a physical therapy session to talk with him. It turned out to be a good thing. He was a cop posing as a newsman.

When I found out about the incident, I posted a sign: NO
ONE IS ALLOWED TO INTERVIEW THIS PATIENT WITHOUT HER LAWYER
PRESENT.

A doctor tore it off the door. "Don't be putting signs up," he
ordered.

"Then don't let strangers in to see her," I said.

After tapering her off the drug overload, Dr. Salazar told me,
"Terri is showing definite improvement, and we're ready to proceed with the skin grafts. She's more rational now and in much
better spirits."

"How long will it take to do the grafts?"

"It's hard to say for sure, but barring any complications, such
as infection or rejection, we should be able to finish in three or
four surgeries. If all goes well, I'd think you can take Terri out by
the end of July. That is, of course, if you agree to care for her."

"I love her. Of course I will. But, frankly, it's scary."

"I know. You'll be surprised, however, at how well the two
of you will manage to cope with the problems. The staff will give
you plenty of pointers for in-home care. We don't expect you to
become Dr. Kildare overnight."

"Is there anything I should do now?"

"Yes. After surgery, which begins tomorrow morning, she'll
need exercise, especially supervised walks. Since she responds to
you better than to the physical therapist, get her out of bed, get
her moving around."

When Terri was overcome by smoke and collapsed on our bedroom floor, she landed on her side, and flames from her burning
nightgown consumed all three layers of skin on the entire left
side of her back and left arm. If only the outer and middle layers
had been burned, I was told, the skin could have healed itself.
But with third-degree burns, healthy skin must be harvested from
another part of the body, in this case the right side of her back,
and placed over the exposed fatty tissue.

Hence Terri's whole back became raw flesh. It reminded me
of meat-market round steak.

I had never seen a skin graft before. I thought the surgeon would skin one side of her back and slap it, like wallpaper, over the burned area.

I felt stupid when a technician explained the procedure to me while Terri was in the operating room. I learned the doctor uses a roller instrument to shave off small pieces of healthy skin only one one-hundredth of an inch thick. Then what's called a mesher perforates the sheets of tissue with a fishnet pattern.

"Sort of an ultra-refined version of how I put meat through a machine to make cube steak when I worked in my father's grocery store as a kid," I joked.

"Exactly," said the technician with a smile. "The doctor will drape patches of tissue over the prepared area where she was burned. Tripling in size, they connect with each other, and blood vessels underneath, to form Terri's new skin."

The next day I started walking Terri up and down the halls. Bandaged over most of her body, dragging one foot in what is called the "burn ward shuffle," she held her left arm bent at the elbow, out in front of her. Her pace was agonizingly slow, like a zombie. My heart was breaking for her.

We stopped at a blackboard near the nurse's station. I took a piece of chalk and wrote in big letters: T. L. YODER, P.I.

"Terri, what does that say?"

She looked at it for a long time, concentrating hard, and finally said, "I don't know."

After minutes of repeating that she didn't know what any of it meant, she said, "That's my name."

"Right. Now, what does the p.i. mean?"

"I don't know."

"Sure you do."

We stood there, talked about it, discussed it, fooled with it, and I asked, "What kind of work were you interested in? What did you want to be?"

"A private investigator."

"What's the p.i. stand for?"

"Private investigator!" she said triumphantly.

"You're coming along all right. See? We'll beat this, honey."

Before Lake returned to Las Vegas, he and I went shopping for Terri, anticipating the day she would be released. Bulky bandages and pain from the burns would make getting into any of her clothes impossible. Lake helped me select an assortment of brightly colored, loose-fitting muumuus that would be cool and not restrict movement. We hoped Terri's new wardrobe would help cheer her up. It did.

The grafts took and Terri got better.

More skin was grafted. Her body and spirit continued their gradual mend.

Twice a day I went to the hospital and we walked the corridors. We'd taken the steps so many times we could have done it blindfolded. Terri begged me to let her outside.

"The doctors won't allow it; you might pick up an infection."

"Please let me go outside. Please, just for a minute. I want to be out of here."

She had been so strong and endured so much pain that finally I could no longer deny this simple request. "Okay. But not for very long."

I opened the door on one of those odd Phoenix days when the sun shines through a light drizzle.

Terri shuffled away from the building. She lifted her head and right arm skyward and said, "I love the rain. This feels wonderful." Her tears and mine mixed with the rain on our faces as she radiated the pure happiness of a little kid.

Checkout day finally came, as Dr. Salazar had predicted, at the end of July. Terri had spent five weeks at Maricopa County General and was overjoyed to get out.

As we drove away from the hospital, she said, "You know what I'd really like?"

"Name it, honey."

"A Big Mac."

When we stepped up to order at McDonald's, the girl behind the counter asked Terri, "What happened to you?"

Terri started crying.

I led her over to a booth, sat her down, and finally managed to calm her.

"Why did she ask me that?"

"Look at you, all bandaged up. She's just curious, and feels bad for you."

"I don't want anyone to pity me."

This went on all the time. Even much later, after the bandages came off, she wouldn't wear short sleeves. People often asked, "Were you in a fire?" or, "What happened to your arm?"—questions she continued to have trouble answering or ignoring.

We moved into a guest bedroom at George and Nancy Vlassis's house, which had never been air-conditioned. Knowing Terri couldn't survive there in the late summer heat, George had a window unit installed to cool our room.

That evening Terri grew very restless and wanted to see our apartment. I said, "Why don't we forget that? I'll take you over there, if you insist, but I don't think you ought to go. It won't make you feel any better to see our place destroyed."

"No. That's okay. I need to see it."

She wouldn't let up. Got very fussy about it.

"Okay, if that's the way you feel, I'll take you right now."

I pulled into the parking lot in back of the apartment and set the headlights on high beam. The electricity in the apartment had been disconnected, but by the car lights we could see everything in the kitchen and living room.

We got out and walked to the back door. When I unlocked it, I asked one more time, "Are you sure you want to go in here?"

"No."

She dissolved into tears and we left.

The next morning we piled into the car to make our "hospital rounds." I still had to stop at my doctor's office once a week for a quick exam and chest X-ray, and Terri went to the burn center every day to soak and remove bandages and have her skin grafts checked.

On this day, after two weeks of our trekking to the hospital, a nurse said to me, "It's time *you* start removing the bandages and redressing her wounds."

"Ma'am, you're talking to a man who flunked Band-Aid in army first-aid training. I know nothin' about none of that. I doubt I'll be able to do it."

"Sure you can. We'll show you how."

They did. The hospital loaded me up with half a dozen shopping bags full of medical supplies.

At the Vlassis home, Terri and I used the large spare bathroom, ideal for her soaks. Nancy helped me maneuver her in and out of the deep old-fashioned tub. At first all three of us were clumsy, slow, and exhausted by the time we blundered our way through. But after a few assisted runs, I became quite adept at doing it alone.

Soaking off the bandages took a long time. They were practically glued to her skin by dried blood and fluids oozing through the gauze. I'd help Terri out of the tub and lay her face down on the bed to dress the wounds. First I covered her raw back and arm with Silvadene ointment—to guard against infection—and medicated gauze pads. Then I rewrapped her in yards and yards of stretchy gauze strips.

We had a helluva time getting the wrappings to stay on her frail legs. In good shape Terri weighs about 120. After the fire she dropped down to 90 pounds and looked as if she had just left a concentration camp. Occasionally she'd go through McDonald's withdrawal and have a Big Mac Attack, so I'd take her there for a burger and fries; she'd eat two or three bites and push it aside.

Every morning after the soak-and-bandage routine, I drove Terri out to the mall, where she could walk around, not feel so cooped up. We window-shopped, drank coffee, people-watched, anything to get her mind off the pain. We tried going to the mall cinema, but she couldn't sit on her burned backside to the end of a movie.

The mall visits stopped. She didn't like people staring at her.

I'd say, "Come here and look at this dress." She would move slowly, like a robot, and say, "Yeah, that's nice. But I'll never get into another dress like that; I'll go to my grave wearing one of these damn muumuus." And then she'd cry. Lots of tears.

We stayed at George's house for three weeks. Mike Stuhff, who visited us frequently, suggested, "Why don't you bring Terri up to Flagstaff? It's a lot cooler than Phoenix. And I got my new office going, with plenty of work for you."

We put what could be salvaged from the apartment into storage and moved to Flagstaff.

23

Two Open Hot-Water Faucets

Helmer and I, on the day of my release from Phoenix Baptist, had gone to the burned-out apartment to take a look.

The place had been totally destroyed by the blaze. If I hadn't known otherwise, I would have thought a bomb had exploded inside.

In the living room we saw the sky through a hole ten feet in diameter in the ceiling. The TV set had folded in on itself, and the telephone resembled something out of a cartoon: a black blob of plastic that melted and ran down onto the table.

The strangest thing happened as we surveyed the destruction: the telephone rang.

"You going to answer it?" Helmer asked.

"No. You go ahead." I put my hands in front of my face and took a step backward, feigning fear.

The apartment looked like a war zone. In the kitchen everything had been destroyed, even pots and pans. A total loss.

The dining area also had been wasted. Charred cookbooks, dishes, and boards littered the floor. Terri's beloved plants had been obliterated.

In the hallway, starting about three feet above the floor, the walls had been scorched to black when the fireball roared out of the kitchen, wheeled around, and hurtled toward our bedroom.

Terri, to reach me, had run through a boiling, churning hell of heat and fire.

Sheets were still on our bed, and burned onto them was an outline of me, a ghostly white impression against a dark gray background, like the chalk figure of a body the homicide detective draws at a murder scene.

"I don't know why you're still here," Helmer said, eyeing the bed and sniffing the stale, water-soaked odor of dead smoke permeating the ruined clothes in our closet.

Smoke had discolored papers on a table where Terri and I had been working. The top sheets were singed black, and any exposed edges of those underneath had curled into distinctive patterns.

Still, the living room ranked worst of all. Its ceiling featured that fire-made skylight, blackened beams, and boards scorched nearly to soot. Sheetrock had been burned off the walls, and exposed studs had metamorphosed to charcoal crumbling onto the floor.

Helmer kept shaking his head. I suggested we get away from the place and asked where he intended to spend the night.

"Are you kidding? I'm getting out of Phoenix, and if you've got a lick of sense you'll be on the plane with me. I mean, what has to happen for you to get the message? Can't you see they don't like you in this town? Get the fuck out while you still can."

In the official fire department report, a fire fighter named Rodman stated that after Terri and I were removed from the rubble, he witnessed Phoenix police detectives removing files from our apartment. I discovered, when I checked for myself, that documents I had been keeping there relating to the Bolles investigation were missing. They also had grabbed my pistol and a jar into which Terri and I tossed loose change.

George Vlassis accompanied me to the police station, where with a minimum of hassle they returned the gun and the money jar. But no files. They denied files had been taken, though I knew better.

Fire fighter Rodman "modified" his report. Originally he wrote that he had *seen* police removing files and putting them into a squad car but later changed this to hearing them *discuss* taking the documents.

No matter. They *were* missing and I knew the police had burgled them.

Really, it was no matter. I always retain several copies of important reports and never keep all of them in the same spot. What would have surprised me was if someone *hadn't* made a grab for those files. With Dunlap and Robison unlikely again to face prosecution, people who already had proved themselves adept at "purging" evidence likely were very concerned about what material we'd unearthed in more than a year and a half of investigation.

What concerned me most, of course, was the possibility that someone had tried to kill Terri and me. Nine months earlier our apartment had been burglarized; valuables were completely overlooked, but several Bolles case interview tapes had been taken. Then, two months after the fire, just a few weeks after we moved to Flagstaff, a *third* burglary occurred: someone broke into a storage locker I maintained in Phoenix and stole an entire box of Bolles investigative material. The owner of the storage facility said a master key, lock pick, or bolt cutter had been employed in the break-in. The lock itself was never found.

After the fire in our apartment, I didn't think myself paranoid to suspect arson. The first fire fighter on the scene had found two hot water faucets running. Neither Terri Lee nor I had turned them on, and they would prove significant to an explanation for the fire.

Devereux, concerned about the possibility of a murder attempt, himself the intended victim of a hit-and-run in that alley, sought an opinion on the fire from Anthony Joseph Pellicano, a Chicago private investigator ranked by author and former CIA agent George O'Toole as one of the nation's four best (O'Toole listed me in this same elite company). O'Toole, using uncharacteristic praise, described Pellicano as having "the perceptiveness of Sherlock Holmes" and "the tenacity of the Royal Canadian Mounted Police."

More important to Devereux, however, was Pellicano's acknowledged expertise on arsons and bombings.

Pellicano studied the fire at our apartment and said it featured many characteristics of a classic method of arson. The arsonist, he pointed out, opens a container of ether near a hot water heater, closes the door to concentrate the evaporating fumes, and turns on one or more hot water faucets. When the draw on the hot water tank becomes sufficient, the gas flame comes on, igniting the ether fumes and triggering the fire.

Interestingly, the fire department determined that the blaze had begun in a pantry right next to the compartment housing the hot water heater.

I saw this as the bottom line: *no* explanation other than Pellicano's accounted for those hot water taps having been turned on.

I studied the fire from every angle I could think of, concluding that the arsonist probably didn't try to kill us, though he wouldn't have been unhappy with that result. I believed, and Devereux agreed, that someone thought there were incriminating documents in the apartment that needed to be destroyed.

Terri, right up to the present, doesn't remember anything that happened during the three days prior to the fire. Not the party for the Navajos. Not the work we did for Stuhff the next day. Nothing.

There was talk about having her hypnotized. Dunlap Committee member Dr. Ken Olsen, a clinical hypnotist, volunteered his services. Terri asked me what I thought, saying "Dr. Olsen thinks I might remember something that will help identify who started the fire."

"I wouldn't fool with it," I said. "It doesn't matter, anyway. They'll say an identification made under hypnosis isn't admissible in court, and anyway, no matter what the proof, there would never be any prosecution."

"Don't you want to know?"

"Sure. But it's not worth it, sweetheart. I believe you can't remember these things because your mind has put up a defense mechanism to block out memories that would be very painful."

Before leaving Phoenix I wrote a long letter of appreciation to the fire fighters and paramedics, making it clear my quarrel was with the police department, not them. I thanked them for saving my life and Terri Lee's, and requested the fire chief to place a copy of the letter in each of their files.

When we moved to Flagstaff, Terri and I rented the cheapest housing available, in a ghetto of house trailers. Each regular-size trailer was sectioned off into a large and a small unit, and we took the less expensive, about one-third of a trailer, with a tiny bedroom and bath. Switching to a roomier one, which we couldn't afford until a couple of months later, did little to facilitate our ninety-minute-a-day soak and bandage.

After several weekly trips to the burn center in Phoenix, the bandages were removed and Terri was measured for a Jobst garment, a skintight suit made from special steel-reinforced elastic. A technician took hundreds of measurements, noting each contour of her torso, legs, and arms, so the garment could be tailor-made to apply equal pressure on every inch of skin covered. She had to wear it all the time, day and night.

We ordered two suits: one to wash and air-dry while she wore the other. The garments were knee-length, and fit closely around her neck, with long sleeves to both wrists.

Dr. Salazar told her the Jobst suit would apply continuous pressure to her skin grafts, making them heal flat and white rather than discolored and grotesquely knotted. He warned Terri that the garment, which resembled a diver's wet suit, would be very tight and somewhat uncomfortable, especially in hot weather, but it would help relieve her constant itching from scar tissue forming and contracting over the grafts.

"Now I can wear clothes that fit," she said happily, "and not look like a mummy draped in Hawaiian print all the time."

We expended God knows how many calories pulling and tugging, stretching and squeezing her into the Jobst suits, but they were an improvement over the miles of gauze we'd previously wrapped around her. With the Jobst under her clothes she could move more freely and not be the target of pointing fingers and curious stares.

When we went back to Phoenix to have her overstretched Jobst replaced, Terri asked, "Why do I have a long sleeve on my right arm? I don't have any burn there. And does it have to come up so tightly around the neck?"

The technician measured her again and altered the design.

It was a big day for her when the new body stockings arrived with a V-neckline, shorter legs, and no sleeve on the right side.

Through a daily process of mental and physical therapy, Terri gradually became able to function more normally and to talk and carry on an intelligent conversation.

And she did her best to make our small home cozier: matching curtains and throw pillows, cross-stitch samplers, macramé wall hangings, and, naturally, plants on every windowsill.

In the mornings I drove to Stuhff's office, fooled around, talked to him about his cases, even did some work. At noon one day when I came home for lunch, I found Terri sitting on the couch crying her eyes out.

"What's the matter, honey?"

"Look, on the TV."

I glanced at the live news report on the screen.

"The MGM hotel in Las Vegas is burning down," she said through gasping sobs. "People are jumping out of windows. It's just awful."

I turned off the television.

To this day, anything relating to fire, or people burning, unnerves her totally.

Unlike the first weeks of her stay in the burn center, with more bad days than good, Terri was now in fine fettle most of the time. But occasionally she sank into depression.

I came home one evening and she said, "We're not ever going to get married, are we?"

"Sure we are. We already talked about that. We're gonna go
to Vegas. Why are you into this now?"

"Well, how do I know you won't find somebody else?"

"Good grief, Terri. How do I know *you* won't ditch me?"

"Oh, yeah!" she said through watery eyes. "Fat chance. Look
at me. Who'd want me?"

She spent a great deal of time crying; and I spent a lot of
time drying her tears.

Terri remembered very little about her stay in the hospital,
but things became less fuzzy for her in Flagstaff, and after several months she was able to find and hold a job. I was proud of
her when she worked her way up from waitress to bartender to
manager of a bar. I encouraged her—you're doing great, stick
with it, keep working—more for the therapy than for the money
she earned. I think she knew, after what happened, that if she
told me, "I need your left arm," she'd get it.

Winter's first snow fell on the trailer park. The wind howled
outside, and we settled in for a warm night in our snug little
home.

"I wonder if he has a warm place to sleep," said Terri.

"Who?"

"An orange tomcat I've seen prowling around the past few
days. He's probably cold and hungry."

"If he comes again, don't feed him. If you do, he'll move
right in. We don't need a cat."

She went to the kitchen sink and was startled by a thud
against the window, caused by the scraggly creature leaping atop
an icy fuel oil tank and losing his footing.

"Lake! Here's the cat. Come see."

Through reflections of Terri and me looking out, I saw two
golden eyes peering in.

"Poor thing," Terri purred. "He must be freezing."

"Yeah," I said, and walked away from the window.

"Lake, can't we bring him in out of the cold?"

"No," I said, heading to the bedroom to get my coat.

And so began our long friendship with a guy we named Oliver.

TORONTO, CANADA. JUNE 14, 1981

Like an old fire horse, I answered the bell one last time for the Bolles investigation.

We were still living, albeit in more commodious housing, in Flagstaff—me working with Stuhff, Terri managing the bar—when I got a call from Don Devereux.

"I heard from McVay," he said.

The man I'd interviewed in Laredo.

"What did he have to say?"

"Said to tell you hello. Recalled your coming to Texas. The place where he was working got burglarized, and the night watchman killed. McVay claims he's innocent, but they convicted him up there in Toronto. Anyway, he told me he's been thinking about the Bolles case, and maybe has something that will help."

"What's he got?"

"He says he knows the location of a murder weapon. Another Adamson murder. He didn't feel comfortable talking on the phone, but said if one of us would come to Canada, he'd give us his information. I guess you're pretty busy looking after Terri Lee. How's she getting along?"

"She's healing up. It's been slow, and her mental condition still isn't always as good as it could be. But she's a brave lady, and each day she gets closer to her old self."

"Tell her I said hello. That Naomi and the kids send their love. We're all pulling for her."

"Thanks, I will. She misses Naomi, and this will mean a lot to her. But about McVay. Are you going to see him?"

"I'd like to, but you know Jonathan. He won't spend the money. I was hoping you could find a way to go."

"I dunno, Don. I'm not crazy about leaving Terri. I *would* like to hear what McVay has to say."

"Talk to Terri Lee, then get back to me. McVay's lawyer, Stan AvRuskin, says he can get you into the prison."

Terri thought I should go. "I need to start taking care of myself," she said. "You've hardly let me out of your sight since this thing happened."

AvRuskin met me at the Buffalo airport, and we drove to Toronto, a short trip.

McVay told me that while he'd been in Maricopa County jail with Adamson, the con man indicated that he had murdered Helen Marston, an elderly Scottsdale woman killed during a burglary at her home. Adamson told McVay he had stolen a gun from Marston and later threw it away in "a stock tank out in the desert, a water runoff for cattle" west of Phoenix.

McVay said he had personally searched for the place, and had found it. He drew me a map.

Devereux and I also found the pond. We thought it important to find the gun, to use the murder of Helen Marston against Adamson should he ever again testify against Robison and Dunlap.

But though we located the spot, we didn't find the gun. Prospectors who lived and worked in the area told us the pond may have accumulated as much as six inches of silt since that day in 1975 when Adamson allegedly threw the gun away.

We used metal detectors and dredging equipment, but came up empty.

"This is it for me," I said to Devereux, when the search was at last abandoned. "No more Bolles case."

He knew I meant it, but asked anyway, "Don't you want to see prosecutions?"

"Sure I do."

But I was just as certain I ought to get away from the madness of the investigation. I thought of Arizona and its file-purging police, its hardened-in-amber attorney general, the terrible price Terri Lee had already paid, those two open hot-water faucets.

"Sure I'd love to see some of those 'law-abiding citizens' brought to trial," I said. "But I don't think that will ever happen. Besides, getting prosecutions wasn't my job."

24

Covering Ass
Through the
Eighties

LAS VEGAS, NEVADA. AUGUST 1989

I was reviewing manuscript pages of this book when the telephone rang.

"Lake, old buddy! How have you been?"

"Do I know you?"

"Oh, yeah. I'm George Weisz, an investigator with the Arizona attorney general's office. We met while you were here working the Bolles case. What have you been doing?"

"Same thing as always. I'm a private investigator."

"Well, *we're* working on the Bolles murder . . ."

Jesus. The reporter had been dead thirteen years, two months.

"That's great," I said, almost choking. "How you coming with it?"

"We'd like to ask you some questions. I've been going over the material you sent to the attorney general and the U.S. attorney. And we know you made a lot of tapes with Robison. We'd like, as part of our investigation, to get together with you and listen to those tapes. We can come to Vegas, or if you'll be in Phoenix soon, we can meet here."

"I'll tell you what you do. Call my attorney, George Vlassis, and set up an appointment through him. We can talk in his office. I'll fly down when I get the word from Vlassis."

"Let's make an appointment while I've got you on the phone."

In a hurry, huh? I thought. Now I remembered Weisz. Like Schafer, Corbin, and the rest, he'd ignored everything we provided his office.

"I can't make an appointment," I said. "I don't know my lawyer's schedule. Give him a call."

I hung up, sure that Vlassis wouldn't allow me to answer their questions. Wise had nerve, I'd give him that.

Still investigating? Now, in 1989, they wanted to talk to me?

I wondered if the real reason for the call was to find out how the book treated them. Or, more ominous, since they wanted to listen to tapes, if they fantasized about retrying Jim.

I had prepared myself to hear "more arrests are expected" spilling out of Weisz's mouth.

Though I kept my pledge to stay away from active involvement in the Bolles case, I closely followed its many twists and turns throughout the 1980s. Cover Your Ass—Robison's description of the police/prosecution motive for ineptitude and worse— became more pronounced, laughable and, ultimately, ludicrous. Here are some examples from the time after we left Phoenix.

- Phoenix organized-crime police officers, after first purging their files on Emprise to remove any reference to John Adamson, created a new, sanitized Emprise file to mollify the curious.

- By hiding the index cards needed to locate the files, police made it impossible to study their dossiers on Adamson, Barry Goldwater, Bradley Funk, and others.

- The police shredded all surveillance reports relating to the murder of Bolles.

- Organized-crime officers kept all the information they gathered on the Bolles murder in a secret file not listed in any official record. Once *five inches* thick, it shrank to virtually nothing after its existence became publicly known.

- Phoenix police still didn't bother to interview Nicole DiVincenzo, who said he had been offered a contract to kill Bolles (which he turned down), and later a contract on John Adamson's life, even though DiVincenzo *was in the Phoenix jail* on another charge.

The Phoenix weekly *New Times* concluded, in an issue printed on the tenth anniversary of the Bolles bombing: "The Phoenix police department deliberately sabotaged its investigation into the murder of Don Bolles."

The saddest part of all is that, except for residents of Arizona who have lived with the case, most Americans have only sketchy knowledge of the tragedy. Many, if they know of Robison and Dunlap at all, believe they got off on a legal technicality—a terrible injustice to these men, who unfairly suffered for so long and conceivably could *still* be tried again by the same state that railroaded them in the first place. Almost as bad, Corbin and Schafer, viewed from a distance, have emerged as heroes in the eyes of some writers for "standing up" to John Adamson and prosecuting him to the fullest extent of the law after he made those outrageous demands in exchange for his testimony.

Cover Your Ass. Here's *Attorney General* Bruce Babbitt in 1977, after his office convicted Dunlap and Robison: "The convictions reaffirm the fact that the [Phoenix police] department is one of the outstanding law enforcement agencies, not only in this state, but in the nation." And here's *Governor* Bruce Babbitt in 1986, after the destruction of almost everything he claimed to be true in the Bolles case: "Police work in this city and this state has come a long way since 1976. We were not in a modern law enforcement situation. At the time, we had not made the evolution into complete police work."

Complete police work? Robison had been right. Even *incomplete* police work didn't encompass purging files, creating phony new files, and shredding documents.

Corbin and Schafer did indeed go after Adamson. In 1980, the con man was tried and quickly convicted of first-degree murder, receiving the death sentence. Adamson had expected the sentence, betting everything on an appeal that said he'd been subjected to double jeopardy.

In 1986, Adamson missed winning his desperate gamble by an eyelash. The U.S. Supreme Court, in a 5–4 decision, held that double jeopardy wasn't applicable and that Adamson must die.

Still, it wasn't over. In 1988 a federal appeals court ruled that Arizona's death penalty law was unconstitutional. The state appealed, and there the matter stands, with the lives of Adamson and several dozen others hanging in the balance.

Max Dunlap nicely picked up the pieces of his life. With the help of his loving family, he reestablished himself as an honest, successful businessman, traits there had never been cause to question.

In July 1983, Max filed a $605 million lawsuit against the city of Phoenix, the Phoenix police department, and nine police officers. Mainly Max wanted the day in court that had been denied him.

It took until 1987 to reach a court, where a mistrial was declared when it turned out several of the defendants had retained the same lawyer. Clearly, what was good for one defendant might not be helpful to another, but whose fault was this? Not Max's. The mistrial smelled to me like a deliberate stalling tactic. During the brief period the case did appear in court, Dunlap's lawyer, Murray Miller, charged that the authorities were still withholding vital evidence.

It was worse than that. *With the trial pending*, the police destroyed additional files relating to the Bolles case, information evidently overlooked in the first waves of purging.

Max's lawsuit was thrown out entirely on February 14, 1989, by Superior Court Judge Robert Gottsfield, who ruled that under state law the lawsuit should have been filed within two years of the June 2, 1980, "temporary dismissal" of the murder charges. In other words, the statute of limitations had run out (Judge Gottsfield held) despite an earlier ruling before the 1987 mistrial that held it had not.

So once again Max was victimized, and guilty parties went unpunished. Said Murray Miller: "He wanted his day in court to show what police did to him to put him on death row. I think it's just a travesty for the Dunlap family not to have had their day in court."

Jim Robison still resides at Arizona State Prison, serving a twenty-six-year sentence for the assault he claims he didn't commit. Long ago he should have been granted parole, but some of the same people who framed him for murder cannot forgive him for assault.

I have never heard of any first-time offender serving this much time for assault. The average time *a convicted murderer* serves is half the number of years Jim has been locked up.

Thanks largely to the efforts of attorney Victor Aranow, who faced a prosecution eager to see his client pay for that twenty-dollar hash sale, Michael JoDon, in my opinion the most important witness of all in the Bolles case, received a suspended sentence.

Robert Corbin remains as attorney general of Arizona, assisted by William Schafer III. I wonder if they are there forever, permanent sentinels, guarding against some replacement who might in the name of justice demand what has always been needed: the convening of a grand jury with the power to force answers.

. . .

Bradley Funk died December 31, 1989, of a heart attack. In its tenth anniversary review of the Bolles case, *New Times* had headlined an article about him: "He Was the Perfect Suspect ... and the Cops Ignored Him."

Neal Roberts practices law in Phoenix.

Terri Lee and I were married December 27, 1982, in Las Vegas, with Lake III serving as best man, and my other sons, Anthony and Rod, in attendance. We moved to Vegas permanently the next month.

Terri is okay now, as good as ever physically and mentally, with only those scars on her back and arm to remind her of our investigation of the Bolles murder. She wanted to work as a p.i., and that's one wish I was able to grant her.

Terri, surprisingly, views our work in Phoenix in a more positive light than I do. "We did good," she says, referring to the conviction reversals. She keeps hoping the real killers will be prosecuted.

But I have arrived at the point where I don't care if they solve the Bolles homicide. I know who did it, but Bradley Funk is dead and I can't drive myself crazy agonizing over the fact that he and others responsible haven't been or likely ever will be punished.

Epilogue

I didn't think anything Attorney General Robert Corbin could stoop to would surprise me, but I underestimated this politician. The action he took on November 27, 1989, was not just surprising; it was sickening: he recharged Jim Robison in the Bolles murder.

A grand jury didn't recharge Robison. I don't believe Corbin could have gotten a grand jury to do it. Instead, he used George Weisz—he of the "Lake, old buddy" greeting—to file a "complaint," which this prosecutor contended was all that he needed. Since the charges against Robison (and Dunlap, for that matter) had never been dropped—a Sword of Damocles dangling over their heads—they could be reinstated whenever the attorney general chose.

He chose a time propitious for himself. Corbin faced a stiff reelection challenge in the Republican primary from David Eisenstein and Grant Woods and, if he survived that, from the winner of the Democratic Party primary—expected to be prominent Phoenix lawyer Georgia Staton. *All* the candidates let it be known that Corbin's total lack of progress in the most important case he ever handled—the Bolles murder—would be a major campaign issue. Thus, when Corbin recharged Robison, many observers felt it represented a desperate gamble to establish that he genuinely sought justice for Don Bolles and merited reelection.

These observers probably underestimated Corbin, as I had. As this is being written, it appears Corbin is about to launch a run for the *Governor*'s seat.

And what about George Weisz? He had relinquished a safe seat in the Arizona legislature to work for Corbin, a self-imposed demotion, a seemingly inexplicable career move. But maybe not. Will Weisz try to ride a Robison prosecution to the attorney general's post?

I learned what Weisz wanted when he called me earlier: tape recordings I had made with Robison. I received several subpoenas—one to a grand jury looking into the matter (it didn't indict) and another to a preliminary hearing—but refused to turn over the tapes. I believed strongly that I had both a defense investigator/client privilege and a journalist/source privilege with Robison. For a few days it appeared I might go to jail, but the judge compromised and said I could hand the tapes over to Robison's lawyer, Tom Henze. I did so, since it was agreeable to Jim.

Don Devereux wrote in *The IRE Journal*, Winter 1990 issue:

> Old notions are obviously hard to give up. After years of promising a new look at the June 1976 bombslaying of Phoenix reporter Don Bolles, Arizona Attorney General Robert Corbin finally has taken some action.
>
> But it certainly would be premature to celebrate.
>
> All that he has done so far is to re-charge Jim Robison in the crime.
>
> The action just taken on November 27 was not a product of last month's sudden flurry of state grand jury interest in the Bolles case.
>
> Rather, it came in the form of a brief "complaint" signed by state attorney general's office investigator George Weisz. . . .
>
> Rumors suggesting such a possibility have been circulating for weeks.
>
> Although it may not have been unexpected, it never-

theless is a disappointing development for those of us still
hoping for a real breakthrough in the case.

I find it very doubtful, in fact, that Robison is guilty
of the Bolles homicide.

There are other much more plausible candidates out
there.

Until 1979 I had assumed that Robison indeed was the
killer as officially alleged.

Yet, after spending many hours with him in repeated
interviews—perhaps the only journalist to do so—and examining other evidence, I gradually changed that opinion.

Corbin's decision to go after Robison again not only
may be terribly unfair to him.

It also may force the state's investigation back along a
familiar, time-wasting path that leads to the same old dead-
end. . . .

Corbin has denied any political considerations in either his actions or their timing.

It is a curious coincidence, however, that he selected
the exact same day to re-charge Robison which Woods
had scheduled to announce his candidacy for the state
attorney general's job.

The renewal of the charge against Robison left me shaking
my head for days, then I reverted to the old fire horse role and
took a look at what Corbin had.

He had nothing—*zero*—that he hadn't had in 1980 when the
supreme court overturned the convictions. *No new evidence at
all.* Two witnesses were presented at the preliminary hearing
that bound Robison over to a new murder trial: convicted land-
fraud swindler Howard Woodall and building executive Larry
Welton, currently serving time in a federal prison for fraud. Each
said Robison had "confessed" to him. Neither would say, nor
would Corbin, what he was receiving in return for testimony.
Both these witnesses were known to Corbin *before* Robison originally was tried in 1977, but were so suspect he used only Woodall—in a minor role—during the original trial.

Books could be written about jailhouse snitches and how they attempt to buy their way out of serious sentences with perjured testimony. Perhaps a sign of Corbin's incompetence, and worse, was that in the many years—nearly ten—since the supreme court overturned the conviction, he hadn't come up with anybody new.

I found it damnable that Robison, an old man now at sixty-seven, had to go through this ordeal again. Forget that it was unconstitutional: the Sixth Amendment promise of a "speedy" trial surely applied here, and by waiting almost ten years, Corbin made a mockery of the Fifth and Fourteenth Amendments, which guarantee "due process."

Things would have been less outrageous had Corbin waited eight, or even nine. But two key witnesses, potential *defendants*, died shortly after Robison was re-charged. One of these, Corbin should have known, was about to pass away: Monte Kobey, whom Michael JoDon said he heard discussing the Bolles bombing before it took place, died in December 1989, after a long bout with AIDS.

More important and damaging to Robison, Bradley Funk died of a heart attack on December 30, 1989.

A living Bradley Funk would have posed a big obstacle to the conviction Corbin hopes to obtain against Jim Robison. The attorney general may even have breathed a sigh of relief, given another problem he has: a $55,000 campaign contribution he accepted from Charles Keating—head of Lincoln Savings and Loan, which became the largest S&L bankruptcy in history—for a campaign in which Corbin ran *unopposed*. Corbin, incidentally, while persecuting Robison, never went after Keating's banking empire, though it was his job to keep tabs on it. When asked if he intended to return the $55,000, Corbin said, "I never promised him anything and have never done anything for him. And I'm just hardheaded enough to think that if you give something back to the man, then it looks like you did something wrong."

E. J. Montini wrote in the *Arizona Republic*, February 16, 1990, "If Corbin runs for governor, however, he'll need a war chest. And Arizona law says that money collected during one campaign can be carried over to the next. Meaning that Corbin could, if he wanted to, take Keating's $50,000 [sic] and run for governor."

Tom Fitzpatrick in *New Times* wrote a revealing article about what he witnessed at Bradley Funk's funeral:

> Sometimes, you can tell something about a man by who shows up at his funeral. . . .
>
> This was a furtive, secretive bunch at the Funk funeral. Their cars were showy and their necks and wrists were covered with gold jewelry. Their clothes were flashy.
>
> There was a Rolls Royce Corniche with the license plates "PRESH."
>
> There were a half dozen Mercedes-Benz four-door jobs and a scattering of BMWs and a trio of the newest darling yuppie vehicle, the Jeep Wagoneer.
>
> They were monied types, these funeralgoers, the kind who clearly reveled in demonstrating their bank accounts.
>
> The fleshy, overdressed men and the women in their pancake make-up and fur coats were here to say good-bye to Funk.
>
> Funk died of a heart attack while attempting to negotiate his glittering Jaguar into a Biltmore-area parking space.
>
> His death puts us just one step farther from ever solving the case.
>
> I would like to believe Attorney General Corbin is sincere about this new grand jury he has formed to study the Bolles matter.
>
> But I can't believe anything Corbin says. To him and his ilk, the Bolles case is kept on hand to be trotted out when there's need for some good ink.
>
> To my way of thinking, Corbin could do himself a lot more good if he would pay Charles Keating back the $55,000 from the last campaign. Corbin accepted the money even though he was running without opposition.
>
> If Corbin performed that one simple act.

Perhaps then, I wouldn't feel it necessary to keep asking why Corbin, with all the vast resources of his office,
never lifted a hand against Keating.

Doesn't that bother anyone else?

"Despite Funk's involvement with both Bolles and Adamson,"
Fitzpatrick pointed out, "Funk never was questioned by police. . . . Add to this the fact that just before the bombing, Bolles
told friends he was heading to San Diego where he hoped to
uncover charges of child molesting made in a sealed deposition
by Funk's former wife."

And add so many other things that pointed to Bradley Funk,
like his sudden flight to that rehab center, like his showing William Wright the type of device used to blow Bolles up, like . . .
What's the use? Funk is dead, and it's well known that juries
don't like to hear a defense attorney implicate a deceased individual, who can no longer defend himself, in a murder.

I'd like to think Corbin doesn't have a chance to convict Jim
Robison, but who knows? He convicted him before. Corbin says
he won't use John Adamson, but like Tom Fitzpatrick, I don't
believe anything Corbin says.

Here's what worries me most: that the jurors judging Robison
won't hear all the facts about the Bolles case. I spent an afternoon in front of that grand jury, mainly presenting them with
the highlights this book contains, and they knew virtually none
of them. They didn't know about Neal Roberts's three "stolen"
vehicles, his "loud and clear" remark, the role of Gail Owens,
nothing. Many of the grand jurors evinced genuine shock at what
I told them. But what if a judge rules all this irrelevant? What if
all the jurors hear is the testimony of those two convicts?

Perhaps I'm too pessimistic. Even if Corbin gets his conviction—against a poor working man, not the Phoenix elite who
were truly behind the crime—it will surely again be thrown out
on appeal: with the complete absence of new evidence, the more
than ten years that will have elapsed before the trial do not fit
anyone's definition of "speedy."

Don Devereux has asked me to come to Phoenix, to go

through it all over again. The last time they almost killed us, I think. But then I think of Jim Robison, *an old man*. God, I hate what Corbin, to advance his own career, has put him through.

I talked to Jim at the pretrial evidentiary hearing where the judge held that the testimony of the two jailbird snitches was sufficient to bind him over for a jury trial. He said that before all this had happened he had been counting on the mandatory release date he had been given—July 4, 1991—from the draconian sentence he'd already served on that bogus assault charge. This had kept him strong, he said. Given him hope that part of his life still remained to be lived. He didn't go any farther, but I could see the concern in his eyes. I think he wonders, as I do, whether his nightmare will ever end.

As I shook hands with Jim, I imagined what Max Dunlap must be thinking. If they convicted Jim, surely the prosecution would come after him next. The strategy was to go after the weakest first, the one with no friends, before taking the risk of tangling again with that army of Max's supporters and associates.

They wove a tangled web. Once the decision was made to protect the powerful, all that remained was a sordid vendetta against the innocent.